This book addresses the number one development priority for so many coaches and mentors – the work-life balance of their clients and themselves. As the world of work changes, enabling organisations and individuals to become more agile, achieving work-life balance is the new ideal for so many of our clients. Extensive research shows that a balanced lifestyle will result in maintaining and sustaining good physical and mental health and effective relationships, boosting productivity and ultimately performance. Julie and Eliot have produced an excellent resource for coaches and mentors. Taking an evidence-based approach, they present some of the latest thinking on this topic, underpinned by their unique perspective and model with supporting tools and techniques. I am delighted to recommend this book as an invaluable resource for those engaged in leadership, coaching, mentoring, and supervision.
—*Denise Whitworth*, EMCC International Vice President Accreditation

This book is timely and highly relevant for those who lead, manage, and support others to improve their health and well-being. For professional bodies like the Chartered Institute of Personnel and Development and educational institutions, such as Middlesex University, health and well-being is a key challenge and we all need to focus our efforts on building healthier workplaces. This resource provides a thorough and comprehensive exposition of the key dimensions and issues within work-life balance and well-being. Full of theoretical insights, tools, techniques, and case studies, I envisage this will become a core text on any human resource management, learning and development, coaching and mentoring programme.
—*Anna Kyprianou*, Pro Vice-Chancellor and Executive Dean of the Faculty of Professional and Social Sciences, Middlesex University

This is a well-researched and easily digestible guide to support coaches with one of the biggest challenges their clients face – work-life balance. Theory, examples, and exercises are brought together in a simple model which provides coaches and mentors with the benchmark reference for supporting their clients. Bravo!
—*Dr Nicolas Anderson*, Managing Director, QinetiQ

In today's constantly changing world, with 24/7 global access, we are seeing an increasing need for coaches and mentors to be alert to the demands of their clients, who may be facing mental, physical, and emotional turmoil and stress. With the advancement in technology and social media, there is inordinate pressure for people to 'keep up', 'keep ahead', achieve, and be liked. So what part can the growing number of coaches and mentors play in attending to this with their clients? In this book, Julie and Eliot have identified the pivotal role that professional practitioners can play to support their clients in finding work-life balance. Here they have explored how practitioners can contribute to clients' awareness of the huge demands each of us may be facing and then help them to manage and influence the factors that may be causing harm and thus work towards finding some balance. I am delighted to recommend this book, as it provides an invaluable contribution to the coaching and mentoring literature that provides practical resources, coupled with the theoretical underpinning, to coaches and mentors in diverse contexts that will enable them to work effectively to support their clients' well-being. At the same time, the coaches and mentors themselves may be facing some or all of these work-life pressures, both personally and through the impact that the lives of their clients have on them. Here, too, is an excellent resource for the practitioner to explore and identify the most appropriate strategies and methods for their own self-care, without which they cannot be of best service to their clients.

—*Dr Alison Hodge,* Coaching Supervisor

Re-examining what is meant by work-life balance is critically important in today's society, given the new and different pressures we find ourselves facing. As coaches and mentors, it is vital that we engage with these issues, not only to support our clients but also to engage in effective self-care, as helpers. In this text, the authors make a useful contribution to this endeavour by critically engaging with this dual focus and offer a useful framework through which we are able to reflect on our own frameworks for examining these issues. They helpfully get the balance right in terms of blending research evidence, theory, and practice, which makes their contribution accessible but rigorous in its approach. An important text at this moment in time.

—*Dr Paul Stokes,* Coaching & Mentoring Research Unit,
Sheffield Business School, Sheffield Hallam University

Coaching and Mentoring for Work–Life Balance

The coaching and mentoring profession is facing a major challenge – helping clients cope effectively with life's complexities and conflicting demands in a rapidly changing environment. Conversations around work-life balance need to address not only the interconnectedness of work, leisure, home, and social life but also the fact that these elements are in flux and require continuous rebalancing. This book is a practical and evidence-based resource to help coaches and mentors in supporting clients to achieve greater work-life balance.

Written by an experienced academic-practitioner team, this book provides coaches and mentors with a way of addressing work-life tensions with their clients. It is grounded in research and practice and offers a wide range of tools and techniques which are supported with real-life case studies illustrating how they can be employed. On top of this, readers are also supported with reflective questions to enhance understanding and a series of downloadable worksheets for practical use.

Coaching and Mentoring for Work-Life Balance is essential reading for professional coaches and mentors who are helping their clients to develop personal resilience and will also be a valuable resource for students in postgraduate coaching and mentoring courses. The authors present some of the latest thinking on this topic, underpinned by their own research and model for work-life balance, making the book indispensable to all those engaged in leadership, coaching, mentoring, and supervision.

Dr Julie Haddock-Millar is a Visiting Professor at the International University of Monaco and Associate Professor (Practice) of Human Resource Management and Senior Teaching Fellow at Middlesex University Business School. She is the European Mentoring & Coaching Council (EMCC) UK Executive Board joint Director for Professional Development and leads on the International Standards for Mentoring and Coaching Programmes (ISMCP) for EMCC International.

She is an EMCC accredited Senior Practitioner Coach and Mentor and EMCC accredited International Programme Manager (IPMA) Master Practitioner.

Eliot Tom is a Coaching Psychologist (MBPsS), and a member of the Special Group of Psychology within the British Psychology Society. She is a psychology graduate and a qualified, practising Coach. She has a Diploma (with Distinction) in Coaching and Mentoring, accredited by the Association for Coaching. Eliot is a Management Consultant at Accenture in their Innovation Centre working with c-suites to plan their innovative company strategies.

Routledge-EMCC Masters in Coaching and Mentoring
Series Editors: Prof David Clutterbuck and Irena Sobolewska
Associate Series Editors: Dr Julie Haddock-Millar and Agnieszka Bajer

This series is published in collaboration with the European Mentoring & Coaching Council (EMCC).

Routledge-EMCC Masters in Coaching and Mentoring provides critical perspectives in coaching and mentoring. It aims to avoid the overcrowded basic coaching/mentoring textbook market and focus instead on providing a toolkit for topics that are outside of core theory but that are necessary to become a mature practitioner.

The series will appeal to those studying to obtain certificates, diplomas, and master's in coaching and mentoring, alongside experienced practitioners who wish to round out their practice using selected essential reading as part of their continuous professional development.

Coaching and Mentoring in the Asia Pacific
Edited by Anna Blackman, Derrick Kon and David Clutterbuck

Coaching Supervision
Advancing Practice and Changing Landscapes
Edited by Jo Birch and Peter Welch

The Art of Listening in Coaching and Mentoring
Authored by Stephen Burt

Coaching and Mentoring for Work-Life Balance
Authored by Dr Julie Haddock-Millar and Eliot Tom

Coaching and Mentoring for Work-Life Balance

Dr Julie Haddock-Millar and Eliot Tom

Routledge
Taylor & Francis Group

LONDON AND NEW YORK

First published 2020
by Routledge
2 Park Square, Milton Park, Abingdon, Oxon OX14 4RN

and by Routledge
52 Vanderbilt Avenue, New York, NY 10017

Routledge is an imprint of the Taylor & Francis Group, an Informa business

British Library Cataloguing-in-Publication Data
A catalogue record for this book is available from the British Library

Library of Congress Cataloging-in-Publication Data
A catalog record has been requested for this book

ISBN: 978-0-367-23560-4 (hbk)
ISBN: 978-0-367-23562-8 (pbk)
ISBN: 978-0-429-28040-5 (ebk)

Typeset in Bembo
by Deanta Global Publishing Services Chennai, India.

Visit the eResources: www.routledge.com/9780367235628

Printed and bound by CPI Group (UK) Ltd, Croydon, CR0 4YY

To my incredibly patient and adoring husband, James, and my exuberant and loving children, Isabella and Tyler – you are the centre of my world.

Julie

To my inspirational, caring, and supportive parents, Deborah and David Tom – I love you!

Eliot

Contents

Figures

Tables

About the authors

Julie Haddock-Millar is a Visiting Professor at the International University of Monaco and Associate Professor (Practice) of Human Resource Management and Senior Teaching Fellow at Middlesex University Business School. She is the European Mentoring & Coaching Council (EMCC) UK Executive Board joint Director for Professional Development and leads on the International Standards for Mentoring and Coaching Programmes (ISMCP) for EMCC International. She is an EMCC accredited Senior Practitioner Coach and Mentor. She is one of two EMCC accredited Master Practitioner Coach and Mentor Programme Managers. Julie is a Chartered Member of the Chartered Institute of Personnel and  Development (CIPD) and CIPD Academic Membership Assessor, Member of the International Mentoring Association (IMA), and Advisory Council Member of the Harvard Business Review (HBR).

Julie gained her Doctorate of Professional Studies (DProf) from Middlesex University in the field of strategic organisational development and mentoring and was nominated for the Ken Goulding Prize for Professional Excellence. She holds a Master of Arts (MA) in Human Resource Development (HRD), won the CIPD outstanding student award, and was a finalist at the CIPD national awards for her postgraduate studies in work-based learning and mentoring. She studied her Postgraduate Certificate in Coaching and Mentoring with Oxford Brookes University. Julie leads and teaches on a number of postgraduate programmes including the flagship Master of Business Administration (MBA) and Doctorate in Business Administration (DBA) programmes. She supervises and mentors doctoral students engaged in research associated with mentoring, coaching and professional development.

Julie has a wealth of experience in mentoring and coaching practice in different sectors and organisations, having led the design and delivery of coaching and mentoring programmes including, amongst others, United Kingdom (UK) Cabinet Office, Financial and Legal Skills Partnership, First Division

Association, The Access Project, and the UK National Health Service. Some of Julie's current projects include the design and delivery of the first NHS Leadership Academy EMCC European Quality Award (EQA) Bespoke Practitioner Mentor Training Programme; the design and delivery of the first EMCC EQA Bespoke Practitioner Coaching and Mentoring Programme Manager Training Programme; and the design and delivery of the first EMCC EQA Bespoke Human Resource Professional Training Programme. Julie is currently leading two large-scale action research mentoring and coaching projects with Youth Business International (YBI) and Médecins Sans Frontières (MSF), involving the ongoing analysis and evaluation of entrepreneurial mentoring, mentoring in the humanitarian field, and coaching field teams in situations which involve armed conflict, natural disaster, endemic and epidemic disease, and/or social violence and healthcare exclusion. In addition, she has been working with Khulisa since 2017 to understand the mentoring landscape in the criminal justice system and beyond.

Eliot Tom is a Coaching Psychologist (MBPsS), and a member of the Special Group of Psychology within the British Psychology Society. She has a Diploma (with Distinction) in Coaching and Mentoring, accredited by the Association for Coaching. She is a psychology graduate, with first-class honours. For her dissertation, Eliot conducted an empirical study using a brief intervention to reduce stress amongst psychologists, coaches and counsellors.

Eliot started her career as a Junior Consultant for three years at a boutique consultancy, Human Systems (Business Psychologists Ltd), specialising in coaching and leadership development. She helped with the design of a 9-month leadership development programme for directors at a global investment bank which was delivered in London, New York, and Singapore. This sparked Eliot's interest in coaching and led her to become a qualified coach with the Institute of Learning and Management (Level 5). Since then, she has coached senior leaders at Barclays Investment Bank and high-flying graduates at Diageo.

For the past five years, Eliot has been working in the Management Consulting Practice at Accenture with a number of FTSE 100 clients. In her first few years, she specialised in the Human Capital practice that houses their Change Management, Learning, and Human Resources (HR) practitioners. She was the lead workshop designer for a number of projects: to name a few, visioning, culture change, and collaboration projects. Eliot is now working in Accenture's Innovation Practice, where she guides and coaches client teams on their innovation journey. She helps clients tackle fundamental questions around how they respond to disruption and shift their mindsets to explore the art of the possible. This role has given Eliot exposure to a wide variety of industries and cutting-edge trends, such as the future of work and the workforce.

Outside of work, Eliot mentors unprivileged children at Depaul, a charity that helps people who are homeless, vulnerable, and disadvantaged. She works with her mentees with the aim to support them more holistically to achieve a variety of goals around general employability, engagement, and confidence building.

Foreword: Balancing act

My wife tells me I am a workaholic. I say I just enjoy and get great fulfilment from almost everything I do.

Who is right? We both are.

If you are lucky enough to live a life where work and play are mostly the same thing, there are potentially even more challenges than if you hate your work. If you also have multiple interests, it's even more difficult. Living a full life can so easily become an over-full life, where there is never enough time for all the things that matter and priorities can become just as confused and distorted.

Achieving balance is the single most complex challenge for people in 21st-century developed societies. The challenge is fuelled by a number of trends. In particular:

- Overwhelming choice. In the 1950s a large grocery store carried perhaps 250 lines of goods. Now a superstore may carry 250,000, or more. The human brain is not designed for evaluating more than a handful of options. Making choices can be stressful, especially if you are a Maximiser (someone who wants to get the best possible solution), rather than a Satisficer (someone prepared to accept a good enough solution). The more choices we have, the more time we expend in choosing, or worrying whether we made the right choice.
- Overwhelming information. The neologism 'infoxication' expresses the problem well. Modern life is a constant bombardment of information, much of which we can do better without. For example, having your genome analysed may allow you to take preventive action against a long-term health threat, but it may also burden you with a heap of worries about 'might be' scenarios.
- Overwhelming pace. Whether it be the time it takes to get a passport, or genetic modification in agriculture, the focus of change is to do more in less time and at less cost. In the workplace, the concept of pacing work has largely been lost. Yet truly productive work has a natural cadence of work, rest, and play. Employers who seek to reintroduce play (fun) back into the workplace are still seen as outliers.

- Overwhelming responsibility. The network of people who depend on us to perform in some manner is growing. Our lives are no longer our own (if they ever were). Instead, they are constrained by perceived obligations towards more and more others. The sense of being 'over-obligated' leads to being over-extended and is a source of compassion fatigue – losing the capacity to empathise and act for the welfare of others.

In my role as a coach supervisor, I often find myself asking coaches who worry for their clients, 'How much caring is "just enough"?'. It's so easy to care too much. In almost every other aspect of life the criterion of 'just enough' appears to be associated with well-being, happiness, and prosperity. How much wealth is just enough; how much happiness and how much status is just enough? What are the costs of going after more and more? Well-being is associated with finding an acceptable balance and knowing that the constant vibrations of a dynamic environment require us to constantly rebalance.

Achieving balance requires frequent attentiveness, self-honesty, and a fair amount of skill. Knowing how to step back and recalibrate against what really matters – and having the discipline to do so – has become an essential survival kit for the digital age. It's not a skill often taught in school, nor in the workplace.

Timing is also important. When a trained diver meets a difficult situation, he or she avoids panic by remembering to Stop, Think, Breathe, and finally Act. Taking time and space to recalibrate in a similar way helps restore perspective to an overloaded life.

To achieve and maintain a sense of balance, we must regularly revisit core questions, such as:

- What would a fulfilled life look like for me?
- What gives meaning to being me?
- What do I want to contribute that is unique to me?
- How much control do I want and need over my choices?
- What are the values I want to adhere to in the choices I make?
- Who can support me in achieving the balance I want, and how?

And this is where this book comes into the picture. With theory, practice, and case examples throughout, this book will assist coaches or mentors in any context to help their clients navigate the complexity of the world we live in today. The authors have brought into one volume a great deal of practical guidance on how to recognise the challenges of achieving a fulfilling life, both for ourselves and those we care about.

David Clutterbuck 2019

Abbreviations

ABCDE	Adversity or Activating event, Beliefs, Consequences, Disputing rational thoughts and beliefs, Effects
AC	Association of Coaches
ACR	Active Constructive Response
AI	Artificial Intelligence
APECS	Association for Professional Executive Coaching and Supervision
BREXIT	British Exit from European Union
CBT	Cognitive Behavioural Therapy
CIPD	Chartered Institute of Personnel and Development
CPAP	Continuous Positive Airway Pressure
CPD	Continuing Professional Development
DBA	Doctor of Business Administration
DEAL	Describe the situation, Express your concerns, Ask for perspective and ideas, List the benefits
DPROF	Doctor of Professional Studies
EI	Emotional Intelligence
EMCC	European Mentoring & Coaching Council
EQA	European Quality Award
FCA	Financial Conduct Authority
FD	Finance Director
FMCG	Fast Moving Consumer Goods Company
GP	General Practitioner
HBR	Harvard Business Review
HR	Human Resources
HRD	Human Resource Development
HQC	High-Quality Connections
ICF	International Coach Federation
IMA	International Mentoring Association
ISMCP	International Standards for Mentoring and Coaching Programmes
MA	Master of Arts
MD	Managing Director

MBA	Master of Business Administration
MBSR	Mindfulness-Based Stress Reduction
MSF	Médecins Sans Frontières (Doctors Without Borders)
NGO	Non-Governmental Organisation
PESTLE	Political, Economic, Social, Technological, Legal, Environmental
PhD	Doctor of Philosophy
SMART	Strength-focused and Meaning-oriented Approach to Resilience and Transformation
SWOT	Strengths, Weaknesses, Opportunities, Threats
YBI	Youth Business International
UK	United Kingdom
USA	United States of America
VUCA	Volatile, Uncertain, Complex Ambiguous
WHO	World Health Organisation

Glossary

Artificial Intelligence   The theory and development of computer systems able to perform tasks normally requiring human intelligence.

Belief   An assumed truth (often not justifiably true).

Burnout   A reaction to chronic stress and is a state of physical mental and emotional exhaustion.

Emotional mastery   Our ability to understand and manage our own emotions, and understand and respond to the emotions of others.

Environmental mastery   Our ability to analyse and manage our environment, appreciate potential resources, access resources, navigate complex external routes to help meet our needs, and address all aspects of our lives.

Flexible working   A way of working that suits an employee's needs, for instance having flexible start or finish times, or working from home.

Generation X   The generation born after that of the baby boomers (roughly from the early 1960s to late 1970s).

Learned helplessness   A behaviour that occurs when the subject ensures repeatedly painful or otherwise aversive stimuli which it is unable to escape from or avoid.

Locus of control   An individual's sense of potency: how much they feel and think they can affect a situation, other people, and govern the outcomes of events.

Mastery   Comprehensive knowledge or skill in something or an accomplishment.

Mental health   A person's condition with regard to their psychological and emotional well-being.

Mental mastery   Our ability to self-enquire, develop self-awareness, self-insight and reflectivity skills.

Millennial   Denoting people reaching young adulthood in the early 21st century.

Physical mastery   Our ability to manage our health and energy levels.

Presenteeism   The practice of being present at one's place of work for more hours than is required; showing up to work when one is ill.

Resilience The degree to which we are able to withstand and recover from challenges, pressure, or stressors, and the extent to which we are adaptable and our capacity to remain flexible in our thoughts, behaviours, and emotions when under stress.

Resilience protective factors Factors that provide a 'buffer' when someone is experiencing difficulties.

Resilience risk factors Adverse conditions or challenging situations which can apply in any context.

Self-care The practice of taking an active role in protecting one's own well-being.

Self-esteem Confidence in one's own worth or abilities; self-respect.

Social mastery Our ability to develop strong relationships and good support networks, at home, work, and within our broader network.

Social networking The activity of sharing information and communicating with groups of people using the internet.

Spiritual mastery Our ability to seek and express meaning and purpose and to understand the way we experience connectedness.

Stress The state of mental or emotional strain or tension resulting from adverse or demanding circumstances.

Thinking errors Irrational thinking that impacts judgements and our decisions.

Well-being The state of being comfortable, healthy, or happy.

Wellness The state of being in good health especially as an actively pursued goal.

Work-life balance The relationship between work and other areas of life.

Acknowledgements

This book would not have been possible without the large number of people who have supported and advised us over the last two years.

First and foremost, we would like to thank our mentors, Professor David Clutterbuck and Deborah Tom. We feel so lucky to have such inspirational role models that have provided support and encouragement throughout. Their experience and insights have helped to shape the direction of this book and crystallised the key messages in a concise and compelling way.

We are grateful to the many coaches, mentors, clients, colleagues, and friends that shared their stories and experiences to help bring the book to life.

We would like to thank our family and friends for their support and encouragement. We have spent many a day and evening mulling over our lives with our partners, discussing our work-life balance, how we care for each other and tend to our needs and the needs of others.

We are incredibly grateful to have so many loved ones in our lives.

Thank you.
With love,
Julie and Eliot

Introduction

Over the last few decades, we have seen a surge in regulatory and policy activity intended to address and improve our well-being and physical and mental health. Yet health issues in developed societies have never been more severe. Affecting all families, groups, teams, and communities, the costs of the society we live in today are widespread and leave no aspect of our lives untouched. Modern life stressors are multifarious. Changing family structures, political/economic uncertainty, concerns about standards of living, inequality, community breakdown, and competition and insecurity at work have resulted in increased adult ill health. It is estimated that one in five adults live with a mental illness and 50% of those go untreated; for children and young people, one in ten is impacted by mental health issues.

In both practitioner and academic literature there has been a surge of interest in physical and mental health. Of particular interest are the factors which influence mental and physical health and evaluation of the interventions which are most effective in supporting children and adults. Subsequently, there have been many studies, publications, and interventions in the areas of work-life balance, work-life integration, well-being, wellness, and happiness explored from multiple perspectives in a variety of disciplines. A common theme has emerged: how to balance work with other areas of life. Our services as coaches and mentors are pivotal to supporting our clients as they develop their capacity to cope, adapt, and thrive. By helping our clients gain self-awareness, self-insight, capability, and the capacity to influence their work-life balance, we influence their physical, mental, and social well-being.

This book is intended to:

- Provide a practical resource which contains tools and techniques you can use in your day-to-day practice.
- Provide insight into some of the significant conceptual and theoretical debates on work-life balance.
- Provide empirical evidence which illustrates the different ways in which coaching and mentoring can support clients' work-life balance.

We know that coaches and mentors draw from many different philosophies and approaches, adopting different methods and ways of working with their clients. This book is designed to support coaches and mentors, regardless of approach, methodology, or specialism.

The style and structure of the book

We present an evidence-based, practical resource which will inform your coaching and mentoring practice. Each chapter presents both theoretical and empirical literature which underpins a specific topic area. Our combined experience in coaching and mentoring spans 30 years; we weave in our own reflections, experiences, and research findings throughout.

The book comprises seven chapters. The first chapter explores the environment we live in today, the sources of pressure, and the costs of today's world to our well-being. We identify the degree to which expectations are shifting and how attitudes towards work-life balance have evolved and will continue to do so with cultural, generational, and economic changes. Consideration is given to the global, international, national, regional, and local actors in the system in which all have a role to play in supporting work-life balance and well-being. We introduce our four-stage model for work-life balance in the context of coaching and mentoring and explain each of the stages within that model.

In chapter 2, we share with you the importance of your clients developing a positive view of self and the relationship this has with work-life balance. We present research which explores what it means to develop a positive view of self and the impact this has on clients' mental and emotional well-being.

The chapter is split into two parts. The first focuses on self-esteem, which is the overall value one places on oneself as a person. The second part looks at 'locus of control', one's sense of potency and ability to influence others, and considers the extent to which one believes one has power over events in one's life. In both parts, we explore how each of these constructs develops, how to spot whether your clients have high or low self-esteem and an internal or external locus of control, and the consequences of these, as well as tools and techniques to develop healthy self-esteem and locus of control.

In chapter 3, we explore the knowledge and the science to address what success is to your clients. We review the academic literature on the predictors and components of success to give you evidence on the subject. We provide you with some tools on how to uncover your clients' beliefs around success in general and how to analyse their level of success and satisfaction. Finally, we cover goal-setting and planning strategies to enable them to realise their ambitions.

The relationship between coaching, mentoring, and resilience is explored in chapter 4. We begin with an overview of the origins of the term resilience. We then look at how it is defined in a variety of contexts and at the relationship between work-life balance and resilience. Next, we explore the impact of stress on resilience levels and the concept of and precursors to burnout. To achieve greater work-life balance, we propose six masteries that all require tending to. These are mental, emotional, social, physical, spiritual, and environmental mastery. We describe each mastery, the theory and evidence underpinning each mastery, and how these important building blocks enhance your clients' resilience and ability to respond positively to setbacks. We invite you to reflect on the six masteries and help your clients to understand where they may need to focus their energies.

The aim of chapter 5 is to support you in helping your clients to improve the quality of their decision-making, negotiation, and influencing skills, because these skills will impact on the work-life balance they can achieve. We introduce the concept of 'critical conversations' and how they are vital in the decision-making process and are a prerequisite to taking the right actions. We then consider how you can support your clients in developing their negotiation and influencing skills to help address an imbalance of power, maximise their impact, and achieve a positive outcome for all. We present a number of tools and techniques, illustrated with case studies.

Chapter 6 explores self-care for you, the coach and mentor. Coaches and mentors engage in the sort of work that can leave us feeling exhausted, over-whelmed, or even burnt out. We explore why self-care is necessary, the common pitfalls, and the strategies for managing self-care; moreover, we offer a number of tools and techniques to develop a self-care plan. We discuss the commitment to self-care within the context of both the nature of the role and the guidelines from a range of professional bodies. We consider the importance of the six masteries in the context of self-care and look at what we can learn and take from the preceding chapters to support the practice of coaches and mentors.

The final chapter draws together the areas reviewed within our Four-Stage Model for Work-Life Balance and considers the degree to which the elements combine to enable clients to achieve the success and well-being they wish for.

Terminology

Practitioners and organisations do have different definitions and interpretations of coaching and mentoring. This book, our research, and our practice are informed by a number of different professional bodies, including the Association of Coaches (AC), the European Mentoring & Coaching Council (EMCC), the Chartered Institute of Personnel and Development (CIPD), and the International Coach Federation (ICF). The roles of the coach and mentor are described differently by the aforementioned professional bodies.

We acknowledge the overlap and similarities in the knowledge, skills, competencies, and behaviours of coaches and mentors. We also acknowledge the differences. Many practitioners, including ourselves, are both coaches *and* mentors, and others may be mentors using coaching skills, competencies, and behaviours.

The approach, tools, and techniques in this book can be applied to both the coaching and mentoring context and your practice. Therefore, the terminology we use in the book is as follows:

- When referring to the practice of coaching and/or mentoring, we refer to coaching or mentoring.
- When referring to coaching and/or mentoring practitioners, we refer to the coach or mentor.
- When referring to the coachee or mentee, we refer to the clients.

1 Work–life balance

Context and meaning

Introduction

The environment we live in today

Pressure, for people within the workforce, has been intensifying in recent decades. Factors such as advances in information technology and information load, the need for speed of response, the importance attached to the quality of customer service and its implications for constant availability, and the pace of change with its resultant upheavals and adjustments all demand our time and can be sources of pressure. With all the pressures and demands, as well as the competition for top jobs, it is all too easy for your clients to want to do whatever it takes to deliver. They see a culture of long working hours and presenteeism, their boss working day and night and the top executives doing the same, and they think that it is required. Yet the evidence is out: That is a way to burnout. Overwhelming information, pace, responsibility, and choice all impact on our well-being and, in particular, our mental and physical health.

By helping your clients see the way they can be effective *and* maintain a healthy work–life balance, you will be doing them and their family, friends, and society a lot of good. It all starts with their mindset. How can you help them shift from thinking of themselves as someone who is 'willing to do whatever the job asks' to someone who 'does great work and is happy, healthy and has happy, healthy relationships and interests outside of work'? Finding the right balance, an acceptable balance which will inevitably change as our lives and the world around us changes, requires purposeful and continuous attention.

What are the costs of the world we live in today?

The human cost of the world we live in today is immense. The costs can be seen at all levels of society: individual, group, team, organisation, and community. The negative effects of society impact all areas of life and our physical, mental, and social well-being. Government, institutional, and research statistics have brought into sharp focus the poor state of our health. In 2017, the UK Government commissioned an independent review into how employers can better support the mental health of all people currently in employment and help them thrive at work (Thriving at Work, 2017). The study presented the following key findings in the area of mental health:

- There are more people at work with mental health conditions than ever before.
- Each year, 300,000 people with a long-term mental health problem lose their jobs.
- Those that do lose their jobs because of mental health problems lose them at a much higher rate than those with physical health conditions.
- At work, 15% of people have symptoms of an existing mental health condition.

The financial costs of poor mental health were also assessed in the study at the level of the organisation, the UK Government, and the economy:

- The annual costs of poor mental health at work is between £33 billion and £42 billion.
- Over half of the annual cost comes from presenteeism, where individuals are less productive due to poor mental health.
- Poor mental health costs the UK Government between £24 billion and £27 billion annually.
- Poor mental health costs the economy between £74 billion and £99 billion in lost annual output.

The costs of stress and burnout are also disturbing. An article by Eric Garton (2017) published in the *Harvard Business Review* claimed that the psychological and physical problems of burnt-out employees cost an estimated $125 billion to $190 billion a year in healthcare spending in the USA. Michael Blanding (2015), writing for the Harvard Business School, claimed:

> Our work can literally make us sick. Long hours, impossible demands from bosses, and uncertain job security can take their toll on our mental and physical well-being, leading to stress-induced aches and pains and anxiety. In extreme cases, the consequences can be worse – heart disease, high blood pressure, alcoholism, mental illness.

Mental ill health amongst workers continues to rise; the main causes include heavy workloads, managerial style, and difficult work relations (CIPD Absence Management survey, 2016). The impacts of poor mental health include lack of concentration, difficulty making decisions, a rise in colleague conflict, and difficulty dealing with challenging situations and meeting deadlines and objectives. The UK has the longest working hours in Europe; some professions are well known for working more than 48 hours a week, as the intensity of work has increased and a culture of long working hours has emerged (Institute for Employment Studies, 2018).

There is a growing concern that the quality of home and community life is deteriorating. There are various explanations, including the growth of the single-parent family, the increased cost of living, more self-containment and isolation, and the lack of local resources and facilities. The pressures and demands of work, reflected in longer hours, more exhaustion, and growth of evening and weekend work, leave less scope for 'quality' family time. The consequences include increases in juvenile crime, more drug abuse, reduction in concern for the local community and in community participation, and less willingness to take responsibility for the care of elderly relatives and the disadvantaged. Whilst steps to redress these concerns transcend work and employment, it is nevertheless argued that the demands of work contribute to reduced participation in non-work activities, resulting in an imbalance.

Shifting landscape and shifting expectations

Attitudes towards work-life balance have evolved and will continue to do so with cultural, generational, and economic changes. The world of work is changing; new organisational models, structures, cultures, ways of working, specialisms, roles, knowledge, and skills are developing to adapt to the shifting landscape. The increasing use of artificial intelligence (AI) and automation will dramatically change the landscape. By one popular estimate, 65% of children entering primary school today will ultimately end up working in completely new job types that don't yet exist (World Economic Forum). How well prepared are we for the future of work?

Recent organisational initiatives have challenged the historical view of 'occupational' health. Interventions now encompass a more holistic approach to wellness and comprise any condition which could potentially impact employee performance. The trend incorporates a broader spectrum of interventions to include work-life balance initiatives which are believed to contribute to greater employee well-being.

Employees' expectations are changing; there is a call towards greater flexibility in the workplace; and many employees are looking to change their work hours, work from home, and have flexible schedules in order to accommodate a better work-life balance. In addition to a better work-life balance, employees are also beginning to expect services beyond the traditional mould, such as improved personal and career development and support, and a range of health promotion services.

Tulgan (1996) suggests that Generation X give greater priority to the balance between work and other areas of life. Millennials are less driven by the pursuit of making money; they want to feel appreciated, have an active voice, have autonomy, have the opportunity to make an impact, and have a sense of self-fulfilment.

What is being done to address the challenges we face?

We know that not enough is being done to support people's health in or outside of the workplace. Globally, the World Health Organisation (WHO) uses its international presence and profile to work towards promoting good mental health, including mental and psychological well-being, the prevention of mental disorders, and the care for those affected by mental disorders. World Mental Health Day, on 10 October 2018, focused on the mental health of young people in a changing world. The WHO shone a light on the early origins of mental illness in teenagers and how many receive little or no support to treat their illnesses. Much of WHO's work focuses on building mental resilience amongst young people and developing the psychosocial support that can be provided by parents, teachers, schools, and communities to help young people cope with the challenges of today's world.

In the UK, industry groups and trade unions have started to develop information on mental health for their members. Some are beginning to champion change in recognition of the need to address mental health issues. Professional bodies and accrediting organisations, such as the Chartered Institute of Personnel and Development (CIPD), have proactively promoted the mental health and well-being of their members. Occupational health providers and employee assistance programmes and insurance provide a source of support for employees. Workplace regulators such as the Financial Conduct Authority (FCA) have heightened their involvement in driving mental health up the agenda. Non-profit organisations and charities such as Mind and the Samaritans offer a number of training and support programmes that focus on raising awareness about emotional health, coping strategies, the value of listening, and building resilience. The programmes are often targeted at the early years age group, employers, and at-risk groups in the community. However, advice and support are open to anyone that is in need.

Strategies, policies, and processes have developed incrementally, resulting in a fragmented approach to work-life balance and well-being. Only in recent years have international and national organisations attempted to move towards an evidence-based, comprehensive, integrated approach to well-being which involves all stakeholders and addresses the challenges people face in today's society. Our clients live within an ecosystem which is often highly complex and always influenced by the interaction between the different layers and actors within. Our ecosystems require a high degree of navigation skills. Our ecosystems are never static; they are constantly changing, as we change, those around us change, and the nature of work, systems, processes, and structures change. We aim to provide support and guidance to help your clients understand and recognise their ecosystems, how they are positioned within them, and how they can navigate their ecosystems whilst at the same time constantly assessing, re-assessing, and addressing their needs.

Why work-life balance?

We consider work-life balance to be the relationship between work and other areas of life. Typically, areas of attention in the lives of our clients which need continuous care in order to maintain a sense of work-life balance include work, social, community, private/home life, finances, and health. In the 1980s and early 1990s, the concept of work-life balance received significant attention. However, the concept was often construed too narrowly, suggesting an equilibrium, matching, or evenness between different areas of life. Many practitioners and academics have found the term work-life balance divisive, an elusive ideal, and have suggested that the separation of life's domains and achieving equilibrium is not always possible or desired (Groysberg & Abrahams, 2014). This is because achieving work-life balance is a never-ending journey, and our needs are different at different times in our lives. For your clients, to make it through some events in life, they might choose to temporarily downplay some of these areas, but doing so for an extended period usually produces negative effects in other areas of life and can cause strain. This has been documented as the case for people who concentrate most or all of their energies on work and career. When we have seen this occur in our own research and practice, in a variety of sectors, where the risk of dissatisfaction is magnified, sickness, work absence, and ultimately resignation are a common occurrence and burnout a possible reality.

Four-stage model to support work-life balance

Work-life balance requires the ongoing assessment and evaluation of all areas of our lives to achieve well-being. But where do we start? In our research and practice we have found that the following themes have the greatest impact on clients' work-life balance and well-being:

- View of self and degree of self-insight, knowledge skills, and behaviour.
- Degree of life satisfaction and view of success.
- Ability to seek and express meaning and purpose, and to understand the way they experience connectedness.
- Ability to understand and regulate the emotions and understand the emotions of others.
- Ability to manage the health and energy levels.
- Ability to cope with pressure and adversity, to bounce back in the face of adverse conditions, change, or pressure.
- Ability to analyse and manage the environment, appreciate potential resources, access resources, navigate external routes to help meet their needs and support all areas of their life.
- Presence of support networks at home, work, and broader network to meet their needs.
- Making informed choices and negotiating with self and others.

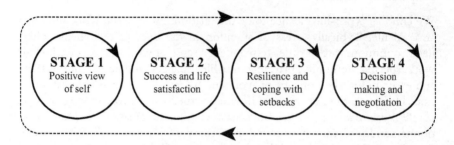

Figure 1.1 Four-Stage Model for Work-Life Balance

Our Four-Stage Model for Work-Life Balance (see Figure 1.1) is an approach that enables coaches or mentors to focus on four specific themes, each of which is essential in supporting clients as they work out how they want to live their lives:

- Positive view of self.
- Success and life satisfaction.
- Resilience and coping with setbacks.
- Decision-making and negotiation.

The model enables you and your clients to focus on specific areas of need which require constant attention and review to achieve the desired work-life balance and well-being. The stages are interconnected and are mutually beneficial; progress in one area will positively impact other areas. The model, tools, and techniques in this book will provide resources that you can use in the long term, regardless of your clients' current work-life balance situation.

Developing a positive view of self

The first stage of the model focuses on the importance of developing a positive view of self and the relationship this has with work-life balance. We first focus on self-esteem, which is the overall value one places on oneself as a person (Baumeister et al., 2003). We also consider the 'locus of control', which is the extent to which one believes they have power over events in their lives (Fournier, 2016).

We consider how self-esteem develops and how our early experiences affect feelings about self, safety, and security, as well as our ability to form bonds with others (Bowlby, 1988). We explore the research that shows self-esteem tends to increase throughout adolescence and stays relatively stable in young adulthood and middle adulthood, before reaching its peak at around 60 years of age, and then shifting into decline in the latter years (Erol & Orth, 2011). We consider other factors that affect self-esteem throughout life, such as major life experiences, traumatic events, lack of money, or use of drugs. We consider the importance of self-esteem in regard to work-life balance, including success, happiness, and well-being. We help you to recognise and identify varying levels of self-esteem and provide a case study exemplar which shows the impact of low self-esteem and how the client's coach started to build self-esteem with several different tools and techniques.

In exploring the causes of low or high self-esteem, we discuss ways to move to a more optimal level of self-esteem and suggest ways in which you can explore with your clients the consequences of their current level of self-esteem. We provide some tools to help your clients improve their self-esteem, including a Cognitive-Based Therapy (CBT) technique, the value and benefits of self-appreciation, self-reflection on achievements and strengths, positive affirmations, and positive role models.

We consider the relationship between our internal locus of control and work-life balance. We explore how the construct develops over time, from childhood, and how early life impacts on an adult's life perceptions, choices, personality, and behaviour. We distinguish between those that have an external locus of control orientation and those who tend to maintain an internal locus of control. We help you to identify if your clients have an internal or external locus of control and consider how you might support and develop their awareness. We provide some tools and techniques to improve your clients' internal locus of control, including challenging their self-limiting thoughts, addressing and breaking habits that negatively impact on their work-life balance, broadening their thinking regarding their lifestyle choices, developing a problem-solving mindset, and building confidence, assertiveness, positivity, and optimism. We provide case exemplars to illustrate some of the challenges clients face, including organisational and country culture; and we offer a range of tools and techniques to support the development of clients' internal locus of control.

Success and life satisfaction

In the second stage, we consider ways in which you can investigate and work with your clients' sense of success and satisfaction. We start by understanding how beliefs are formed and how they impact on our goals and actions. Our clients' definition of success will be influenced by their life stages, culture, values, and gender, and the definition of success is hermeneutic. Thus, their assumed truths about success affect how much success they think they can expect. In particular, we explore two mindsets that may limit your clients' views of success – pessimism and dealing with limited beliefs.

We then explain the universal clusters of components of success that most people find important and draw attention to some of the most prominent theorists and empirical studies. We touch on the areas of having good health, security, achievement, happiness, connection, autonomy, and living a life based on values, faith, and principles. Having this evidence-based knowledge can inform your work whilst staying client-centred, and following the thread of what they are saying will allow you to cover the ground thoroughly.

We look at several ways to uncover your clients' views of what they want and how close they are to achieving success. We provide some tools and techniques which will enable your clients to make choices and will guide their decisions in the light of what matters to them and help them live an authentic, full life.

We then cover goal-setting and the design of strategies to guide you in helping your clients set realistic goals and take committed actions. By helping clients not only think through what they want but take full responsibility for their autonomy and freedom within their goal-setting and execution of goals, we help them make great decisions. We provide our recommendations on maintaining forward momentum and ensuring our clients are going forward in the right gear – not too high nor too low.

Resilience and coping with setbacks

The third stage of the model is resilience and coping with setbacks. Research on resilience focuses on risk and protective factors alongside individual and internal resiliency factors, resiliency processes, and outcomes. Some studies have found that coaching or mentoring can act as a protective factor, a known buffer of stressors, providing protection in situations of immense change, particularly in the organisational setting where restructuring and downsizing are commonplace. Coaching or mentoring can help to develop positive self-concepts, self-regulation, and management of emotions, self-confidence, good decision-making, empowerment, and relational and social skills. We take a holistic approach to resilience, implicit in our model of 'six masteries of resilience'. The model states that:

- An individual's development is influenced by the surrounding environment.
- As individuals change, they also influence their home, work, and the broader environment.
- Individuals are connected with others in a community network.
- Strategies, tools, and techniques work together as an integrated approach to help build an effective system of resilience.

To achieve work-life balance, we propose that all the six masteries require tending to. The six masteries of resilience are:

- *Mental mastery*, which relates to our ability to develop self-awareness, self-insight, and reflectivity skills.
- *Emotional mastery*, which relates to our ability to understand and manage our own emotions and understand and respond to the emotions of others.
- *Social mastery*, which relates to our ability to develop strong relationships and good support networks, at home, work, and in our broader network.

- *Physical mastery*, which relates to our ability to manage our health and energy levels.
- *Spiritual mastery*, which relates to our ability to seek and express meaning and purpose and to understand the way we experience connectedness.
- *Environmental mastery*, which relates to our ability to analyse and manage our environment, appreciate potential resources, access resources, and navigate complex external routes to help meet our needs and address all aspects of our lives.

Each mastery is an important building block in enhancing clients' resilience and developing their ability to respond to setbacks. We can play a critical role in helping our clients work towards and maintain good physical and mental health, cope with life's stressors, and learn and adapt so that they are fit for the future.

Decision-making and negotiation

The fourth stage of the model is decision-making and negotiation. As a coach or mentor, our role, amongst others, is to assist our clients with major changes in work and life outside of work. In reaching decisions, we help our clients think through the options available, consider alternatives, understand the consequences of action or inaction, and move forward in achieving the clients' short-, medium-, and long-term aims. Coaching or mentoring helps people develop greater awareness and achieve a deeper understanding of their internal and external contexts. To gain an understanding of context, it is critical for people to have purposeful, critical conversations with a wide range of stakeholders, often referred to as our developmental network. A significant part of our role is to help our clients identify what types of conversations need to take place, with whom (their stakeholders), and when. In turn, this will involve helping clients prepare for the conversations that need to take place to move forward. In exploring the nature of critical conversations, we present four types of conversations:

- Internal dialogue.
- Systemic dialogue with immediate stakeholders.
- Colleague/organisational dialogue.
- Social networking dialogue.

Another crucial role of the coach or mentor is to help clients develop the ability to address their work-life balance by effectively negotiating and influencing. This stage involves helping your clients to effectively navigate their path to achieving greater control and influence towards greater work-life balance and ultimately their life satisfaction. We cannot underestimate the critical importance of negotiation as a core skill in achieving work-life balance. Supporting your clients to successfully negotiate, whereby all parties' interests are considered and relationships are preserved, is a key role of the coach or mentor. The impacts of poor negotiation or, at the extreme, avoidance and absence of negotiation may negatively influence pay, career trajectory, and promotion and employment conditions. In family life, their ability to negotiate will influence other important factors of work-life balance and life satisfaction such as discussing mutual financial responsibilities, how they wish to raise their children, and the sharing of domestic responsibilities with their partner.

Self-care for coaches and mentors

In Chapter 6, we also invite you to consider your own self-care practices as a coach or mentor. We aim to provide you with a preventative practice that can mitigate the known negative stressors embedded in the work of a coach and mentor. We explore why self-care is of importance to our profession and the consequences of not engaging in self-care, the common pitfalls, and the necessity to prioritise our self-care. We identify the degree to which self-care is multidimensional and multifaceted; no single intervention will cater for all the aspects that need attention. We invite you to choose the self-care strategies that reflect your needs from your analysis – choose the ones that you think will work for you, ones that will have the most value and keep you at your best. We recognise the value of supervision as an essential method for increasing self-awareness in coaches and mentors and monitoring self-care. Supervision provides a developmental function, resourcing function, and qualitative function, all of which are important aspects of the continuing professional development (CPD) of the coach or mentor.

Closing remarks

In the chapters that follow, we explore how coaches or mentors can support clients in becoming aware of the tension and conflict between different parts of their lives, and in addressing those conflicts. We look at the causes of conflict and the barriers clients face in taking control over their lives. We share theory, evidence, and practice to underpin each stage of our model, and provide practical tools and techniques that you can use with your clients to work towards achieving their desired work-life balance.

References

Baumeister, R.F., Campbell, J.D., Krueger, J.I. & Vohs, K.D. (2003). Does high self-esteem cause better performance, interpersonal success, happiness, or healthier lifestyles? *Psychological Science in the Public Interest*, 4(1), pp. 1–44.
Blanding, M., 2015. Workplace Stress Responsible for Up to $190 Billion in Annual Healthcare Costs. *Forbes Online*: January 26, 2015.
Bowlby, J. (1988). *A secure base: Parent-child attachment and healthy human development*. New York: Basic Books.

CIPD, *Absence Management ANNUAL SURVEY REPORT 2016* https://www.cipd.co.uk/ Images/absence-management_2016_tcm18-16360.pdf.

Erol, R.Y. & Orth, U. (2011). Self-esteem development from age 14 to 30 years: a longitudinal study. *Journal of Personality and Social Psychology*, 101(3), p. 607.

Fournier, G. (2016). Locus of control. Psych Central. Accessed on 28th July 2017 at: https://psychcentral.com/encyclopedia/locus-of-control/.

Garton, E., 2017. Employee burnout is a problem with the company, not the person. *Harvard Business Review*. Available at: https://hbr.org/2017/04/employee-burnout-is-a-problem-with-the-company-not-the-person

Groysberg, B. & Abrahams, R. (2014). Manage your work, manage your life. *Harvard Business Review*, 92(3), pp. 58–66.

Thriving at Work. The Stevenson/Farmer review of mental health and employers Stevenson D and Farmer P. The Independent Review of Mental Health and Employers. (October 2017). Accessed on 14th January 2019 at: https://assets.publishing.service.gov.uk/ government/uploads/system/uploads/attachment_data/file/658145/thriving-at-work-stevenson-farmer-review.pdf.

Tulgan, B. (1996). *Managing Generation X: how to bring out the best in young talent*. Oxford: Capstone Publishing.

World Economic Forum, Jan 2016. The future of jobs: Employment, skills and workforce strategy for the fourth industrial revolution. In *Global Insight Report*, World Economic Forum, Geneva. Accessed on 20th January 2019 at: http://reports.weforum.org/ future-of-jobs-2016/chapter-1-the-future-of-jobs-and-skills/#view/fn-1.

2 Stage 1

Positive view of self

Introduction

Self is the term used by psychologists to describe a construct of how we define ourselves, how we believe ourselves to be. Those who have a positive view of self are emotionally resilient, able to assert themselves, and are able to generate and maintain a robust mental state (Baumeister, 1993). To develop a positive view of self, individuals first need to dedicate time to gain self-insight, which can be done through receiving feedback and through deep reflection. This is where coaches or mentors can be helpful: in slowing down their clients and encouraging them to 'hold up the mirror'. In this digital age, it is so easy to keep ourselves occupied and distracted with our lives on autopilot, acting mindlessly and responding from habit. The coach or mentor can inject a pause in between stimulus and response, inviting exploration of self and accessing wisdom, giving time to think and decide before responding. This process allows our clients to become more mindful of their unique take on the world and to choose their behaviour. In this way, they learn from their experiences so that they thrive in a fast-changing world. In this chapter, we explore the first stage of our model for Work-life Balance, illustrated in Figure 2.1.

Clients' 'presenting problems' are often about their problematic boss or colleague. If we focus on that issue, our and their attention is often diverted from their self. We know that the real work is often about the self and that people frequently divert focus away from this very subject. We suggest that no discussion about the boss or colleague should take place until you have covered an exploration of their self. By taking the time to help our clients understand their sense of worth, how assured they are in their ability, their power, you lay the foundation for more courageous conversations. Understanding self is the priority, and it takes conscious effort, courage, and willingness to explore. Your clients might not want or feel able to go there, but through your coaching or mentoring relationship, you can engender their cooperation. Through your equanimity, your openness, and your unconditional positive regard, you give them the courage and motivation to look at their part in the scenario they bring to coaching or mentoring.

As coaches or mentors working in a global economy, sensitivity to cultural variances is important: The construct of the self varies in different cultures

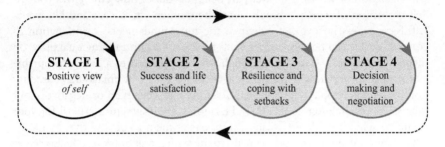

Figure 2.1 Four-Stage Model for Work-Life Balance

(Heine et al., 1999). Research shows that North Americans often have a positive view of self (Diener and Diener, 1996) and tend to enhance the positivity of their self-view (Taylor and Brown, 1988). This is compared to the Japanese, for example, who have a more self-critical focus (Heine et al., 1999).

Reflecting on your own practice:

- Do your clients have the same understanding of the constructs of self as you?
- If not, how are you flexing your approach?
- How would this affect your work together?

In this chapter, we will focus on two aspects of self – self-esteem and locus of control. Self-esteem is the overall value one places on oneself as a person (Baumeister et al., 2003). Locus of control is the extent to which one believes one has power over events in their life (Fournier, 2016). Research shows that addressing these two areas of self leads to higher job satisfaction (Judge and Bono, 2001). We will therefore explore how each of these constructs develops, how to spot whether your clients have high or low self-esteem, or an internal or external locus of control. We look at the consequences of low self-esteem and external internal locus of control. We will then introduce you to some tools and techniques you might like to use to develop healthy self-esteem and internal locus of control in your clients. Should you find that your clients' self-esteem is damaged and/or they have a poor locus of control, you can focus on reparative work, helping to rebuild these essential components of self. The exercises we will show you in this chapter, to help move someone from good to great, can also be used to move someone from poor to good.

Self-esteem

What is self-esteem?

Self-esteem is the overall value people place on themselves as a person (Baumeister et al., 2003). It has two significant parts: Self-evaluation of competence and self-evaluation of worth, the latter part being devoid of how efficacious you are. Self-evaluation of worth is simply about how much you accept and like yourself. Researchers believe self-esteem is the most fundamental manifestation of core self-evaluation because it represents the overall value an individual place on themselves (Judge & Cable, 1997). High self-esteem refers to a highly favourable evaluation of the self, whereas low self-esteem refers to an unfavourable evaluation of the self. People with low self-esteem will be uncertain or negative about themselves (Baumeister et al., 2003). Having high self-esteem is crucial for your clients to achieve work-life balance, as it enables them to be assertive, to ask for what they want and need, and to say no to the wrong task or project. It also acts as a buffer, providing protection from experiences that would otherwise be harmful to their sense of self (Longmore & DeMaris 1997) and improving resilience. As you help improve your clients' self-esteem, they will value themselves more and spend time doing things that are a priority to them. Self-esteem will also affect how others perceive them, and they will be better at 'impression management' and influencing others' decisions. So, for example, how worthy your clients feel for the next role within their company will be expressed by their demeanour, and their confidence in themselves will give confidence to those making decisions about them. The benefits of high self-esteem are innumerable (Baumeister, 2013): Happiness and initiative are the two spurs of a host of positive outcomes. As you become adept at understanding and enhancing clients' self-esteem, you exponentially affect their lives positively.

How does self-esteem develop?

The known antecedents of self-esteem are how one is valued and accepted as growing up; no opinion is more sought than their parents', and so it is found that our self-esteem is directly related to the experiences we had as a child (Leary et al., 1995).

According to the Attachment Theory, it is the care we receive in the first 18 months of life that affects our self-esteem the most: That level of care also affects our feelings about other aspects of self, our safety, our security, and our ability to form bonds with others (Bowlby, 1973). Those people who had a primary caregiver who showed them consistent love and care and who encouraged them to develop a sense of ownership will have 'stable' self-esteem. They know what they can and can't do, and they know what they like about themselves. For those whose primary caregiver was either dismissive of them or delivered inconsistent care, then the sense of self-esteem will probably be damaged. These individuals tend to worry, ignore emotions, find it difficult to trust people, and constantly look to others for reassurance. They may have self-worth based on obtaining others' approval, having love and support from family, or having God's love (Park, Crocker & Mickelson, 2004). People often develop narcissistic traits if they have been spoiled as a child with parents worshipping the ground they walk on or if they have suffered neglect or emotional abuse during childhood (Johnston & Smith, 2017).

Reflecting on your own practice:

- How well do you know your clients' early parental care?
- How well do you recognise symptoms of poor self-esteem, such as your client not being assured, feeling uncomfortable with their emotions and/or having a neurotic need for approval?

These early patterns can be exceedingly difficult to change. Dr Ulrich Orth and Dr Richard W. Robins distilled insights from two longitudinal studies with large, diverse samples (Orth, Robins & Widaman, 2012; Orth, Trzesniewski & Robins, 2010). They found that self-esteem increases throughout adolescence to middle adulthood and reaches its peak at around 60 years of age (Orth & Robins, 2014). They found that self-esteem decreases at an accelerating rate into old age, as people lose their health, autonomy, status, and power.

Other factors affect self-esteem throughout life, such as significant life experiences, traumatic events, workplace intimidation, bad luck, lack of money, use of drugs, or how much rejection or social acceptance one receives. Self-esteem is lowered by negative experiences like failure, criticism, and rejection. There is a concern about the effect of social media on young people's self-esteem. Self-esteem and self-acceptance are often injured by comparison to one's peers, a phenomenon we see in young people, particularly those who compare themselves to others on social media. Those who engage in frequent social comparisons report guilt, regret, and blame (White et al., 2006).

Consequences of low and high self-esteem

Psychologists have argued that self-esteem is a fundamental human need (Allport, 1955). We all tend to try to protect, maintain, and enhance our feelings of self-worth (Crocker & Park, 2004). Having self-esteem acts as protection: It strengthens our resilience and coping strategies when we encounter stressors (Zeigler-Hill, 2013; Arndt & Goldenberg, 2002) and negative feedback (Koole & Kuhl, 2003). High self-esteem is strongly linked to long-term happiness (Baumeister et al., 2003). It is also linked to levels of felt affection, energy, alertness, calmness, and singleness of purpose (Epstein, 1979). Those with high self-esteem are significantly less likely to develop depression and anxiety (Whisman & Kwon, 1993). Moreover, individuals with high self-esteem are more likely to act on their beliefs and values, be more likely to speak up in groups, to challenge others, and to start conversations with others (Baumeister, 2013).

Low self-esteem has consistently been linked with poor health, such as higher body fat mass (Trzesniewski et al., 2006), heart disease (Forthofer et al., 2001), and smoking (Yang & Schaninger, 2010). Individuals with low self-esteem are more likely to experience an increase in psychological and somatic problems in connection with ordinary stressful daily events (DeLongis, Folkman and Lazarus, 1988; Whisman and Kwon, 1993). So if your clients seem to react to normal amounts of stressors with disproportional psychological stress or physical ill-health or come across as a pushover, you might want to investigate their self-esteem, as this may be impacting their work-life balance.

You can see that self-esteem is a critical component of success, happiness, and well-being. As your clients understand themselves more, they will be more likely to stretch outside of their comfort zone, try out new behaviours, and therefore, grow. In the process of that growth, it is likely they will feel inauthentic for a while because they will be doing things that are 'not like themselves'. You can reassure them that 'feeling fake' is often a sign of growth; it is merely stepping outside of what they usually do. Soon the new behaviour will feel normal and will be incorporated in a revised and refreshed authentic self.

The good news is that self-esteem can be learned and developed, even in adulthood, as it is built on our thoughts of ourselves. In this chapter, we will show how to look out for those with either high and low self-esteem and provide you with some techniques to help increase self-esteem. This knowledge and skills will set you up for enhanced professionalism and potency.

How can you recognise and identify varying levels of self-esteem in your clients?

As you become more aware of the level of your clients' self-esteem, you will understand the rationale behind a number of their behaviours, and you will reach the core of their mental or behavioural issues, finding the pivotal essence for their ongoing success.

Low self-esteem

If your clients have low self-esteem, you may find that they:

- Make lots of statements about what they are not good at, where they have made mistakes, and what they don't know and can't do.
- Regularly mention that other people are better than they are.
- Are unsure of their ability.
- Have doubts about whether they can do what is expected of them.
- Have received 360-degree or other feedback and have overreacted.
- Have said in so many words that they feel insignificant.
- Have had feedback from others that they lack interpersonal skills.
- Accentuate the negative.
- Appear reluctant to take on experiments and rehearsals in the coaching or mentoring sessions.
- Are also hesitant in taking on challenges or new tasks.
- Continuously make harsh or unfair comments of themselves.
- Are awkward at the beginning of each coaching or mentoring session.
- Have a lack of eye contact.
- Have a soft handshake or a too hard handshake.
- Avoid discussions about emotions.
- Have closed body language.

CASE STUDY

Lucy was working in a multinational FMCG company on the graduate programme. A coach was asked to coach her, as she had just got promoted, and the organisation wanted her to realise her potential as she was recognised as one of the high flyers. When the coach first met her, she walked into the room with her eyes mostly averted to the ground. The coach greeted her with a big warm smile and her hand, which she shook with a low grip and very softly said hello. During the first coaching session, Lucy informed the coach that she had received negative feedback recently about her presence in meetings and some of the work she had been producing. She explained to the coach that she doesn't believe that she deserved the promotion and that she was well outside of her comfort zone. She then went onto explain how there are so many other graduates who are better and worthier of the promotion than she was. Following the feedback, she started dwelling on the comments and making an assumption about what people thought about her, which wasn't necessarily true.

It became apparent to the coach that Lucy had low self-esteem. When the coach explored this further, it stemmed from her childhood, where she battled for many years about the way that she looked. During our sessions, they focused on thinking through the consequences of her self-esteem on her performance and building her self-esteem through reframing, running a 360-degree feedback that focused on her strengths, positive visualisations, acting, and understanding her values. Over time, her whole manner, body language, and voice changed, as did her opinion of herself and her abilities; she increased her responsibilities and ownership, to the delight of her boss and friends.

Give some time now to think through how you would approach this client if you were their coach or mentor?

High self-esteem

If your clients have high self-esteem, you may find that:

- They will readily tell you what they are good at and aren't so good at.
- They talk about their work as being valuable and valued in the organisation.
- They can articulate with assurance their strengths, capabilities, developments, and hopes.
- They appear to have a good social and family life, with solid relationships.
- Their boss says that in meetings, they are appropriately visible and verbal.
- They do not get worked up/are not oversensitive about work or personal issues.
- They are comfortable with asking colleagues how they feel.
- They tell you about when they have given praise to others, with fluidity.

- Any feedback received from others is considered and worked on where appropriate.
- They appear to have a collaborative approach, where they appreciate diversity and allow people they work with to be their true self.
- They sit erect and hold themselves well.
- Their voice is nicely audible and not too loud.
- Their handshake is firm but not crushing, nor is it weak.
- Their face is relaxed in repose.
- They smile appropriately.

Excessively high self-esteem

It is likely if you are working with executives that you will come across narcissists, and it is not uncommon to find them at the top of organisations. Narcissism is when self-esteem becomes inflated. It originated in Greek mythology, Narcissus fell in love with his image reflected in a pool of water. Those with narcissism are thought to be self-centred, have an unrealistic view of their accomplishments, preoccupy themselves with thoughts of success, and need to seek excessive admiration from others (Kernis, 2013). Often successful people engage in narcissistic behaviour; for example, politicians or even entrepreneurs can exhibit narcissistic behaviour. Narcissists may be charming, so you don't notice them at first, but it is important to understand the condition of narcissism so you can do good work not only for that person but for the people who work with them also. Narcissists are usually insecure, a trait that they hide through bravado. They usually have an inner conflict of inadequacy and a need for attention. If your clients have too high self-esteem and are narcissistic, you may find they:

- Constantly talk about themselves as pivotal in every aspect of every project.
- Have high and urgent ambitions, suspiciously grandiose with unlimited fantasies of success, power, and their own brilliance.
- Respond to feedback with anger.
- Expect a lot from you in between sessions.
- Are not interested in or considerate about others.
- Change appointment times of coaching or mentoring sessions with little regard for the inconvenience doing so causes.
- Say that their direct reports are incompetent.
- Do not appear interested in people that are not directly going to serve them.
- Are not sympathetic to others.
- Seek to take advantage of others.
- Responses to other people's difficulties that show a lack of empathy.
- Rarely praise others or talk about who they admire.
- Have been accused of being arrogant by others.
- Command too much space.
- Fill the room with their voice.
- Crush your hand on a handshake.
- Stare into your eyes or look through you.

CASE STUDY

Luke is the CEO of a medium-sized business in the UK. There had been a recent run of resignations from people who had been with the company for over 20 years; indeed, most of the senior management had left. His Finance Director suggested he come for coaching. In the first coaching, he came across very charming, driven, and engaging. However, the coach was quite shocked to hear him speak about his team, which he did in a very derogatory manner. As the sessions progressed, the coach kept noticing some recurring patterns of behaviours: He lacked empathy for his team, and he spoke very highly of himself and proclaimed outlandish expectations of his future breadth of success such as 'to be a billionaire from a global business within five years'. Therefore, it became apparent quite early on that Luke was, potentially, a narcissistic.

Because of these warning signs the coach was receiving, the coach thought it would be good to do a 360-degree feedback with his peers and direct reports. This generated such rich insight. His peers and direct reports claimed that 'he's very self-centred – the business revolved around him', 'his rules don't apply to him', 'he wants everything done his way', 'he wouldn't keep to his processes', and 'he does not take feedback well'. The coach decided to follow Luke round for a day. In the team meeting, the coach observed he had an overpowering presence in the room, he interrupted and spoke over his team and cancelled the agenda to follow a topic he was interested in. The coach also witnessed two outbursts in the day, which aligned with the 360-degree feedback that said he wanted everything his way. When the coach reviewed what they had witnessed, being careful to avoid any judgement, just using description language, he became very defensive and denied that was what happened.

There came an opening for change when Luke described how he would like to expand into new territories in China. The coach had just read a study that showed humility was a character trait of successful Western leaders in that country. They discussed that humility could be demonstrated by asking for feedback and acting on it, learning from criticism, making it safe for people to criticise, admitting mistakes, and being committed to the success of your team. When the coach framed our ongoing work as helping him be successful in China by working on those things, he relaxed and was amenable. What he learned in those sessions, even though it was aimed at his work in China, became fodder for change in his behaviour with the UK team.

Give some time now to think through how you would approach this client if you were their coach or mentor?

How to explore the causes of low or overly high self-esteem

Trying to understand the cause of low self-esteem or overly high self-esteem before discussing ways to move to a more optimal level of self-esteem may be revealing. As previously discussed, low self-esteem often derives from child-hood, when a person in authority (usually a parent) neglected, abused, or bul-lied the person. Excessive high self-esteem can develop as a result of parents spoiling the person when they were younger: Failing to set adequate discipline and giving excessive praise to the child (Ramsey et al., 1996). If it turns out to be a deep-rooted problem, stemming from childhood, it might be that clients could benefit from counselling simultaneously or going to counselling before resuming coaching or mentoring.

We believe there are helpful questions that will enable your clients to under-stand their drivers and some of their inhibitors, and these questions can also help you both unpack the origin and underlying cause of their low or overly high self-esteem. This discovery of the clients' world is essential, but of course most of us are not therapists, and our focus is on the future. We outline a few prompts to help you with this conversation below:

- If it's all right with you, rather than just taking a snapshot of where you are right now, I would like to appreciate the context by looking at the whole movie of your life, going right back to when you were born, your family, your early life, and school life.
- So tell me when you were born?
- Who was in the family and where were you all living?
- Tell me something about your mother – how would you describe her character? Did she work?
- What was her relationship like with your father?
- Tell me something about your father?
- What was your relationship like with him?
- Tell me about your brothers and sisters. When did they arrive? How close are you with them?
- Who looked after you the first couple of years?
- How was school? What were you good at?
- Did you have any ambitions or daydreams about what you wanted to be?
- Talk me through senior school.
- How did your parents respond to your success?
- And how did they discipline you?
- What were the two most significant things that happened to you before you were 21?
- Talk me through the next few years and your career choices.
- What do you do for fun?
- What effect has marriage/partner relationships had on your life?
- [For clients with children] How has being a parent been?

- What more do you think, feel, or want to say?
- What do you need more or less of in your life to have optimal self-esteem?

Asking your clients to draw out their timeline can also be powerful. Invite your clients to draw a horizontal and vertical line on a blank sheet of paper. On the horizontal line, the left-hand side signifies their birth, and the right-hand side means their age now. On the vertical line, the top end signifies feelings of joy, happiness, contentment, and energy and the bottom end of the line signifies feelings of despondency, isolation, unhappiness, grief, and misery. Step 1 involves inviting your clients drawing the key events that have shaped their lives, both positively and negatively. Encourage them not to overthink it and to do it spontaneously. A blank example of the template can be seen in Figure 2.2.

Step 2 involves reflecting on their pictures. Assure them that they can say as much as they would like to disclose at specific points in their life. We provide a number of prompt questions (see Table 2.1) which your clients may wish to record their answers so they can reflect at a later stage.

Whether your clients' self-esteem is derived from adulthood or childhood, as a coach or mentor, finding out the underlying cause before working with your clients to identify behaviours to change is mandatory. Very often you need to do no more than finding the cause, as knowing the cause can be curative because your clients will most likely be able to work out what they need to do. We have one client who, when they realised their poor self-worth was from the comments of one teacher, some 45 years earlier, was able to see the folly in carrying it around with them and simply dropped it, there and then. They were clever enough to move forward immediately without that drag of negative criticism damaging their sense of possibility.

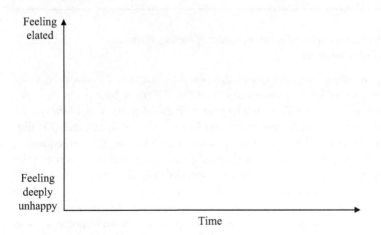

Figure 2.2 Your timeline (step 1)

Table 2.1 Exploring your timeline (step 2)

What patterns or themes do you notice?
Describe what made the high points so positive. What did it feel like?
What was it really like to be at those lows? What actions did you take to make them better?
What contributed to your highs and lows? (For example, your attitude, personality, skills.)
What do you need more or less of in your life to have optimal self-esteem?
What do you want to create that hasn't happened yet? What do you want to bring back into your life?

How to help clients explore the consequences of having their current level of self-esteem

Enabling your clients to understand the benefits, costs, and consequences of having their current level of self-esteem is useful. Clients who have been experiencing low self-esteem will see it affecting their life in some negative ways; for instance, low self-esteem is a predictor and a consequence of burnout (Dahlin, Joneborg & Runeson, 2007). You may help your clients see the consequences of low self-esteem. For example, if they don't ask for resources and they take on too much work, they might become overloaded; they might find it too hard to say 'no' to colleagues and bosses and end up with too much work to do. They also may sacrifice important aspects of their life, they might not speak out in meetings or conferences, they might be passed over on opportunities to work on interesting projects, and they might miss out on promotion.

When you explore the consequences of changing their self-esteem you will drive up their motivation to change. As they start to value themselves more realistically, what will it be like for them to be able to ask for help or resources?

Or say 'no' to requests? What will change for them when they are not over-loaded from taking on too much work? What will change for them if they feel their voice is valuable and they speak out more? Some coaches or mentors literally co-create with their clients a picture, an image of how, by having optimum self-esteem, the clients can carve out a more balanced life or one that meets their needs better. To encourage your clients to think through a variety of consequences, you might like to use some of the following questions as prompts:

- How is your self-esteem affecting what you really want to do?
- How is your self-esteem impacting your career progression?
- Are you true to yourself or are you ignoring your own values?
- If you were totally comfortable with yourself and everyone else was very comfortable with you, what would change with respect to what you felt and what you did?
- If you knew you were or could get competent, what would you do?
- What would be better in your life if you had a more realistic view of your self-worth?
- When you are able to manage your sense of self-worth better, what will be different?
- How would you like to be more socially skilled?
- How would you like your body or appearance to change?
- How will having the right balance of self-esteem change your work-life balance? What would change at work? What would change in your personal life? Who would benefit? How important is that to you?

Coaching or mentoring those with extremely high self-esteem who display narcissistic traits is challenging. A conversation about their self-esteem must be managed carefully, and to do this you need to gain their trust by showing acknowledgement of their need to be recognised. Good practice suggests that we should neither collude and reinforce grandiose self-perceptions nor accentuate weaknesses, as this could frighten the narcissist (de Vries, 2014). If your clients have traits of narcissism, you may find that they have a predisposition towards workaholism and consequently, burnout (Schwarzkopf et al., 2016). Since they often have high expectations, research shows that emotional exhaustion and depersonalisation (characterised by alienation from work) may follow when goals aren't achieved (Maslach, Schaufeli & Leiter, 2001). If your clients are experiencing this, help them understand the consequences on their work, family, friends, and physical and mental health, as well as what their loved ones may feel will be valuable.

Some questions to encourage reflection on the consequences for those with excessively high self-esteem are:

- How might others view you if you continue to underestimate their needs/abilities?
- What do you think is going to happen if you do not show them empathy?

- How do others see you and how could this affect your future?
- How may acting in a way that affronts others affect your relationships?
- If you are so focused on achieving, how may it affect your work-life balance and your overall success?
- Are you being true to yourself and sticking to your values? Or are you ignoring your values?
- When did you last celebrate the successes of others? Praise them?
- What do you appreciate about your team? How could you show your appreciation more?

Be aware that narcissists often struggle to ascertain how and why they annoy others as they often believe they are not in the wrong. So when the time is right to start confronting their dysfunctional behaviour, be sure not to be overly critical, as this is when narcissists often respond with anger. To add to this, people with excessively high self-esteem are often not aware they have a problem, nor the detrimental impact they may have on people surrounding them (Lubit, 2002). Helping them gain insight may stabilise their inflated self-esteem. Consider running 360-degree feedback and observing them at work; doing these two things may be revealing, because in sessions, they may just appear confident.

As mentioned previously, coaching or mentoring a narcissist is challenging and can have a draining effect on you as the coach or mentor. In chapter 6, we talk about the importance of self-care and tangible things you can do to take good care of yourself.

Tools and techniques to help your clients improve their self-esteem

The ABCDE method of helping clients reframe

Psychologist Albert Ellis created the ABC model (1957) to explain how beliefs caused emotional and behavioural responses. This model can also be called the ABCDE model, wherein the last two steps are made explicit. This model can be used to help clients reframe how they think about a situation. It can also guide them to create new patterns of thinking, reinforce positive patterns, and inhibit negative ones. Ellis used the term 'find the insane part' of their story in amongst the sane part: What part is not true, is a thinking error, is a cognitive distortion, is a wild assumption? The five elements of the ABCDE method are:

- Activating event – the event that triggers the stress or worry (i.e. a conversation with their boss regarding negative feedback, a presentation or job dissatisfaction). Help your clients be objective and specific about the event, specifying the who, what, when, and where of the situation.
- Belief system – the cognitive component in the clients' reaction to events (i.e. I'm never good enough or I think my boss is trying to manage me out). Inquire about their self-talk at the time of the adversity; what were they saying to themselves? What is the underlying belief?

- Consequences of A and B – emotional consequences of these irrational beliefs (i.e. rumination). Draw out how they were feeling and what they did.
- Disputing irrational thoughts and beliefs – challenge the clients' irrational beliefs as directly as possible by asking them to point out any inaccuracies in their beliefs. Then encourage them to think about the problem event in a more realistic and helpful way by generating a more accurate belief about the event.
- Effects – cognitive and emotional effects of changing one's interpretation of the event (i.e. cognitive restructuring and thus anxiety decreases). Ask clients to see what's happened to their state of mind and the lessons they've learnt.

To bring this alive, an example is below:

- Activating event – a client, who was working in an investment bank, was unsure of her boss's perception of her, as he had cancelled her performance review for the second time.
- Belief – she believed that her lack of academic qualification was hindering her promotion.
- Consequences of A and B – having these beliefs, meant that she was not putting herself forward for stretching roles, so she was unable to prove that she was ready for promotion.
- Disputing irrational thoughts and beliefs – the coach asked the following questions to help dispute these thoughts: Are there people without other qualifications at the next level? Has your boss ever said this to you or is this an assumption you are holding? What would it be like for you to ask your boss outright if this is an inhibitor? Having dropped the negative thought, what does that energise you to do?
- Effects – this questioning gave her confidence to ask her boss outright whether she needed other qualifications, to which he responded no. This gave her the confidence to believe that she could take a position at the next level. Now she just needed to prove that she could be stepping outside of her comfort zone and start to lead a team.

This technique can help clients have a rational and realistic voice and thus constructive self-talk. You may want to reassure your clients that this is something that needs practice. As your clients practice this technique, they would do well to monitor their beliefs and the accuracy of their beliefs; this makes the work generative.

Self-appreciation

Self-acceptance and self-appreciating are crucial to mental health. The absence of them can lead to uncontrolled anger or depression (Carson & Langer, 2006). We are each a 'work in progress', and coaching or mentoring can help clients gain perspective and take actions in line with the values they hold and what is important to them even in the midst of compromises and difficulties.

There are many ways to helping your clients gain self-acceptance and self-appreciation. Here are few that you might not have tried:

- Write down all the people they spend time with and think about why these people like them.
- Write a list of all the reasons why they would like themselves if they were someone else.
- Reframe difficulties as positives (for instance M15 and M16 are now actively recruiting those with autism and Asperger's syndrome because they are brilliant at focusing and spotting patterns that most other people miss).
- Write a list of their top seven qualities and carry them around with them, reading them occasionally to remind themselves why they are unique and what they can easily exhibit.
- Try mindfulness with them and as a practice in between sessions because it develops the capacity to notice things without judgement.
- Look back at a 360-degree appraisal or generate a 360-degree appraisal with only positive comments. This exercise could take the form of asking a few people to write about 'their possibility': what would they love to see their person growing into that is entirely feasible yet also inspiring? This latter exercise works best as team coaching or mentoring activity or in a situation where you can brief the participants well.

This technique is not appropriate if your clients display narcissistic traits.

Self-reflection on achievements and strengths

Sometimes in the telling of the stories of difficulties, we can lose focus on the positives. To remind your clients of their achievements, ask them to:

- Look back through performance appraisals, feedback, or boss's references and remember the good things people have said about them.
- Reflect on all their achievements, pulling out their key strengths.
- Reflect on what they want (we can hear a lot about what is happening that they don't like) in the situation.

This technique is probably not appropriate if your clients display narcissistic traits.

Positive affirmations

You probably know that positive affirmations are a technique focusing on the positive rather than the negative and involves repeating a positive statement, such as 'I can make my own choices and decisions'. The idea is that by repeating these statements twice a day, the brain reconditions itself and changes the way you feel and think. You might not know, however, about a particular form of positive affirmation that is thought to be superior to ordinary positive affirmations in its effectiveness in changing behaviour, and that form is called Implementation Affirmation. It has a specific structure, with two parts 'When x happens, I will do y'. For example, if you have clients with low self-esteem who don't speak out in meetings enough, a pertinent implementation affirmation might be:

- 'When I have an idea in a meeting, I will not wait until the idea is perfectly formed but I will speak out and offer my suggestion at the earliest opportunity.'

Or, if you have clients that you suspect have low self-esteem and who keep taking on more and more work without any new resources, the affirmation might be:

- 'When I'm asked by my boss to do yet another task, I will say, "Of course. But let's prioritise together my workload now".'

You might like to generate a few ideas for clients' Implementation Affirmations and work on making a couple for yourself to describe to your clients.

Source information from others

Since our beliefs largely affect our self-esteem about how much other people value us, a simple way of raising self-esteem is to help your clients feel comfortable about performing what for some is an embarrassing act – to ask several people what they like about them. Have them dare to ask their family and friends what they see as their strengths. They might prefer you did it for them but resist. Ideally, you will practice with them how to ask friends or family and how to receive a compliment. Rehearsing how it might be done can soften their resistance, and if they do it, it makes the experience/what is said more memorable. Then they are equipped to do the same thing in an ongoing way, long after your relationship with them has ended. In the rehearsals, we have found that helping them receive a compliment is just as important as asking for feedback. Most people tend to brush off a compliment with a dash of humour or look down and shuffle their feet: By helping them practice merely standing their ground, looking at the other person in the eye and saying, 'thank you' slowly and clearly and loudly, you are prepping them for a good experience. We ask our clients to prepare to tell the other person what they also like about them, which adds a surprise to the conversation that the other person isn't expecting. This has been found to be a very bonding exercise and deepens the relationship. It also has opened the way, in many cases, to other honest and positive feedback encounters between the people involved.

Experiment with your clients

Ask them to experiment in their day-to-day life through 'acting as if' they already have the optimum amount of self-esteem. Have them notice how it felt, what was different and what outcome was achieved. You can explore with them their views and imaginings: What would you be like if you had a different upbringing? How would you sit differently? How would you sound? How would you be with me? What might have you worn? Where might you be prepared to go? How might you respond differently? What work might you do? Where would you live? You may like to consider the following exercise.

On pieces of paper or cards, write 10%, 20%, 30%, and so on until 100%. If there is space in the room you are in, put them down on the floor in order. Invite your clients to step on 10%. Ask them if they had 10% more self-esteem what would they do? Then ask them to step on 20%; if they had 20% more self-esteem what would they do? Continue until you get to 100%.

If the space you are working in isn't big enough, hand them the pieces of paper one by one.

Alternatively, they could fill out the following template (Table 2.2) and keep it as a reminder.

Positive role models

You might want to help your clients consider people who seem to have an optimistic and positive sense of self about their ability and worth. You can begin by asking your clients what it is they like, respect, and value about them.

Table 2.2 Building self-esteem

If you had…	What would you do that would be different?	What would you see that would be different?	What would you feel that would be different?
10% more self-esteem			
20% more self-esteem			
30% more self-esteem			
50% more self-esteem			
100% more self-esteem			

You could explore what these people do that your clients don't do, what they sound like, and what attitudes they have. Encourage your clients to spend time with them (i.e. watching them on video, thinking about them, or asking others about them). Ask your clients to think about their body language, what words they used, and what actions they've taken. Ask them to 'try on' that behaviour, to mimic them even in your sessions, so that they adopt their persona in a safe space. We all learn through imitation (the psychological term is imprinting). They might like to role-play with you in a session. From there, you can ask your usual debrief questions around what they thought of doing, what they noticed, what option they had in their head, and how they feel. It is a short extrapolation from there to seek what aspects they might be willing to try out in real life, as an experiment.

Journaling

Writing a diary of thoughts is a common reflective tool. The mere act of writing down thoughts and feelings can be cathartic, can release tension, and can change behaviour. By going over what was written and analysing the content, one can gain greater insight. Many clients might be willing to share with you their journaling or at least their reflections about journaling and what it throws up for them about their sense of confidence, worth, and potency. We will go into more detail about this in chapter 4.

Assertiveness for personal power

Many people with low self-esteem have issues with assertiveness. Assertiveness has been defined as a socially acceptable assertion of rights and feelings (Eisler, Miller & Hersen, 1973). Many clients with low or high self-esteem may veer between submissiveness through to passiveness to outright aggression. They may not have learned to discern the differences nor develop the skills to self-manage. You can work with their past critical experiences and tease out where they were on the continuum, or you might like to role-play a forthcoming situation and work out with them how they acted on the continuum. Following on from that, you could explore with them their ideas on behaving differently along the continuum and role-play again to see how they did and how they felt about it. You can lead discussions with them on the repercussions of acting in any particular way and explore alternative assertive ways of responding. Then role-play with them again so that they can practice in a safe environment. You may keep the role-plays focused around asserting their work-life balance rights and wishes.

Active Constructive Response (ACR)

This is a methodology you may not be used to – it comes from the military training in social skills. It is called ACR, and it aims to strengthen relationships through active, constructive responding (Gable et al., 2004). You could explain the four styles:

- Active constructive (offering authentic, enthusiastic support).
- Passive constructive (mildly offering understated support).
- Passive destructive (ignoring the event/person/issue).
- Active destructive (pointing out negative aspects of the event, suggestion, person).

You could act out several scenarios and discuss the four styles. When someone acts in ACR, they feel better about themselves, and the other players they are engaging with have better relationships.

You could also invite your clients to use the following template (see Table 2.3) to reflect on their behaviour.

Adopt a growth mindset

Based on the work of Professor Carol Dweck (2008), you could imbue in your clients to praise their effort, strategy, or skill (with less focus on the outcome, more focus on the input). This is a counterculture approach; most organisational appraisals are outcome-oriented, but it has been found to foster a 'growth mindset' where the person feels inspired to keep trying and develop. It acknowledges the detail and effort made. You could experiment with your clients giving and taking praise focused on effort, strategy, or skill rather than outcome.

Use of imagery

Visualisation is a proven technique for helping people change behaviour. A simple form of this would be to ask your clients to imagine themselves in a past situation but this time having optimal self-esteem. Ask them how they stood, sat, walked, talked, responded, and initiated conversations. Ask them

Table 2.3 Reflecting on how you respond

What was the scenario?	In what style did you respond?	How could you have responded better?	If you responded in ACR, what would you do, feel, and see that would be different?

how they felt. Now ask them to visualise themselves with optimal self-esteem in something coming up immediately after the coaching or mentoring session. The more detail they see and hear the better; encourage them to imagine the visualisation is life-sized, directly in front of them, full colour, and surround-sound – check in with them how it feels to have that optimal self-esteem.

As a coach or mentor, you might lead them through a visualisation. To get comfortable with this, listen to a few experts in visualisation on YouTube, such as Paul McKenna (2016). Then I would recommend that you create your visualisation examples and rehearse and hone them before using them with your clients.

Research shows that self-esteem may be a predictor of internal locus of control (Faitz, 2012), so we shall next work with locus of control.

Internal locus of control

What is locus of control?

Internal locus of control is an individual's sense of potency: How much they feel and think they can affect a situation, influence other people, and govern the outcome of events (Nowicki & Strickland, 1973). People with an internal locus of control (called 'internals'), believe in their ability to control a situation and influence those around them. People with an external locus of control (called 'externals') believe they have little control over people or situations – that people, luck, or fate will predict the outcome. What do you think you are? Whichever you are as a coach or mentor will impact on the coaching or relationship with your clients, how you see their situation, and their options. We will investigate this further as we explore the construct.

Psychologists view locus of control as a crucial construct, which originated from Rotter's (1954) Social Learning Theory. This theory posits that people learn from one another through direct experience or observing the behaviour of others and that rewards and punishments form their behavioural patterns. Internal locus of control was developed to explain why some individuals ignore rewards that reinforce behaviour and punishments that inhibit behaviour (Manz and Sims, 1980). The reason why some people do not respond to rewards and punishments is attributed to their locus of control, which gives them a 'generalised expectancy' that, if they are internals, they have control over others' behaviour, a situation, and outcomes, and if they are externals, they don't have control over these things.

How does locus of control develop?

The end of childhood usually shapes this construct. Carton and Nowicki (1994) found four things:

1. Children who developed an external locus of control tended to have parents who were very controlling, whereas children who developed an internal locus of control had parents who gave them more autonomy.

2. Children developed an external locus of control if they experienced some life stressors (such as father's absence due to divorce or death or by intense marital breakdown).
3. Children developed an internal locus of control when they had parents who were warm, emotionally supportive, and nurturing.
4. Internal locus of control was developed when parents gave firm, consistent, and fair responses, rewards, and punishments.

It is worth knowing that if you are a coach going for accreditation with the International Coaching Federation (ICF), you need to be careful in how much you dwell on the past, as applicants do not receive a pass score if they frequently ask information that relates to their past. Other governing coaching or mentoring bodies like the European Mentoring & Coaching Council (EMCC), Accreditation for Coaching, and the Association for Professional for Executive Coaching and Supervision (APECS) do not have this restriction. We believe that there is enough research to prove that early life impacts on adult life perceptions, choices, personality, and behaviour, and therefore early life is not only an acceptable topic but an essential topic. You will, of course, want to move the focus into the future at an appropriate stage in the session.

When we look at how locus of control develops, forms and manifests in the population, we see an interesting story. Locus of control is spread along a normal distribution continuum in the population, with around 68% falling into the external or the internal category; 27% being highly one way or another, and 5% having an extreme external or internal locus of control (Johnson et al., 1998).

Like many of our personality traits, we tend to change in middle-age: People tend to have a more internal locus of control as they develop the skills, strategies, and capabilities to deal with life. However, in old age, as individuals become more dependent on others, they tend to move towards an external locus of control orientation. Those seniors who do maintain an internal locus of control, however, are considerably healthier than those who move to external (Johnson et al., 1998).

No one will either have a fully internal or external locus of control, as people swing along the continuum according to the situation and influences around them. Some people are more internal at home but more external at work (or vice versa). Unfortunate life events totally outside of people's control, like hurricane disasters or sudden death of close loved ones, may increase an external mindset and behaviour. Extremes of either end of the continuum can be detrimental, for instance, if someone is extremely internal they might ignore facts, fail to listen to sound advice, and disregard those in power, to their later chagrin. Men, in particular, tend to veer to extreme internal mindsets in the face of uncontrollable life events (Sherman, Higgs and Williams 1997).

Consequences of having an internal locus of control

Internals believe they can shape the future through making the right choices and decisions. As you can imagine, this, in turn, makes them more confident and often more successful at work. This was confirmed by a meta-analysis by Judge et al. (2001), who found that locus of control was one of the key factors that are correlated with more satisfaction and success in job performance (Judge et al., 2001). Internals tend to aim higher and strive for achievement. This is because they believe they have the power to accomplish what they set out to do and they tend to be resourceful, actively seeking information and support from others who will help them influence the situation and other people. They understand that the outcomes will be a result of their effort and attitude. If they succeed, they take the credit, and if they fail, they take ownership. It is because of these factors that internal locus of control has been found to be a key contributor to the success of new business start-ups (Brockhaus, 1982).

There does seem to be a gender split, with females being more external than males (Sherman, Higgs and Williams, 1997). This gender split can be explained by Bronfenbrenner's (1979) ecological theory of human development, which describes how events and perceptions are affected by family, community, and culture. Traditional conditioning of women doesn't value their autonomy and control. Therefore, women end up perceiving of themselves as having less control, and thus this may explain why so many women develop an external locus of control. In the UK, the pay gap was unearthed in an infamous BBC exposure of women doing similar jobs to their male counterparts and having far less pay. Just over half of the BBC staff are men; yet amongst the high earners, two-thirds were male. Moreover, the average woman's salary in Britain is 29% lower than the average man's (The Economist, 2017). This trend is seen across many industries in most countries. Individualistic cultures (like the USA, Australia, Canada, Germany, the UK,) tend to develop and value internals, whereas collectivist countries (Japan, China, South Korea, Spain) value externals (Mueller and Thomas, 2001). So you need to be prepared to adjust your approach if your clients are from a collectivist country.

Consequences of having an external locus of control

Externals, on the other hand, are liable to feel hopeless; they give up easily and are prone to feel like a victim. They also tend to be more passive and accepting – they conform to the concept developed by Professor Martin Seligman called 'learned helplessness'. This is a phenomenon named following an experiment where Seligman & Maier (1967) exposed dogs to unavoidable shocks and found that when dogs learned that they still received shocks regardless of how they responded, they gave up trying any new strategy to avoid the shocks. The dogs simply became deflated and whined when they were shocked. Learned helplessness has a knock-on effect on motivation (Maier & Seligman, 1976).

It has been found that lower goal expectation is related to externals (Strassberg, 1973), and externals tend not to be as motivated as internals (Spector, 1982). This leads externals to set lower goals, exhibit lower proactivity, and consequently, attain fewer achievements. It has been shown that there is a relationship between anxiety and locus of control: Externals have higher levels of anxiety (Archer, 1979). Externals are less aggressive and tend not to be overly focused on achieving at all costs. They are usually humble, easy-going, and quick to praise others. Humility has been found to be one of a handful of key traits in leaders of successful companies (Collins, 2007) and is seen as a virtuous character trait (Peterson & Seligman, 2004). Externals often work well with others, share the credit, and don't brag.

Like self-esteem, although one's upbringing shapes locus of control, it can be developed in adulthood. The following section will provide you with tips on how to work out where your clients are on the locus-of-control spectrum and give you tools and techniques to use with your clients to help them develop a healthy internal locus of control. This will empower your clients to do the things they deem important and want to do, and will affect the situations they feel need changing. The execution of what your clients want to change is dealt with in chapter 5 (decision-making and negotiation with others).

How to spot whether your clients have an internal or external locus of control

If your clients have an internal locus of control, you may find that they:

- Take ownership for success and failure.
- Have a can-do attitude.
- See the possibility in how things can be changed versus accepting the status quo.
- Believe they can persuade and influence people to bend a little to their needs.
- Are confident they can be successful in their own way, on their own terms, if they exert the effort and gain new abilities.
- Have a mindset which seeks to learn and stay ahead of the curve.
- Do not like others having control over them.
- Take personal responsibility for how they spend their time and what they spend their time on.
- Deal with challenges and setbacks in a proactive way.
- Are less likely to bow down to authority.

If your clients have an external locus of control, you may find that they:

- Are demotivated with their work.
- Look for others for direction.
- Blame others or situations.
- Feel like a victim because of bad luck or fate.

- Are conforming and compliant.
- Don't like to rock the boat.
- Focus on the external obstacles to their success.
- Are less self-reliant and rely on others for assurance and justification.
- Give up easily when they meet obstacles they think can't be overcome.
- Are comfortable with being led by others.

How locus of control might impact on work-life balance

The conflict of managing work and personal life causes stress for a large body of people, and those with higher levels of conflict suffer higher levels of psychological distress. Stressors, as we briefly touched on in chapter 1, contribute to the deluge of anxiety and depression and other illnesses. Work stress interferes with personal life (Karkoulian, Srour & Sinan, 2016). The level of perceived stress at work impacts on the relationship between our potency and how much our personal life interferes with work. So, if your clients work in a highly stressful environment, it will impact on their ability to be potent (i.e. to use their internal locus of control) and will allow their personal lives to disturb the working pace, working environment, and workload. Later in this chapter, we will discuss ways to help your clients become potent in these situations. Because people who can balance their work and personal lives report experiencing lower stress levels than those who lack this balance (Ross & Vasantha, 2014).

There are very particular impacts on work-life balance, on those with an external or an internal locus of control. It has been found that internals experience less conflict between work and family demands and have lower perceived job stress (Chen & Silverthorne, 2008). This is because they can cope more effectively with stressful events (Gray-Stanley et al., 2010). When people start to move along the continuum and move from internal to external or external to internal, their work-life balance will be impacted. When externals start to exert more control over their lives i.e. exhibit more internal locus of control, then, they often decrease the interference of work on their personal lives (Karkoulian, Srour & Sinan, 2016). Research indicates that externals have greater work-life-family conflict than internals (Clarke, 2002) and more work and life stress (Noor, 2002). This is unsurprising when you unpack the characteristics of those with an external locus of control, because they believe power lies in the hands of others and they have little autonomy to decide about their work-life balance.

Locus of control affects the mental, emotional, and physical health of your clients. Internals tend to understand that the only thing they can control is themselves – both by what they proactively do and don't do and by how they react to adversity; they can be more emotionally resilient. Many researchers have found that internals also avoid burnout more easily than externals (Schmitz, Neumann & Oppermann, 2000) because they do not feel helpless and are proactive in finding coping strategies or plans to deal with stress.

Research shows that internals have higher job satisfaction and satisfaction with their work-life balance (Spector, 1982). This may be because internals tend to take value-directed and goal-directed actions more frequently than externals and as a result, they perform better and have the benefits of their performance. This, in turn, may lead them to advance quicker, receive more promotions, and have greater satisfaction. In addition to this, according to the Cognitive Consistency Theory (Spector, 1982), internals are more likely to leave a situation if they are dissatisfied, and if they decide not to leave, they re-evaluate the situation favourably to retain consistency between their attitudes and behaviours. Externals, who do not perceive they have control, tend to remain in a dissatisfying situation because they feel helpless about external constraints. They often blame and moan and show little desire to change their attitudes and beliefs into more positive ones or affect the situation to improve it (Spector, 1982).

The key point for you as the coach or mentor is to remind yourself and your clients that people have more choice than they at first think they do; people underestimate their options. Even if they can't change the situation or others, they can work on changing their relationship with the situation or others, i.e. their attitude, beliefs, and behaviours. We find that people undervalue the power of this choice. The importance of recognising and utilising choice is that for those who perceive they have control of a situation, they engage in more proactive coping strategies, reduce conflict, and find more balance in work and life. Your clients are likely to resist the belief that they have more than a binary choice: 'I have to adhere to the way things are done around here, or I leave.' 'If I were run over by a bus tomorrow, no one would miss me.' 'I'm just a cog in a machine to them; they don't care about my wish to be home to put the kids to bed. I've worked this long and hard, and I want that promotion now'.

Effect of gender on work-life balance

It is well documented that women take on 40% more of the household chores than men, with women averaging 26 hours a week and men 16 hours (Office for National Statistics, 2016). Given these facts, running a home and family obviously impacts on women's work-life balance more than men's. Furthermore, gender biases exist in the workplace (Rehman & Roomi, 2012) which affects men's and women's work-life balance differently. Culturally, it is easier for women to ask for time off to look after children or parents than it is for men. Male self-esteem and self-identity are more directly attributed to their work (Karkoulian, Srour & Sinan, 2016). Women are prey to the cultural conditioning that expects them to spend more time at home with their children and be less committed to paid work than men (Watts, 2009).

Research has shown that there is a gender difference in the relationships between locus of control, work-life balance, and perceived stress. Sometimes work is said to 'interfere' with personal life, such as when people neglect personal needs because of work and personal life suffers because of work. Sometimes personal life is said to 'interfere' with work, such as when personal life drains you of energy for work, when it is hard to work because of personal matters, and when it is hard to work because of tiredness. Internals who are female have less work conflict and are more satisfied at work (Ngah, Ahmad & Baba, 2009).

It has been found that when females, with an internal locus of control, perceive their levels of stress to increase, they allow their work lives to interfere with their personal lives (more than asserting their personal life over their work lives). They will neglect their personal health and social needs.

When men who have an internal locus of control perceive their levels of stress to increase, they find their personal lives interfere with their work lives and they feel drained of energy for work (Karkoulian, Srour & Sinan, 2016). An explanation for these findings is that people in organisations are more forgiving and understanding towards females who request time off for family reasons. When men experience work-life conflict, the attitude towards them is far less understanding because they are culturally expected to put work first as a way of looking after their family (Sav, Harris & Sebar, 2013). Flexible working has been found to decrease conflict and stress regarding work-life balance in women, but in men, it has been found to increase their work-life conflict and stress (Hofacker & Konig, 2013). This is possibly because, as Watts (2009) found, men use work as an escape to a calmer atmosphere.

Coaching or mentoring clients who work in a culture of overworking

Directors/lawyers who are working towards Partnership, or managers wishing to be senior managers, exist in highly competitive 'up-or-out' cultures that imbue in people acquiescence to the norm, which makes it really difficult for people to impart their potency around their private goals and needs. We know of a City law firm where people are locked out of their computer if they haven't clocked 5.6 billable hours in a day, and another law firm where there is a dormitory in the basement for people to sleep a few hours as they work later into the night. The dentist there works throughout the night, doing fillings at 3:00 a.m. How would you help a client who is desperate to make promotion in such a culture? You know, from your education, that continuous long hours and lack of sleep harms decision-making, creativity, and problem-solving. It also makes people brusque and short-tempered, which are potentially damaging to relationships. Long-term sleep deprivation harms health. Whose life is it? Does their company own your client's life? It is a big responsibility for you to interrupt any mindless behaviour and help them discover what is really important to them and their broader options before it's too late. George Valliant, a Professor at Harvard Medical School, showed that being engaged with your family, friends, and community gives you the biggest sense of well-being at the end of your life (Valliant, 1977).

Reflecting on your own practice:

- Knowing this, how do you coach or mentor someone caught up in a culture of overworking?
- How can you help them engage their potency in working smart?

Good practice suggests our ethical duty is to help our clients feel empowered to seek to change customs, systems, rules, and procedures that do not respect what it is to be human. In doing so, we help them consider the short- and long-term cost of attempting to affect the cultural rules and traditions within their organisation rather than blindly accepting the norm when it is harmful to their purpose, values, key relationships, and their mental and physical health.

Tools and techniques to improve your clients' internal locus of control

Identify situations they can and can't control

You can help your clients understand what they can and can't control. The first stage is to invite your clients to make a list of all concerns that are currently on their mind. Then rank the concerns from 1–10, or however many there are, 1 being of most concern and 10 of least concern (Table 2.4). Then populate the matrix in Table 2.5.

In the second stage, you will work with your clients to identify if they feel:

- It is something over which they feel they have control.
- It is something they are not able to control but feel that they are able to influence.
- They have little control or influence and should therefore let the issue go.

The third stage involves identifying specific actions or next steps that clients might take, within a feasible and practical timescale. Table 2.5 might be used to assist with this stage.

Table 2.4 Control, influence, or let go

Mark each concern with whether you are: *able to control, able to influence, or are not able to control or influence and should therefore let go*			
Concern	Able to control	Able to influence	Let go
1.			
2.			
3.			

Table 2.5 Action plan

Action or Next Step	Timescale
1.	
2.	
3.	

Challenge their self-limiting thoughts

Our thoughts profoundly influence the way we feel and behave. Professor Daniel Kahneman found that we are all prone to thinking errors and cognitive bias (Kahneman, 2011). Thinking errors and cognitive bias are irrational thinking that impacts judgments and therefore our decisions. Uncovering biases enables people to make better decisions. Often people are unaware of their irrational thinking, so your role as the coach and the mentor, first, is to help your clients recognise these thought patterns. The common thinking errors are:

- Catastrophising: Magnifying the problem and ruminating on irrational worst-case scenarios, or thinking that the causes of negative events are permanent.
- Over personalising: Thinking that the situation is all about you, or you blame self.
- Externalising: Blaming others. Assuming you know what others think or/ and feel that other people should know how you feel even though you haven't told them.
- Negative thinking: Self-criticism or a voice that suggests things will go wrong.
- Overgeneralising: When people come to a conclusion based on a single situation.
- Optimism/Negative thinking: Only seeing the positives and discounting the negative. Or being over-negative and seeing only the negatives and discounting the positive; seeing it as permanent, personal, and pervasive.
- Confirmation thinking: You jump on information or recall information that confirms your preconception before gathering the facts/other views; ignoring other points of view.
- Hyperbolic discounting: A tendency to go for short-term wins.
- All or nothing thinking: Seeing the thing as all or nothing, one thing or another, there is no middle ground. For example: 'I can't affect anything' or 'I have to stay in the office till ten as all my team are staying'.
- The oughts/musts/shoulds: Feels that people should behave in a certain way, feels 'right'.
- Anchoring bias: An over-reliance on past evidence/experience.
- Attentional bias/effect: The tendency to amplify the effect of one piece of evidence, especially when the evidence was emotional.
- Self-serving bias: The tendency to see or present ambiguous data as being beneficial to themselves.

Once you help your clients recognise these self-limiting thoughts, the second step is to challenge their thinking errors. You will need to challenge their thinking by asking if they are holding assumptions or whether their thought is grounded on facts. For example, something I often hear is, 'I can't do any work in normal working hours as I'm in back-to-back meetings all day'. However, with further analysis and planning, they begin to realise they do have a choice to change the situation. Help them see the consequences of thinking in this way and what actions they display when in the grip of these thinking errors.

Going forward, you can encourage your clients to record their thinking errors so that they are then able to figure out when and why these thinking patterns occur. Understanding why thinking errors pop up makes it easier to address and change them. Table 2.6 provides a template which clients can complete.

When moving through the exercise to the reflection stage, consider the following questions:

- Were they able to confront their dysfunctional thoughts?
- What did that feel like?
- What else did you notice?

Table 2.6 Dealing with thinking errors

Date?	Where did it occur?	What thinking error was it?	How can I respond?	Reflection

Challenge their habits

Identify, challenge, and break habits that leak into their personal life by looking at the cost they have on their work-life balance. For example, we often hear that our clients insist on reading their emails on a Sunday so that they are ready for work on Monday – consider questioning why they are doing this. What is the cost of their doing this on their family life and on their rest and recreation time? If there is too much work to do, they need to be assertive and negotiate more resources or say no; otherwise, they are absorbing the workload at the cost of their well-being and relationships. In chapter 5, you can read the conversations clients need to have with themselves and others when negotiating issues that potentially impact work-life balance.

Drive up their autonomy and responsibility

As coaches or mentors, we are able to help our clients step back and gain a sense of what they can and can't control as well as broaden the art of the possible regarding achieving what success looks like for them.

Many clients become stuck into a routine or a way of looking at things in which they don't exercise their autonomy and responsibility: They just do what everyone else is doing even if it clashes with their values and is damaging their health or key relationships or happiness. We have spent entire sessions just with autonomy and responsibility and what unfolded has always been very interesting. Clients have identified that many of their issues are related to these two topics. You can explore what the terms mean to them, how they are living them, and what alternative stances/actions they could experiment with that would give them more ownership and help them feel better about themselves.

Your role as the coach or mentor is to support your clients to take ownership and responsibility in executing their stated plan. This helps them learn from failures. Some questions that you may wish to use can be found below:

- If nothing changes, what would that cost you?
- How would it be to do your part in making that happen?
- What would be the result if you did x?
- Are you moving forward in the right gear? Is it too high? Is it too low? How could you change the gear?
- What other resources (people or things) can you use to help you find the answer to your issue or problem?
- To succeed your meetings tomorrow, what is the first thing you will make sure you don't do anymore?
- What DO you have the power to do right now?
- How willing are you to do whatever it takes to discover the highest and best of who you are?
- Have you used all the resources at your disposal? Really? All of them?
- What would you do if you knew you couldn't fail?
- Who is in control? Who decides?

Broaden their thinking regarding their lifestyle choices

Some of us assume that clients are living their lifestyle choice, but when we stop to question what lifestyle they want we can be in for quite a surprise. We've experienced quite a few executives who would rather be doing something else – to the extent that they dream and cry about it. In helping clients decide a career path or new role, how well do you explore with them how it will affect their lifestyle? Most clients often just think what career they want, versus what lifestyle they want – until it is too late. We explore this in more detail in the next chapter.

Cultivate their sense of discipline

Jim Collins, the author of *Good to Great, Built to Last* and *How the Mighty Fall*, (2001) found that disciplined people who engage in disciplined thought and who take disciplined action – operating with freedom within a framework of responsibilities – create great results. How comfortable are you that you even know how disciplined are the thoughts and actions of your clients? How planned are your clients? How do they execute their plans? If your clients are either not enjoying working remotely, being unemployed, or without a plan, it could be that this is driving a feeling of being out of control; it isn't good to have too much time unfilled, open, and uncommitted: Encourage them to plan to do something worthwhile every day. When enquiring about discipline, you could ask them where in their life they need to be more disciplined. Why? What gets in the way? What have they tried? What part of being disciplined is difficult for them? Out of their answers will fall your strategy for helping them.

Develop a problem-solving mindset in your clients

You might like to explore with your clients the things they wish were more under their control, the things that they feel they don't have ordered, sorted, or managed. Once you have understood the situation, you could explore where they need your help in partnering them in problem-solving. You aim to move them away from being the victim to being a mover of events. Once they have decided upon what needs to happen, what do they need to do within themselves to execute the steps and what support could they get? By helping them see out the timeline of action, they can learn from the feedback and increase their confidence and sense of potency over time.

Play to their strengths

Make your clients aware of how their strengths could be used in the service of their locus of control. For example, their enthusiasm or resoluteness and fairness or politeness can be used to good effect when using your locus of control. Are they aware of their strengths? How are they playing to their strengths? Ask them, 'What would it look like if you turned the volume up on one of your strengths?'

On the other hand, be sure that your clients are not overplaying a strength regarding their locus of control, as this might make them too task-oriented and annoy others.

Encourage positivity and optimism

Positive emotions lead to expansive and exploratory behaviour (Frederickson, 2013). When we are feeling good, we are more inquisitive, have a desire to gain insight, and are able to think through more options when solutioning. By focusing on the positive, we can make ourselves feel good and be creative. You can help your clients be aware of their thoughts and feelings first (through some of the techniques above) and then using positive thinking will enable them to manifest what they want.

The following are ways to encourage positivity and optimism:

- Remind them what they are grateful for and where they can find joy in their life.
- Have them keep a joy diary – a daily record of things they are grateful for.
- Start their day with a positive affirmation (more can be found about this in the self-esteem tools and techniques above).
- Reframe their self-limiting thoughts (see technique 1 on locus of control above).
- Turn failures into lessons through developing a growth mindset.
- Surround themselves with people who make them feel good.
- Realise that problems are probably not forever – they are not as permanent or pervasive as they might appear to be.

Knowing now what you know about locus of control, have a read of these case studies and think through the questions at the end of each one.

CASE STUDY

A coach was presented with an issue from a female coachee who was from Saudi Arabia and working in an American firm in Scotland. She had a strong internal locus of control, largely because she had a strong mother and strong grandmother, she told the coach. Her assertive style was appreciated in the American company, and she rose through the ranks quickly. She was just 32 when she was made a senior leader in the business. But when was relocated back to her country of birth, she felt her authentic style had to be curtailed. She was put in charge of 250 people, and many of them were men who were older than she was. In this culture, younger women did not cross older men, in any way, shape, or form. She had been successful in turning around a failing part of the business in Scotland and had been sent to Saudi Arabia to turn around 'ways of working'. The issue brought to her coach was 'I feel stressed and my motivation is going downhill. How can I be myself here and operate in the successful way I have done before when culturally, I'm expected to be subservient? I feel impotent here.'

Reflecting on your practice:

- Knowing what you now know about locus of control, what would you need to be aware of or learn?
- How would you prepare yourself to coach or mentor this person?

CASE STUDY

A coach was supporting a leadership programme for a British organisation and was assigned six of the delegates to coach over one year. One of the delegates was a 31-year-old Singaporean woman who was working for a German boss. She was typical of the collectivist culture: she respected those who were older and senior, and she wanted to consult her team in most decisions. Her German boss wanted her to be more 'dynamic' and to 'lead'; by that, he meant she should be more forceful and make unilateral decisions. She explained to the coach that she couldn't be what her boss wanted her to be and that acceding to his request would cause her to act in a way that was contrary to her upbringing and values. She explained further by stating that 'at my father's table, I am not allowed to speak until I am invited to speak'.

Reflecting on your practice:

- What do you need to consider as a coach in this situation?
- How does knowing about locus of control help steer your questions to your clients?

CASE STUDY

The GM of a vital geographical area for a large international company, who was working in Nairobi, consulted a coach. He was Welsh and had married a woman from his hometown. He was very much a family man. At the same time, he was ambitious: He was aiming to become the global CEO. His question to the coach was, 'Can I keep my family as my number one priority and be this global leader? Everyone else around me works all hours and puts work first. Sure, the secretaries and juniors take flexi-time, but I don't know one single man that takes flexi-time. Look, the current CEO took his family on holiday, and he hadn't even taken a holiday for three years, but this year he took them on holiday, and he made the whole family fly to three locations – all so that he could do business in each location. I don't want to do that or be like that. My wife wouldn't stand for it either. Do I have to sacrifice my ambition? Am I faced with work versus my personal life?'

Reflecting on your own practice:

- What thoughts have been stimulated that you might like to take to supervision or a peer group?
- What if anything has resonated with you in relation to your coaching or mentoring practice?

Closing remarks

In this chapter, you have learnt what self-esteem and locus of control are, how to spot high/low self-esteem and internal/external locus of control, the impacts of these variances, and techniques and tips to improve self-esteem and to develop internal locus of control in your clients. The benefits of having self-esteem and an internal locus of control are innumerable and crucial for work-life balance. Although self-esteem and locus of control are shaped as early as the first 18 months of life, they can both be changed.

As coaches or mentors, we have the opportunity to help our clients develop the optimal amount of self-esteem and locus of control. The tools and techniques in this chapter are part of your toolbox, and they are there for you to pick and choose amongst depending on your clients and their situations. Armed with this knowledge and toolkit, you will hopefully feel more equipped to deal with these sensitive topics with your clients; our experience would predict that the impact you make will be deep and profound.

QUESTIONS FOR REFLECTION

- Which of your clients currently could really benefit from an exploration of the consequences of their self-esteem?
- Think of a client you are working with who has low or high self-esteem. How is it affecting them? How is it affecting your relationship with them? How is it affecting what you do with them?
- How can you help your client realise their self-esteem is affecting their work-life balance, well-being and resilience?
- How could you best challenge your clients' perceptions about what they believe they have no control over or impact on?
- How can you help your clients develop their sense of worth so that they aimed higher?
- How can you install in your clients a self-reflective capacity around their sense of competence in the future?

Additional reading and resources

Baumeister, R.F., Campbell, J.D., Krueger, J.I. & Vohs, K.D. (2003). Does high self-esteem cause better performance, interpersonal success, happiness, or healthier lifestyles? *Psychological science in the public interest*, 4(1), pp. 1–44.

Carton, J.S. & Nowicki, S. (1994). Antecedents of individual differences in locus of control of reinforcement: A critical review. *Genetic, Social, and General Psychology Monographs*.

Everett, N. (2013). *Meet Yourself: A User's Guide to Building Self-Esteem*. TEDxYouth@ BommerCanyon. https://www.youtube.com/watch?v=uOrzmFUJtrs

Fredrickson, B.L. (2013). Positive emotions broaden and build. In Patricia Devine, and Ashby Plant (Eds), *Advances in experimental social psychology* Vol. 47 (pp. 1–53). Burlington: Academic Press.

Kahneman, D. (2011). *Thinking, fast and slow*. New York: Macmillan.

McKenna, P. (2016). *Instant Confidence*. London: Hay House, Inc.

Mruk, C.J. (2006). *Self-esteem research, theory, and practice: Toward a positive psychology of self-esteem*. New York: Springer Publishing Company.

References

Allport, G.W. (1955). *Becoming; Basic Considerations for a Psychology of Personality* (Vol. 20). Yale University Press.

Archer, R.P. (1979). Relationships between locus of control and anxiety. *Journal of Personality Assessment*, 43(6), pp. 617–626.

Arndt, J. & Goldenberg, J.L. (2002). From threat to sweat: the role of physiological arousal in the motivation to maintain self-esteem. In A. Tesser, D.A. Stapel & J.V. Wood (Eds), *Self and Motivation: Emerging Psychological Perspectives* (pp. 43–69). Washington, DC: American Psychological Association.

Baumeister, R.F. (1993). Understanding the inner nature of low self-esteem: Uncertain, fragile, protective, and conflicted. In *Self-Esteem* (pp. 201–218). Springer US.

Baumeister, R.F. (Ed.) (2013). *Self-Esteem: The Puzzle of Low Self-Regard*. New York: Springer Science & Business Media.

Baumeister, R.F., Campbell, J.D., Krueger, J.I. & Vohs, K.D. (2003). Does high self-esteem cause better performance, interpersonal success, happiness, or healthier lifestyles? *Psychological Science in the Public Interest*, 4(1), pp. 1–44.

Bowlby, J. (1973). *Attachment and loss, vol. II: Separation (2)*. New York: Basic Books.

Bronfenbrenner, U. (1979). *The Ecology of Human Development: Experiments in Nature and Design*. Cambridge, MA: Harvard University Press.

Brockhaus, R.H. (1982). Psychology of the entrepreneur. In D.L. Sexton, C.A. Kent & K.H. Vesper (Eds), *Encyclopedia of Entrepreneurship* (pp. 39–71). Englewood Cliffs, NJ: Prentice-Hall, Inc.

Carson, S.H. & Langer, E.J. (2006). Mindfulness and self-acceptance. *Journal of Rational-Emotive and Cognitive-Behavior Therapy*, 24(1), pp. 29–43.

Carton, J.S. & Nowicki, S. (1994). Antecedents of individual differences in locus of control of reinforcement: a critical review. *Genetic, Social, and General Psychology Monographs*, 120(1), pp. 31–81.

Clark, S.C. (2002). Employees' sense of community, sense of control, and work/family conflict in Native American organizations. *Journal of Vocational Behavior*, 61(1), pp. 92–108.

Chen, J.C. & Silverthorne, C. (2008). The impact of locus of control on job stress, job performance and job satisfaction in Taiwan. *Leadership & Organization Development Journal*, 29(7), pp. 572–582.

Collins, J. (2007). Level 5 leadership. *The Jossey-Bass Reader on Educational Leadership*, 2, pp. 27–50.

Collins, J. (2001). *Good to Great - (Why Some Companies Make the Leap and others Don't)*. London: Random House Business Books.

Crocker, J. & Park, L.E. (2004). The costly pursuit of self-esteem. *Psychological Bulletin*, 130(3), p. 392.

Dahlin, M., Joneborg, N. & Runeson, B. (2007). Performance-based self-esteem and burnout in a cross-sectional study of medical students. *Medical Teacher*, 29(1), pp. 43–48.

Diener, E. & Diener, C. (1996). Most people are happy. *Psychological Science*, 7(3), pp. 181–185.

DeLongis, A., Folkman, S. & Lazarus, R.S. (1988). The impact of daily stress on health and mood: psychological and social resources as mediators. *Journal of Personality and Social Psychology*, 54(3), p. 486.

De Vries, M.F. (2014). Coaching or mentoring the toxic leader. *Harvard Business Review*, 92(4), pp. 100–109.

Dweck, C.S. (2008). *Mindset: The New Psychology of Success*. Random House Digital, Inc.

Eisler, R.M., Miller, P.M. & Hersen, M. (1973). Components of assertive behavior. *Journal of Clinical Psychology*, 29(3), pp. 295–299.

Ellis, A. (1957). Rational psychotherapy and individual psychology. *Journal of Individual Psychology*, 13, pp. 38–44.

Epstein, S. (1979). The ecological study of emotions in humans. *Advances in the Study of Communication and Affect*, 5, pp. 47–83.

Faitz, L. (2012). Individual Reactions to Adversity: An Exploration of the Relationship Between Self-Esteem, Resilience, and Locus of Control. McKendree University. Issue 19 – Winter 2012. Accessed on 1st December 2018 at: https://www.mckendree.edu/web/scholars/winter2012/faitz.htm.

Forthofer, M.S., Janz, N.K., Dodge, J.A. & Clark, N.M. (2001). Gender differences in the associations of self-esteem, stress and social support with functional health status among older adults with heart disease. *Journal of Women & Aging*, 13(1), pp. 19–37.

Fournier, G. (2016). Locus of Control. Psych Central. Accessed on 28th July 2018 at: https://psychcentral.com/encyclopedia/locus-of-control/.

Fredrickson, B.L. (2013). Positive emotions broaden and build. In Patricia Devine, and Ashby Plant (Eds), *Advances in Experimental Social Psychology* Vol. 47 (pp. 1–53). Burlington: Academic Press.

Gable, S.L., Reis, H.T., Impett, E.A. & Asher, E.R. (2004). What do you do when things go right? The intrapersonal and interpersonal benefits of sharing positive events. *Journal of Personality and Social Psychology*, 87, pp. 228–245. doi:10.1037/0022-3514.87.2.228.

Gray-Stanley, J.A., Muramatsu, N., Heller, T., Hughes, S., Johnson, T.P. & Ramirez-Valles, J. (2010). Work stress and depression among direct support professionals: the role of work support and locus of control. *Journal of Intellectual Disability Research*, 54(8), pp. 749–761.

Heine, S.J., Lehman, D.R., Markus, H.R. & Kitayama, S. (1999). Is there a universal need for positive self-regard? *Psychological Review*, 106(4), p. 766.

Hofäcker, D. & König, S. (2013). Flexibility and work-life conflict in times of crisis: a gender perspective. *International Journal of Sociology and Social Policy*, 33(9/10), pp. 613–635.

Johnson, B. & Smith, D. (2017). How to mentor a narcissist. *Havard Business Review*. Accessed on 11th December 2018 at: https://hbr.org/2017/09/how-to-mentor-a-narcissist.

Johnson, B.D., Stone, G.L., Altmaier, E.M. & Berdahl, L.D. (1998). The relationship of demographic factors, locus of control and self-efficacy to successful nursing home adjustment. *The Gerontologist*, 38(2), pp. 209–216.

Judge, T.A. & Bono, J.E. (2001). Relationship of core self-evaluations traits – self-esteem, generalized self-efficacy, locus of control, and emotional stability – with job satisfaction and job performance: a meta-analysis. *Journal of Applied Psychology*, 86, p. 80.

Judge, T.A. & Cable, D.M. (1997). Applicant personality, organizational culture, and organization attraction. *Personnel Psychology*, 50(2), pp. 359–394.

Kahneman, D. (2011). *Thinking, Fast and Slow*. New York: Macmillan.

Kernis, M.H. (Ed.) (2013). *Self-Esteem Issues and Answers: A Sourcebook of Current Perspectives*. Psychology Press.

Koole, S.L. & Kuhl, J. (2003). In search of the real self: a functional perspective on optimal self-esteem and authenticity. *Psychological Inquiry*, 14(1), pp. 43–48.

Karkoulian, S., Srour, J. & Sinan, T. (2016). A gender perspective on work-life balance, perceived stress, and locus of control. *Journal of Business Research*, 69(11), pp. 4918–4923.

Leary, M.R., Tambor, E.S., Terdal, S.K. & Downs, D.L. (1995). Self-esteem as an interpersonal monitor: the sociometer hypothesis. *Journal of Personality and Social Psychology*, 68(3), p. 518.

Longmore, M.A. & DeMaris, M. (1997). Perceived inequity and depression in intimate relationships: the moderating effect of self-esteem. *Social Psychology Quarterly*, 60, pp. 172–184.

Lubit, R. (2002). The long-term organizational impact of destructively narcissistic managers. *The Academy of Management Executive*, 16(1), pp. 127–138.

Maier, S.F. & Seligman, M.E. (1976). Learned helplessness: theory and evidence. *Journal of Experimental Psychology: General*, 105(1), p. 3.

Maslach, C., Schaufeli, W.B. & Leiter, M.P. (2001). Job burnout. *Annual Review of Psychology*, 52(1), pp. 397–422.

Manz, C.C. & Sims, H.P. (1980). Self-management as a substitute for leadership: a social learning theory perspective. *Academy of Management Review*, 5(3), pp. 361–367.

McKenna, P. (2016). *Instant Confidence*. London: Hay House, Inc.

Mueller, S.L. & Thomas, A.S. (2001). Culture and entrepreneurial potential: a nine country study of locus of control and innovativeness. *Journal of Business Venturing*, 16(1), pp. 51–75.

Ngah, N., Ahmad, A. & Baba, M. (2009). The mediating effect of work-family conflict on the relationship between locus of control and job satisfaction. *Journal of Social Sciences*, 5(4), pp. 348–354.

Noor, N.M. (2002). Work-family conflict, locus of control, and women's well-being: tests of alternative pathways. *The Journal of Social Psychology*, 142(5), pp. 645–662.

Nowicki, S. & Strickland, B.R. (1973). A locus of control scale for children. *Journal of Consulting and Clinical Psychology*, 40(1), p. 148.

Office of National Statistics. (2016). *Women shoulder the responsibility of 'unpaid work'*. Accessed on 10th January 2019 at: https://www.ons.gov.uk/employmentandlabourmarket/peopleinwork/earningsandworkinghours/articles/womenshouldertheresponsibilityof unpaidwork/2016-11-10.

Orth, U. & Robins, R.W. (2014). The development of self-esteem. *Current Directions in Psychological Science*, 23(5), pp. 381–387.

Orth, U., Robins, R.W. & Widaman, K.F. (2012). Life-span development of self-esteem and its effects on important life outcomes. *Journal of Personality and Social Psychology*, 102, pp. 1271–1288.

Orth, U., Trzesniewski, K.H. & Robins, R.W. (2010). Self-esteem development from young adulthood to old age: a cohort-sequential longitudinal study. *Journal of Personality and Social Psychology*, 98(4), p. 645.

Park, L.E., Crocker, J. & Mickelson, K.D. (2004). Attachment styles and contingencies of self-worth. *Personality and Social Psychology Bulletin*, 30(10), pp. 1243–1254.

Peterson, C. & Seligman, M.E. (2004). *Character Strengths and Virtues: A Handbook and Classification (Vol. 1)*. New York: Oxford University Press.

Ramsey, A., Watson, P.J., Biderman, M.D. & Reeves, A.L. (1996). Self-reported narcissism and perceived parental permissiveness and authoritarianism. *The Journal of Genetic Psychology*, 157(2), pp. 227–238.

Rehman, S. & Azam Roomi, M. (2012). Gender and work-life balance: a phenomenological study of women entrepreneurs in Pakistan. *Journal of Small Business and Enterprise Development*, 19(2), pp. 209–228.

Ross, D.S. & Vasantha, S. (2014). A conceptual study on impact of stress on work-life balance. *Sai Om Journal of Commerce & Management: A Peer Reviewed National Journal*, 1(2), pp. 61–65 (Online ISSN 2347-7563).

Rotter, J.B. (1954). *Social Learning and Clinical Psychology*. Englewood Cliffs, NJ: Prentice-Hall.

Sav, A., Harris, N. & Sebar, B. (2013). Work-life conflict and facilitation among Australian Muslim men. *Equality, Diversity and Inclusion: An International Journal*, 32(7), pp. 671–687.

Schmitz, N., Neumann, W. & Oppermann, R. (2000). Stress, burnout and locus of control in German nurses. *International Journal of Nursing Studies*, 37(2), pp. 95–99.

Schwarzkopf, K., Straus, D., Porschke, H., Znoj, H., Conrad, N., Schmidt-Trucksäss, A. & von Känel, R. (2016). Empirical evidence for a relationship between narcissistic personality traits and job burnout. *Burnout Research*, 3(2), pp. 25–33.

Seligman, M.E. & Maier, S.F. (1967). Failure to escape traumatic shock. *Journal of Experimental Psychology*, 74(1), p. 1.

Sherman, A.C., Higgs, G.E. & Williams, R.L. (1997). Gender differences in the locus of control construct. *Psychology and Health*, 12(2), pp. 239–248.

Spector, P.E. (1982). Behavior in organizations as a function of employee's locus of control. *Psychological Bulletin*, 91(3), p. 482.

Strassberg, D.S. (1973). Relationships among locus of control, anxiety, and valued-goal expectations. *Journal of Consulting and Clinical Psychology*, 41(2), p. 319.

Taylor, S.E. & Brown, J.D. (1988). Illusion and well-being: a social psychological perspective on mental health. *Psychological Bulletin*, 103(2), p.193.

The Economist. (2017). Are women paid less than men for the same work? Accessed on 12th December 2018 at: https://www.economist.com/graphic-detail/2017/08/01/are-women-paid-less-than-men-for-the-same-work.

Trzesniewski, K.H., Donnellan, M.B., Moffitt, T.E., Robins, R.W., Poulton, R. & Caspi, A., (2006). Low self-esteem during adolescence predicts poor health, criminal behaviour, and limited economic prospects during adulthood. *Developmental Psychology*, 42(2), p. 381.

Valliant, G.E. (1977). *Adaptation to Life*. Boston, MA: Little, Brown.

Watts, J.H. (2009). Leaders of men: women 'managing' in construction. *Work, Employment and Society*, 23(3), pp. 512–530.

White, J.B., Langer, E.J., Yariv, L. & Welch, J.C. (2006). Frequent social comparisons and destructive emotions and behaviors: the dark side of social comparisons. *Journal of Adult Development*, 13(1), pp. 36–44.

Whisman, M.A. & Kwon, P. (1993). Life stress and dysphoria: the role of self-esteem and hopelessness. *Journal of Personality and Social Psychology*, 65(5), p. 1054.

Yang, Z. & Schaninger, C.M. (2010). The impact of parenting strategies on child smoking behavior: the role of child self-esteem trajectory. *Journal of Public Policy & Marketing*, 29(2), pp. 232–247.

Zeigler-Hill, V. (Ed.) (2013). *Self-Esteem (1)*. Psychology Press.

3   Stage 2

Success and life satisfaction

Introduction

Our definition of success will be influenced by our stage of life, culture, values, and gender. The definition of success is hermeneutic; it is affected by our philosophy and approach. Success can be, therefore, a broad topic to cover with our clients. We all need to be prepared to deal with a myriad of responses to the question 'What is success to you?' Clients' responses to this meta question will drive their behaviour, affect their achievements, and colour their sense of well-being. Their expectations of success will be a mediator in their behavioural choices (Weiner, 1985).

In this chapter, we explore ways in which you can investigate and work with your clients' sense of success and satisfaction, the second stage in our model for work-life balance, illustrated in Figure 3.1.

There could be said to be two main paths to working with clients: One path involves staying with their interpretation, faithfully following their thread, entering into the way they see the world. The other path entails referencing their interpretation to models and concepts from the academic literature. We posit that mastery in coaching or mentoring requires the practitioner to straddle both paths. We believe that the evidence-based practitioner needs to be knowledgeable about what the literature says about success. It isn't enough to merely listen and follow the clients' lead, paraphrasing back what they say and challenging assumptions. As the industry matures into a profession, best practice dictates we adopt professional practices, and in this instance that manifests in knowing and using the evidence in the research on the topic. What does the science say about the factors and predictors of success? What have others found to be critical factors in building a satisfied, happy life and a successful life? This knowledge is your starting point, and it can inform your work with your clients. In this chapter, we give you some of the literature on success to equip you with a flavour of some of the great findings out there on this subject.

We explore beliefs: What the science tells us about how beliefs are formed and how beliefs impact our goals and actions. We consider limiting beliefs and pessimistic beliefs, two ways of being that negatively impact on success and satisfaction, and how to adopt more empowering beliefs.

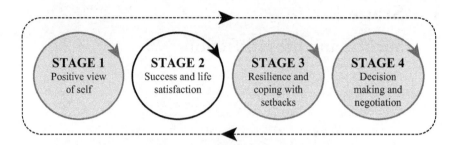

Figure 3.1 Four-Stage Model for Work-Life Balance

Following from there, we focus on the client's view of what they want, how close they are to it, what they have in their favour, and what obstacles might face them. So from the nomothetic generalisations from the science, we move to the phenomenological stance of your clients and explore their very personal view of success. Here we introduce some well-known tools from psychodynamics that have been adjusted to fit our purpose. We merge the two approaches – from the nomothetic seven clusters and the phenomenological stance of your clients into a table that will serve as a gap analysis, to see how your clients' answers fit common frameworks for defining success. Where they are different, you can investigate what the difference means and how your clients' definitions affect their perceptions and choices.

Finally, once your clients have stated their views of where they are on their path to success, you will want to cover goal-setting and designing strategies that will help them be on the right path at the right pace. Our section on goal-setting offers some ways to refine your work in this area. We end by contemplating with you how your clients can keep momentum long after your coaching or mentoring relationship is over.

Beliefs about success

Beliefs are assumed truths (many of which are not demonstrably true). Our clients' assumed truths about success affect how much success they think they can expect. Scientific research has shown that there are known categories that inform our beliefs, and we cover some of them here. A client's beliefs about success will be influenced by some situations: Culture and ethnicity, original and current socio-economic group, gender, and age and stage of life.

Culture and ethnicity

Psychologist Dr Geerte Hofstede (1984) found that there is a cultural difference in the way people interpret the concepts of success, quality of life, and life satisfaction. Hofstede's work showed that countries defined as 'masculine' and in the category of 'strong uncertainty avoidance', such as North America, the UK, and Hong Kong, put achievement and personal satisfaction as highest priorities in their definition of success. It is now well known that different nationalities have different 'need hierarchies'. The USA has a need hierarchy like Maslow's (Maslow & Lewis, 1987), which involves basic food, shelter, social connection, sense of worth, and self-actualisation. Other countries like Denmark, Sweden, and Norway ('feminine, weak uncertainty avoidance' cultures) have needs to satisfy that are based more around the group, the clan, the family, and society (Hofstede, 1984). How is the ethnicity, the nationality, or the country where your clients are working affecting their view of what and how much success is possible?

Socio-economic group

Our socio-economic group has been proven to predict achievements (Sirin, 2005). There are of course multiple reasons for this. Our socio-economic group affects our ambition, expectations, access to educational materials, whether we have a quiet place to study, access to some role models, access to mentors, and how we are influenced by other people's attitudes. Your coaching or mentoring to those of low socio-economic background can help your clients aim higher and navigate upward mobility through perceived or real social boundaries. How has (and is) the socio-economic origins of your clients affecting their behaviour? How does your socio-economic group affect your view of your clients?

Gender

Professor Jacquelynne Eccles' work shows there is still rigid socialisation and differences in expectations between men and women of roles, careers, and what should be satisfying. She argues that we need to encourage girls and women to develop values around achieving, to broaden their views about their options, and to enable achievement-related choices (Wigfield & Eccles, 2002). Once in work, success is often about balancing career and family for both men and women, but women have more focus on raising children than do men; this commitment limits their ambitions in the workplace (Mahdavi, 2010; MacDonald, Phipps & Lethbridge, 2005).

Reflecting on your own practice:

- How might you address the gender issue as it relates to your clients' views of their ambitions, and impact on work-life balance in your coaching or mentoring practice?
- How does your gender affect the way you view male and female clients?
- How does your gender affect your view of success for yourself?

Age and stage of life

Our age and our stage of life affect our definition of success and our views of work-life balance.

Professor George Vaillant's (2001) seminal work showed that successful ageing has known controllable factors such as a stable marriage, keeping within a 'good' weight, exercising, and continuous learning (Vaillant & Mukamal, 2001). He indicated that these have to be embedded and nurtured some 30 years before we grow old and that it does not work out well to neglect relationships or our physical health for large chunks of time. We have worked with a client in IT who was in charge of an investment bank's global infrastructure, who worked 20-hour days regularly, over a year or more, only to find his wife leaving him – and he ended up in hospital. How does this fit with your clients? Are they sacrificing any of these areas to be successful in their current role at work? Are you?

Some of our clients have had an extremely narrow focus on what success is to them, such as one who said to us, 'becoming partner is what matters to me and nothing else matters this year.' The trouble is that other factors do matter further down the line – so how do you deal with this when 'help me become a partner' is the client's goal and your engagement with them is short?

The client's stage of life will tend to be reflected in their goals. Clients in their twenties will say they'd like to find the life partner, buy a house, see their friends, and gain the next promotion. Clients in their thirties are likely to say, 'my main aim is that my family are healthy and well, they have a roof over their head, my work has made a difference, and I'm being paid enough to pay for our family home and lifestyle.' Clients who are near retirement talk of hoping to 'set up' their family – possibly help their children to buy a house, add to their pension fund, keep healthy and perhaps leave a legacy through their work or savings.

Life satisfaction is a judgement where individuals assess the quality of their lives according to their unique set of criteria (Shin & Johnson, 1978). Most clients would say the criteria include feeling competent, clocking up some achievements, being financially secure, having a good home and social life – but we urge you not to assume, as each client is likely to assign a different weighting to these criteria, and you can be surprised by a client's unique set of criteria (Diener et al., 1985).

You have undoubtedly found that your clients are focusing on succeeding in one or two areas of their life, at the expense of other areas. They may be doing this wittingly, with the support of key people in their lives, or they may be on a treadmill or feel forced. Most people who have achieved great things have sacrificed other aspects of their lives. It isn't for us to decide whether that is good, but it is for us to help clients make mindful choices, having been aware of their values, lifestyle wishes, effects on others, and the consequences down the line. Short-term sacrifices might not result in serious implications later, but if those sacrifices are sustained, they will result in loss of some kind: Is that the loss that the person wishes to risk? For some of our clients caught in a corporate role where the culture is up or out, they find their wishes compromised and see their options as very limited. We've known many clients who ignore their families and wear themselves out with a very heavy workload, and when they do see their family, they are irritable or fall asleep in front of the television, giving no effort to engaging well with the ones they say they are doing it all for. It is a common problem. How well are you helping your clients think through how their focus and energy at work is making them ignore, possibly at their peril, other essential aspects of their life?

We have found it useful to consider the psychosocial stage that your clients might be in or be stuck around. Erikson (1963) developed the theory of eight psychosocial life-stages. He believed that failure to master each of these stages sequentially leads to a feeling of inadequacy and failure. We provide a summary here of the stages and how they might relate to your practice.

Trust versus mistrust (the first year and a half)

The first 18 months of life are critical for establishing self-esteem, trust of others, and trust of the world. If your clients had erratic, negligent, or abusive care during this time, they might have low self-esteem and a deep-seated mistrust of people. They are unlikely to be hopeful about their future. This might affect their view of what kind of success or how much they can hope for, given that people will let them down. In such an instance, you could help them look for evidence that disproves that theory: Who has been faithful to them? Who around them relied on someone and that person came through for them? How can you help them reshape their sense of worth and trust?

Autonomy versus shame/doubt (1–3 years)

It is important that toddlers are allowed to experiment and at the same time, given boundaries. If your clients had controlling or nervous parents/carers who hindered their development at this time, they are likely to be fearful and doubt their abilities. They might not remember their upbringing before they were three years of age, but the pattern would have been set, and it is likely that their parents continued to behave in the same manner as they went into their primary years, so you could tell perhaps from how they were parented later in life whether they were encouraged to experiment or not. You might like to explore who believes in them, who has given feedback about their abilities, and to what extent they have built their beliefs around their sense of agency.

Initiative versus guilt (3–6 years)

If you ask your clients how their parents or carers responded to their attempts to do something new, you will gain a sense of how empowered they are likely to be now. Those whose parents or carers supported their choices and helped them safely explore their limitations will likely be adventurous in how they see their options now. Those who were stifled or criticised will need you to help them take small experimental steps, incrementally gaining their belief in themselves and feeling safe.

Industry versus inferiority (7–12 years)

This is the stage where the child develops a belief in applying themselves, achieving things, and feeling proud of those accomplishments. If they were not supported in their youth to pass through this psychosocial stage well, they will develop a sense of inferiority which could drive passivity or aggression. If your clients are passive or aggressive, you might want to inquire about how they were supported during their 7–12th years. You will need to help them see how they can make it in the world.

Identity versus role-confusion (13–20 years)

At this stage, the young adult starts to ask, and hopefully answer, questions like 'Who am I? What do I want to do with my life?' Unless resolved here, this identity issue can crop up throughout adulthood until it is resolved. You might meet clients at any age with this issue and have, perhaps unwittingly, helped many through this stuck stage. What tribe do your clients belong to? What role do they take in their family, teams, at work, and in society? What do they believe about how they should act and what they should achieve? They will need help identifying who they are and who they can be.

Intimacy versus isolation (20s–40s)

This stage is all about our social connections, relationships, and a sense of belonging. Just how well was this stage tackled during these years of your clients' lives? What are the ramifications now? How is their role or workload affecting their social life and key relationships outside of work? Do they believe they can love and be loved?

Generativity versus stagnation (40s–60s)

When someone is at this stage, they are ready to give back. They volunteer, share, teach, and mentor. When Erikson (1963) made this model, people retired by 60; now that the retirement age is later, this stage could be extended. If your clients are towards the latter end of this stage and they are still required to be productive, you might find them weary of it all. They are likely to be less interested in producing at the same volume as they used to and more interested in picking and choosing where they wish to be effective. If your clients feel they have stagnated, this will result in profoundly negative emotions. Can you help them see where they are growing and how their life counts?

Integrity versus despair (60+)

This last stage is about ageing well. It is about reflecting on life and either feeling satisfied and proud – or not. If you coach or mentor people in their sixties, it is likely their focus will be on a legacy piece of work or on helping the next generation. If they are still manic about wanting to achieve, it could be that they are stuck in the identity or even the industry psycho-social stage, and you could focus your work accordingly. Despair can be hidden. The existential question that needs answering is 'Was it OK to have been me?'

Joan Erikson, Erikson's wife and collaborator, worked with him in their later years (80+) on a ninth stage, when a crisis hit all the stages in the reverse order (Erikson & Erikson, 1998). The elderly face loss of hope and loss of trust in their capacities, and they have to trust the younger generation to look after them. They might lose their autonomy, feel inferior, useless, and isolated, and they might despair at the world and their situation. Whilst we might not coach or mentor people of this age, we are likely to be coaching or mentoring people who are dealing with their elderly relatives who are in that age group.

Looking at the various psychosocial stages of life might help you analyse where your clients are and what their existential questions might be, which will be more important than just facing the presenting problem they air.

What do you know of your clients' beliefs about success?

We know that beliefs are assumed truths and that our clients' beliefs about success and satisfaction will guide their ambitions and actions. Can you say with certainty what your clients hold as true about their possibility, their place in the world? Your clients' view of the level of success they deserve or that 'people like them' can expect will affect the choices they make and how they feel about their life. It is their relationship with success that is crucial to find out. Here are some questions to find out your clients' beliefs about success and satisfaction:

- What is success to you?
- What is important for others that isn't important for you?
- What do you think is possible for you and what isn't?
- What do you believe about very successful people?
- What do you believe about moderately successful people?
- What do you believe about unsuccessful people?
- Where do you fit along the continuum of unsuccessful to very successful people?
- What do you think the conditions of success are?
- What gives you or would give you a sense of satisfaction with your life?
- What do you think is the price of chasing achievements?
- What are you willing to sacrifice for achievements? Why? When is it all right in your view to make those sacrifices?
- How much do your past life experiences affect your ambitions today?
- How has your background shaped your values and beliefs around success and life satisfaction?
- What do you hope for?

- What would you do if you knew you could be successful? What fuels that sense of knowing and what inhibits it?
- What success do you believe is out of reach for you? What makes you think that?
- What can 'people like you' not expect?
- What are the 'realities' of success for you (in your country, for your age, for someone with your background, and for someone with your lack of *xyz*)?
- What do you dream of? What are your beliefs about what parts of this dream could be achieved?
- What are you assuming about success?

The two mindsets that will limit your clients' success

Dealing with limiting beliefs

Limiting beliefs constrain our clients. Limiting beliefs are often irrational and illogical, and are skewed generalisations. Once you find a belief that might be limiting, you could work with them to change that belief. Some steps you might like to try with your clients are presented in Table 3.1.

Table 3.1 Dealing with limiting beliefs

Challenge the evidence around this assumed truth.
Ask them to consider the consequences of holding that belief.
Ask them how it negatively impacts their life.
Explore what beliefs might be better to hold that also might be true.
Understand the supporting evidence for that new belief.
Discuss the consequences of holding that belief.

Pessimism

Pessimism is not all bad: We know Olympic gold medallists who swear their pessimism drives them to achieve perfection, but for many, a pessimistic explanatory style is a known contributor to illness (Peterson, Seligman & Vaillant, 1988) and depression (Hu, Zhang & Yang, 2015). A pessimistic stance, when met with difficulties, failure, and disappointment, can result in a fatalistic withdrawal from goal-directed behaviour. If your clients have a negative outlook or hold negative beliefs, they may overemphasise the negatives and discount the positives. They might see things that have gone wrong as having permanent effects or repercussions, they might see a negative situation or trait as pervasive and imagine it affecting their future, and they might over-personalise, thinking that they've been and will be discriminated against. Martin Seligman terms this kind of thinking as 'learned helplessness', and those with learned helplessness are not likely to have inspiring visions of their success (Seligman, 1972).

If you have clients who are pessimistic, we suggest helping your clients compartmentalise:

- What about what they are worried about is really permanent and what is temporary (to stop them thinking that it is permanent)?
- What is an isolated case and where has it or could it spread, and where won't it necessarily spread (to stop them over generalising and to stop the negativity being pervasive)?
- What about what happened by chance or happens to others (to stop the over personalising)?

Which of your clients could do with you working with them in this way?

The science: Seven components of success found in the literature

Now let's look at the nomothetic stance on success, the universal clusters of components of success that most people find important. The literature shows some essential components in a variety of studies over the last 70 years on what makes people happy and satisfied at the end of their life, what needs they have to satisfy, and studies of people who have felt unsatisfied, been unhappy, and have regrets. Having this knowledge can aid your conversation with your clients. There are seven major components and they are:

1. Having good health: Physical, emotional, and mental (Layard et al., 2014).
2. Having security: A home, food, education (Maslow, 1943).
3. Achieving things, feeling competent, and feeling satisfied with those achievements (McClelland & Johnson, 1984).

4. Having moments of happiness, joy, and pleasure (Lyubomirsky, King & Diener, 2005).
5. Feeling connected with others (Sandstrom & Dunn, 2013).
6. Having autonomy and freedom (Deci & Ryan, 1987).
7. Living a life based on one's values, faith, and principles (Moynihan, 2015).

Let's take each of these in turn.

Having good health: Physical, emotional, and mental

Professor and economist Richard Layard and his colleagues at the Well-being Research Programme at the London School of Economics' Centre for Economic Performance concluded that the most important predictor of adult-life satisfaction is emotional and mental health, in adulthood and childhood (Layard et al., 2014). Emotional and mental health are much more important to satisfaction levels compared to intellectual performance when young, and wealth is more important when older. Physical health is also a stronger predictor for happier adult life than wealth and intellectual performance.

We go into these areas in this book when we look at Resilience and coping with setbacks (in chapter 4), but for now, consider the state of your current clients' physical, mental, and emotional health. How are these states affecting their work-life balance and life satisfaction? What do they need to consider, reframe, accept, or change?

Having security: A home, food, education

Psychologist Abraham Maslow (1943) created the concept of a hierarchy of needs. He believed we need to satisfy the lower needs before addressing the higher needs. Our needs drive our behaviour. The most basic needs are the need for shelter, food, water, and air, as well as keeping us safe from harm, which involves having financial security and good health. Ignoring basic human needs creates dissatisfaction. Higher up in the hierarchy of needs we find love, belonging, self-esteem, and self-actualization.

We might expect our executives that we coach to be sorted in the lower areas, but we can be surprised: Some work in countries where there is warfare, have roles that involve some risk, or they may be getting divorced and halving their money. It is always worth checking out with your clients how they feel about these aspects of their life and the effects their current levels of fears are having on them.

Achieving things, feeling competent, and feeling satisfied with those achievements

Harvard Psychologist David McClelland is a significant contributor to the research around the need for achievement and the characteristics and benefits of being a high achiever. McClelland & Johnson (1984) created a set of factors which describes high achievers as people who:

- Like situations where they can take personal responsibility for finding solutions and problems.
- Tend to set moderate achievement goals and take calculated risks.
- Want concrete feedback about how well they are doing.

Pause for a moment and with a client in mind, reflect on the following questions:

- How are their ambitions affecting their choices regarding their work-life balance?
- What is the ongoing cost of their drive towards their achievements?
- How can you help your client see the consequences and work out the risks/rewards?
- Who is involved and influencing their goals? How much of what they are doing is what they really want and how much of it is what others really want?
- How much of what they are going after do they really believe in and really want for themselves?
- How much do they feel they are growing versus stagnating or going backwards?
- How are they gathering useful feedback?
- How are they learning from their successes and failures?

Having moments of happiness, joy, and pleasure

Juggling working life with other commitments can be frenetic and relentless. Just how much fun, rest, pleasure, and joy are your clients having in their life? What are they putting off and at what cost? In 2015, just three in 10 people in the UK were 'happy with their lives' (The Telegraph, 2015).

Dr Sonja Lyubomirsky and colleagues conducted a robust review of the cross-sectional literature and found that happiness precedes success. We need to be happy, to have positive emotions, in order to be motivated to commit to working actively towards new goals and be creative about obstacles we face. This was found to be true across several life domains: Work, relationships, and health (Lyubomirsky, King & Diener, 2005).

Professor Kahneman and economist Deaton (2010) did a study on happiness and life satisfaction with a big data set (some 450,000 respondents), and their findings have attracted much attention. They found that those on incomes less than $75,000 experience greater emotional pain than those on more than $75,000, attributed to worry about their security and basic needs causing a strain on their emotional well-being. They defined emotional well-being as fleeting emotions, positive affective feelings, like joy and pleasure.

In the context of this study, emotional well-being and happiness are used inter-changeably. They tapped into this definition of happiness by asking respondents to rate their mood the day before (not by how happy they thought they were overall, at that time in their history). To look at life satisfaction, they asked, 'imagine you had the best possible life....' and to rank their current life 1–10 relative to that best life. They found that there is no further correlation with individuals' emotional well-being and income above $75,000. However, the higher the individuals' income, the more satisfied they were with their life. The results suggest that more money doesn't necessarily buy more happiness, and that individuals' emotional well-being is constrained by other factors such as life circumstances and their temperament.

Professor Kahneman, who dedicated years to studying happiness, believes that people don't strive to maximise their happiness; they aim to optimise their satisfaction with themselves and with their lives and have more sustainable feelings of contentment. Happiness is a momentary experience and fleeting emotion, whilst life satisfaction is a long-term feeling, built over time. Kahneman (2018) believes life satisfaction is about achieving goals, meeting expectations, and creating the kind of life that you admire. It is important that your clients have both happiness and satisfaction with their life.

Reflecting on your own practice:

- How happy are your clients?
- How satisfied with their life, when they consider the best possible life they hope and expect to have, are they?
- How can they have balance or harmony in striving for both and attending to the other things in life that are important?

Feeling connected with others

We are social animals; all of us need social company. Dr Gillian Sandstrom and Professor Elizabeth Dunn (2014) found that the number of interactions people have can predict their day-to-day sense of belonging and happiness. They found that when people interacted with people close to them, they reported that they were happier, and the more people interacted with strangers (for example a barista in a coffee shop), the greater their sense of belonging to the community. Many clients see less of their friends than they wish – we suggest to just check with your clients to find out the magnitude of the gap in how they are living their life versus how they wish to be living their life, the consequences of this, and what they might see as options to change the situation.

Having autonomy and freedom

Professor Edward Deci and Richard Ryan spent a few decades dedicating their research to motivation. They created the Self-Determination Theory, which posits that we are extrinsically and intrinsically motivated and that both types of motivation influence our behaviour (Deci & Ryan, 1987). Extrinsic motivation is when behaviour is driven by external sources, such as money or good grades, whilst intrinsic motivation is when behaviour is internally driven, because, for example, it is personally rewarding or connected to our values (Deci & Ryan, 1985). All of us share the universal needs for autonomy and a desire to control our lives. When your clients have autonomy they are likely to feel high self-esteem, better physical and psychological health, more cognitive flexibility, more creativity, and a more positive emotional tone (Deci & Ryan, 1987) than if they feel they have little control over their work or destiny.

Autonomy is closely linked to authenticity. Authenticity in psychology is a construct that is about being true and genuine to your own values, and it is also about accepting the burden of having freedom – the responsibility of having choice. An Australian nurse, Bronnie Ware, spent several years in palliative care and asked her patients whether they had any regrets or anything they would have done differently. She recorded the answers and published them in a book called *The Top 5 Regrets from the Dying* (Ware, 2012). The top five regrets were:

- I wish I had the courage to live a life true to myself, not the life others expected of me.
- I wish I hadn't worked so hard.
- I wish I had the courage to express my feelings.
- I wish I had stayed in touch with my friends.
- I wish I had let myself be happier.

Ware (2012) concluded that we all have a choice, and we can choose what success looks like and can choose happiness and life satisfaction. As coaches or mentors, we can help our clients live an authentic life, think through what taking responsibility with their autonomy and freedom means, make mindful decisions, and take actions mindfully

Living a life based on one's values, faith, and principles

There is evidence that those who live a life according to their values, faith, and principles are happier than those who do not (Moynihan, 2015). It is our experience that those clients who have strayed from their values, faith, and principles are often the most lost, the most in conflict with others and themselves, the most unsatisfied, and the most likely to feel they have not been a success. Values are the principles in which we live our life. When people live their values, they feel congruent and comfortable in their own skin, which enables them to be authentic. Whilst it can be a sensitive subject to discuss with your clients, we see great efficacy in doing so.

You may find that if your clients are experiencing a significant life experience, such as getting divorced, a family member dying, or their being diagnosed with cancer, they may suddenly wake up to their values. Which of your clients need to identify what matters to them and build their decisions, behaviour, and time around them?

The benefit of approaching these seven components of success with your clients

Our clients often come to us with specific problems. All good coaches or mentors know, however, that the presenting problem might not be the real problem. The three major reasons why the presenting problem might not be the real problem are:

1. 'The problem', the 'thing', might not be the issue at all; it is likely to be the way our clients are thinking about or relating to or reacting to the 'thing' that is the real problem.
2. The 'issue' or the lens through which they see 'the problem' is the wrong lens, giving them a warped or narrow perspective.
3. The focus is on the wrong problem – something bigger, more resonant, and more important might be going on.

By helping your clients define what success is for them, you can help them break out of any myopic look at the work you do together. There is a trend in the contracting of coaches or mentors that the programme of work be just over six sessions. We wonder if this is enough. In just six sessions the temptation is to deal with the presenting problem only, because there might not be time to gain more perspective. Our role as a coach or mentor is to help them gain self-awareness about what they are looking at, the way they are looking at it, or the way they are approaching it. Often our clients don't allow themselves to just stop and think, and they neglect their own well-being, happiness, and satisfaction as they pursue work goals We can be the pause button for our clients and can help them gain perspective, connect with their feelings, and create robust plans that will meet their needs as a human being

Pause to consider where your clients are placing their focus. We've noticed many clients arrive with tangled up thoughts and energy around something that is happening right now, and unless they can take a wider perspective and a longer view, they might make wrong decisions and take wrong-footed actions. If you both work from a position of the context of their situation and how they are feeling about themselves in relation to the bigger picture of what success means to them and what success they want in various aspects of their life, then you will be in a better position to partner with them in pursuit of the core universal things we all want: a sense of achievement, autonomy, connection, happiness, satisfaction, and wellness. In the previous chapter, we acknowledged how our past life experiences impact and shape us, and it is also worth covering this ground when exploring what success means for your clients.

Exploring and analysing your clients' view of success

Our conversations with clients aim to enable them to make choices and to guide their decisions in light of what matters to them to help them live an authentic, full life. In this section, we suggest some techniques to help conduct these conversations with your clients. This is sophisticated work: You need to gain their trust and ensure you create psychological safety because they could be unnerved about showing their vulnerability and unleashing thoughts – saying out loud what scares them – because they don't yet know the solutions to their problems.

Tools and techniques

Mindful breathing

To help your client relax enough to access their deepest inner fears and share their concerns with you, you will need to set the tone, the atmosphere, and the pace. Talking and thinking fast gets in the way of accessing deep feelings and thoughts. We find that by asking the client to join us in an exercise of mindful breathing, we can quickly create a conducive reflexive space. Mindful breathing, akin to meditation, slows down their parasympathetic nervous system and allows us to gain clarity and insight, and to be more creative with our ideas and the generation of options. We have written the following script that you may wish to learn and practice aloud before trying with one of your clients:

'Start by sitting comfortably, with your eyes closed or open. Notice how you feel right now. Notice how you are breathing. Take a few deep, long breaths. Breathing in through your nose and out through your mouth. Find your own natural rhythm.

Exhale completely, and then as you inhale feel the air come into the lower part of your belly, middle belly, sides and backs of the ribs and only lastly into your chest and throat. Hold your breath for two seconds and slowly exhale to the count of one-two-three-and-four, emptying out your lungs.

Do another two rounds of this breathing exercise. Thoughts may appear, and that is okay. As and when they do, notice them and then draw your attention back to your breath.

Now notice how you feel right now. It is likely you feel remarkably calmer and more peaceful.'

Questions to assess your clients' needs and desires

Here is a series of suggested questions that explore what success means to your clients right now and how much and what kind of success they want to create for themselves:

- What is success to you over the next year – the next five – or the next 10 years?

- What gives you happiness? How much of that are you getting?
- What do you need to feel and what needs to be in your life to be successful?
- What do you need to have accomplished, in order to feel a 'success'?
- How will you know when you are successful? Happy? Satisfied? Well?
- What needs to change about your body to feel successful?
- What will it feel like to be a success (in the kinds of emotions you will have/show)?
- What will it be like to be a success in terms of your mental state?
- What is success for you in terms of your home – next year, in 5–10 years?
- How do you want to be spending your time in five years?
- Who do you want to be around and have around you in 5–10 years' time?
- What will financial success look like to you?
- What is it you would have loved to have achieved by this time next year? In five years? In 10 years?
- What will your relationships be like when they are 10/10?
- How will you see success regarding fun and enjoyment in your life?
- What will your social life be like if it was super-successful?
- How will your family connections be when they are utterly successful?
- How different will things be when you live a life that is more authentic?
- How will you be when you are successfully living your values/faith/ principles?
- If I could wave a magic wand and your heart's highest hope would be fulfilled –what would be fulfilled? What are your beliefs around this ever happening?

Rich pictures

Asking big, open questions may not be the right approach for some people; they might shy away from, or seize up, or make jokes to deflect away from facing serious or disturbing truths. Psychodynamic approaches can be useful because they bypass words and allow them to express themselves, sometimes revealing subconscious needs and values. Rich Pictures is a psychodynamic projective technique. It involves asking clients to draw their life right now and how they want it to be, say, in one year or 5–20 years. The method taps into the subconscious (some say the unconscious) and gives them a chance to confront what is going on right now that they don't want to say or can't find words to say.

To do rich pictures, invite your clients to draw a vertical line in the middle of a blank A4 page (or better still, an artists' sheet of A3 and give them a range of coloured crayons, pens, and inks). On the left-hand side ask them to simply draw, spontaneously, their life as it is now. Reassure them not to worry about their artistic ability and encourage them not to overthink it. Then ask them to draw on another sheet what success looks like for them in the future (you can work out between you what period would be good or do several sheets for several points in the future).

Once they have finished, ask them to write some words to describe what they see as the differences in the two pictures. Once they are finished, ask them:

- What strikes you about the pictures?
- What do you notice about the differences between the pictures?
- What are these differences saying to you about your life and the changes/ developments you might want to make?
- What do the pictures show that is important to you?
- As you look at your picture that depicts where you are today, what would be your biggest regret if you were to die yesterday?
- What is striking you about what is essential that you want to work towards?

Wheel of Life

This is a technique you are probably already aware of and we are using it to identify your clients' criteria of success and where they are with respect to those criteria currently. It is a visual representation of their current success and life satisfaction.

The first step is to brainstorm with your clients about the areas of success and satisfaction they consider important now, in the relative near-future, and in the medium-term future. Looking at our previous components, this might include job, career, mental health, emotional health, physical health, social life, partner, friends, immediate family, wider family, children, their home, engagement with their community, religion, hobbies, financial security, holidays, achievements, accomplishments, autonomy, freedom, living their values, etc. The domains of success that they consider important become the spokes of their wheel.

Invite them to draw a circle and, depending on how many important life domains they have, ask them to draw the equivalent spokes from the centre of the circle and write a title on top of each of them. Their Rich Pictures might inform some of their spokes. Assure them only to write down aspects that are important to them, it can be anything between 5–12 spokes. It should look something like Figure 3.2.

The third step is to ask them to mark on their circle, on a scale of 1–10, how successful they currently feel on each of the elements (10 is very successful and on the outer edge of the circle). Then, ask them to join the dots. This will give them a visual representation of how successful they feel.

Ask them to stand back and look at their wheel for a few moments. Then ask them to consider some questions around the wheel. We've identified a few of our favourites in Table 3.2.

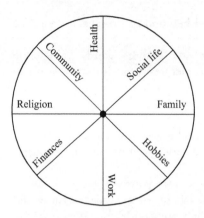

Figure 3.2 Wheel of Life

Table 3.2 Exploring the Wheel of Life

What strikes you about your wheel?
Is your wheel wonky? Is it balanced?
In what area/s are you most successful or satisfied? Why is that?
In what area/s are you least successful or satisfied? What is the background to that?
What are the consequences of the unsuccessful parts in your life?
What actions can you start to take to feel more fulfilled and balanced?
Which is the area that, if it received greater attention, would give you the most sense of success and/or satisfaction that felt meaningful to you at this time in your life?

CASE STUDY

James came to coaching with the issue that he was at a crossroads and didn't know what was next for him. He has spent the past 30 years working in several organisations, working up the career ladder. He recently got diagnosed with cancer, so quit his high-pressure job. He wanted to do a job which allowed for more flexibility. The coach worked with James to identify his values and what was important to him. The coach used the Wheel of Life as a means to help James self-evaluate the current reality. His completed wheel is shown in Figure 3.3.

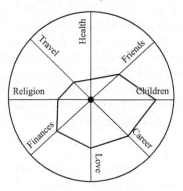

Figure 3.3 James's Wheel of Life

It became clear to the coach that there were some important domains of success that he was not satisfied with. His energies were focused on some areas, leaving other areas bereft of his attention. The coach helped James step back to consider the consequences and benefits of living the life he was currently living. He felt that the area that needed to shift the most, the one that would give him huge joy and satisfaction, was travel. He wanted to go travelling again. He hadn't properly travelled for some 40 years, since his gap year. He was coming to a time in his life where he could retire, semi-retire, or at least redefine his work and working life. He had savings and indeed had received a pay-out due to a critical illness, so money wasn't an issue, although he was nervous about spending and not earning. The issue was his wife – she wouldn't want to go travelling in the way that he wanted to (backpacking, walking, taking bus trips). He explored a few easier options but decided to come back to what would really help him feel wonderful. The coach worked with him on how he might approach the subject with his wife, and they rehearsed several scenarios until he was comfortable having the conversation with her. His quest was to exert his need for freedom and autonomy, adventure and travel, whilst at the same time avoiding upset to his wife. As coaches or mentors, we can help our clients step back and weigh up the consequences and benefits of the way they are living their life, reappraise those choices, and make mindful decisions based on what will work better for them. The wheel can be used as a shortcut for doing just that.

Values

There are numerous ways to guide your clients to uncover what they value. You may wish to ask them to cast their mind back to a positive memory. Invite them to imagine themselves back in that moment of time. Hearing what they heard and seeing what they saw. Ask them what that positive memory says about their values.

The following questions may also be useful for you when exploring this topic:

* What is important to you? What is really important to you? What is really, really important to you?
* What motivates you to get up in the morning?
* What are you doing when you are doing your best?
* What do you admire about people? What do people admire about you?
* When are you at your happiest? What does that say about what you value?
* What principles do you want to be judged on?
* What would make you proud – and what does that say about your values?
* How do you want to spend your time?
* How do you want to be described at your funeral – and what does that say about your values?
* What do you want your colleagues to say about you? How about your friends? Your children? Your partner? Your family?

To help clients face how well they are living their values, you may wish to use the template in Figure 3.3 with your clients. In the first column, you can invite them to populate their values. In the top line of the rest of the columns, they can add the dates they wish to reflect, which may be every day, every week, or every month. After every critical event or at milestones your clients can reflect on how well they were living their values out of 10, with 1 not living at all and 10 living to the fullest. A partially illustrated example can be found in Figure 3.3.

Table 3.3 Living your values

Values	1st May	15th May	29th May	5th June	12th June
Joie de vivre	8/10	7/10			
Honesty	7/10	8/10			
Dedication	5/10	4/10			
Optimism	6/10	6/10			
Passion	7/10	3/10			

Once they've completed this template, they can bring this to the coaching or mentoring session to have an honest, open conversation. You may like to explore:

- Where do you see a pattern?
- What scores most surprise you?
- What scores do you want to address first?
- What would it look like if <insert value> was one mark higher? What would be different?
- Where could you have been more <insert value>?
- What or where could you show more <insert value>?
- When you are being really successful, how will you be? How do you know?
- How is the way you are living your values affecting your career decisions?
- How is the way you are living your values helping or hindering you to feel successful?
- If we were to take your scores as a film script, how is the way you are living your values going to affect the end of the movie? What will be the outcomes?

Analysing their success in line with the academic literature

Having explored your clients' beliefs around the success domains they generated in their rich pictures, Wheel of Life, and values, you will have analysed how they sit alongside their phenomenological view of success. We are now suggesting that you analyse with them how they sit alongside common elements of success academics have found through research.

This is a more structured approach. We've constructed a table you might like to play with (Table 3.4). It takes the seven components of success (you could always add others that arise through your conversations with your clients). Ask them to scale each element, using the same 1–10 scoring system as before.

Having teased out their ratings, you can then explore with them any patterns or anomalies you find. What is standing out for them? What is surprising them? How about you? What are you noticing that you could offer as your observation?

Table 3.4 Analysing the seven elements of success

How well are you…	Scale 1/10	Comments
Making time for exercise and outdoor activities?		
Enjoying a wide range of emotions and able to manage your emotions/mental state?		
Having security, i.e. a home, enough money?		
Putting your time and energy into situations where you can take personal responsibility for finding solutions and problems?		
Setting moderate achievement goals and taking calculated risks?		
Having enough moments of happiness, joy, and pleasure?		
Feeling connected with others; feeling you belong?		
Seeing enough of family and friends?		
Feeling authentic, having autonomy and freedom?		
Living a life based on one's values, faith, and principles?		

Goal-setting

Goals keep us motivated and focused, and they help us achieve (Locke & Latham, 1994). Goals will give big-picture views of success more granularly as your clients think through the possibilities they want to create in their lives. The goals you help your clients create can be turned into statements of what they want to achieve and serve as focal points for their efforts. As goals have been found to regulate behaviour and drive behaviour to reach valued outcomes (Locke & Latham, 1994), you will be helping them be more likely to reach their hearts highest hopes.

We each have the freedom to carve the life we want and with that freedom comes responsibility. As coaches or mentors, we too have freedom and responsibility to in helping our clients work out: whether they are giving sufficient time, space and attention to everything, they consider important; what they want to aim for; what plans they have to accomplish their goals, what actions will they need to take and what might be the consequences for them and others in taking these actions as well as thinking through what outcomes might be reached for them and others.

By helping clients not only think through what they want but take full responsibility for their autonomy and freedom within their goal setting and execution of goals, we help them make great decisions. If they are aiming very low or high – or if they are narrowly focused on one or two aims this year, and we don't challenge them on their plans and consequences of actions, or talk through the potential outcomes – we are not upholding our responsibility in partnering with them. Likewise, if we invite them to aim for goals that are wildly unrealistic, or that impact on others or need others' consent without discussing how they might gain that consent, we are being irresponsible. Knowing what to focus on can be onerous and an ethical issue, something that supervision can help with.

Helping clients make good goals is important. Generally, when our clients set goals, they will be more likely to realise their wishes because:

- Goals will give them a sense of direction.
- Goals help direct their decisions.
- Goals help them focus on where to spend their time, money, and effort.
- Goals can inspire through setbacks and difficulties.

It can be difficult knowing how far to check or work with clients on their goals and planning. Your clients may be brilliant at planning, it might even be their expertise, and so asking basic questions around goal-setting might appear trivial to them and like a waste valuable coaching time. We've experimented with different questions around goal-setting and have found these to be the most useful and the most likely not to cause any negative reaction:

- What level of goal-setting and decision-making have you done around this?
- You've obviously made goals before – what goal-setting method has worked best for you?
- What level of thinking have you done around this? Where does your thinking need help?
- You appear to have made an insight – where else can this insight work for you?
- If that is your goal – what do you know and what do we need to work on together?
- Given what you know about your goal-setting and adherence of focus/ effort to goals, what would be the most useful thing for us to discuss?
- Why is this goal important?
- What are the facets that will make your success likely?

- What do you think the biggest obstacles might be?
- What's bothering you about this goal?
- At what stage do you need or could you involve others?
- Who do you know who might help?
- How good are you at keeping to plans and executing them?
- What resources/strengths do you have, or could you have?
- What will be different when you achieve success?
- How will you be different when you achieve this success?
- How can you be this goal – bring into your presence what you most value?
- What skills will you have to acquire?
- What knowledge do you need?
- What mindset would be best to adopt?
- Where are your freedoms?
- What are you assuming?
- What do you need to do to assume full responsibility when you execute your plan?
- What habits will you have to drop and create to meet these goals?
- How could you draw some of the qualities you want as an outcome of the success closer, in the way you live your life tomorrow?
- How does the way you are working towards your goals impact on you and others?
- To what extent are your goals self-congruent?
- To what extent do your goals match other people's goals and the wills of others?
- What goals are going to be most valuable not for only you but all the key players?

It might help by having your clients make a clear and simple sentence about the success they want. Some clients enjoy working that up into a picture, a collage, a literal vision which can be used as an ongoing reminder to guide them. Begin with the end in mind, said Stephen Covey (2013), and clients find that both useful to keep them focused and help their decision-making, and it can be inspiring. We would add that a vision of the end state can motivate but it can also demotivate because it can feel so far from where they are that they become demoralised. So we've found it important to set out milestones that feel achievable to celebrate success. The goals do not need to be all about achievements; they can be steps of learning, becoming more skilled at something, anything that is heading in the right direction.

Most people know about the SMART mnemonic for goal-setting. They check that the goal is specific, measurable, achievable, relevant, and timely. Below is an extended version of that mnemonic that adds different elements to broaden the check.

- S–specific, significant, serious, stretching.
- M–measurable, meaningful, motivational.

- A–attainable, achievable, agreed, aligned.
- R–relevant, reasonable, rewarding.
- T–time-bound, timely.

A more serious check on clients' goals might be to have them stand well ahead in the future, to imagine they are 90 years of age and having achieved the goal they are striving for – but, have lost various other factors in their single-minded focus. For instance, what if they led a group of people to meet a tough aim on time but in that single-minded focus lost their health? Can you spin that story to see their reaction – imagine they've had an illness that makes them unable to be mobile? Or what if they've lost their spouse? Our experience is that the goals people thought were so important often disintegrate into nothing when they've been diagnosed with a life-threatening illness. We can help our clients gain perspective by testing their goals with provocative questions and sometimes unpleasant thoughts. Some clients act as if their entire life is being judged on whether they are a success on the project they are working on at the moment. There is obviously little wisdom in that but it is easy to become myopic when pressure is upon us and the income we use to support our family's security depends on pleasing a demanding boss. Finding the right way to help clients in such a situation is sensitive work.

Sometimes clients have goals that are so high they are grandiose. Achievement of these goals would take them away from their present life, and therein lies the secret: They don't like their present life. Inquiring into what they want to run away from, who they are not being that they would like to be, and what they need might help ground them. We then help them focus on what is really important and letting go of the attachment to the things that are not. It might be fruitful here to concentrate on goals other than achievements or accomplishments, such as goals around the kind of home they want to live in, goals around the family relationships, and goals around the quality of relationship with their partner.

Designing strategies

Our role is to help our clients make goals that fit their values and will not harm them. Then our role is to design strategies that achieve those goals with minimum effort and maximum enjoyment, and that gain maximum value. Designing strategies isn't just about listing all the actions they are going to do and forcing them to commit to the what, when, where, how. Our work here involves direct communication, giving feedback, and your observations of the tasks ahead, given what your clients have told you or the 360-degree feedback or psychometrics you may have seen on them. If you think the pace is too fast or the aim too low/high, you can, if you've contracted for it, offer your thoughts, again, without attachment; you aren't speaking as a boss or a judge but as a partner. You need to be their faithful frank friend ensuring they are inspired, will notice opportunities, won't take on too much, won't fall down the holes they've fallen through before, will evolve their ability at self-directed learning, will stay focused, and will put in the effort required as well as deal appropriately with obstacles and setbacks.

Most executive clients are confident, diligent, and committed; they can be overly self-reliant and overly independent, and overly conscientious. We've found that we can serve them by forcing them to consider simple questions such as, 'Where could you be asking for help?', 'What could you do to have more enjoyment in life?' You could rehearse with them in the session how they might seek help, encouraging them to stretch themselves in the psychological safety of a coaching space.

In your partnering, you can ask:

- How could you best use me in helping you think through your actions?
- How could you think differently about yourself as a result of this session? How does that impact your view of success/your goals/your planned actions?
- From the work that we have done together, could you create a new habit that would be useful to you as you embark on these actions towards your success?
- What can you do with what we have thought about/experienced/ talked about? What will that look like? What will it enable you to do? How valuable is that to you?

Working through goals and designing strategies can be an anxious time as clients unpack all the things they will need to do and the obstacles they will need to overcome. It is here that through a Rogerian therapeutic relationship and our coaching presence we can imbue calm confidence in them. Through our warm acceptance of their whole self, through our care, and our unconditional positive regard, we can foster their self-belief and realism. As we retain equanimity, they will feel they can access and acknowledge their feelings. This level of honesty helps clients engage with greater motivation and a greater sense of ownership. We can be useful in assisting clients to pause and contemplate the extent to which the actions they are taking and planning to take are in line with their informed decisions. They've thought things through, and it is their choice and their will; they are not being persuaded by anyone else against their volition and wisdom. This will all aid the authenticity of their strategies and commitments to them.

With our objectivity we can help our clients create strategies towards goals that will help them to function better and to have well-being along the way – and this will make the goal-attainment actions more sustainable (Grant & Cavanagh, 2011). We can support our clients in improving their happiness. Part of this work is to help them function better, which might include mini-skill development and instruction in problem-solving, negotiating, or assertiveness. Part of the work to bring about well-being might be to consider with their choices in how they might like to celebrate successful milestones, imposed rest and recreation and fun. We know that happiness precedes success across major life domains (Lyubomirsky, King & Diener, 2005), so do check that they aren't muscling down for a long grind without much payback; where are the opportunities for pleasure, joy, contentment?

Some of your clients are likely to be high-achievers. There are ethical issues to consider when coaching or mentoring high-achievers. Here are a few of them:

- High achievers can work too hard and burn out. To what extent are you colluding with their perverse need to achieve?
- Many high-achievers strive to overachieve, to stand out, and to make more money and gain more status than others. Many writers on society say that it is the very divide between rich and poor and those with a high and low status that causes distress and crime. Wilkinson and Pickett (2010) argue that more equality is better for us all and that feeding high-achievers is morally wrong for the health of society. How could you address the moral issues of greed and avarice?
- High-achievers rarely have pleasure as part of their plan. Overachievement may be their dark side and their crucifix: It brings with it anxiety, depression, and a feeling of never been satisfied or content. Should you help them find balance if the balance isn't what they want?

There have been found to be universal desires, states, and conditions that we all need. Those needs include personal growth/feelings of competence, social connection/relatedness as well as freedom and autonomy (Deci & Ryan, 1985).

If you take time to unpick these, check in with your clients, using the following questions:

- How good is the pace for you with this plan on your personal growth?
- What will you be learning along the way; what competence will you be developing? How relevant to you and the future of work, as well as to others, is it that you develop that competence?
- What opportunities for engaging with others do these actions present? How do or could these actions give you an opportunity to be with the kind of other people you wish to be with?
- How will or can these actions add to your sense of freedom?
- What part of this plan most excites you?
- What part of this plan gives you a sense of autonomy?
- How might you enjoy these actions?

Keeping momentum

When we contract, we ask our clients the role they would like us to play. After helping gain insight and make plans, clients often want us to help them keep progress, be their conscience, monitor their actions, and adhere to their plans. But how do we do that without appearing to judge or without acting like another boss or just another person with an agenda on them? What we have learned is to ask with objectivity and without attachment to any particular answer. You can ask:

- If you didn't do as we planned, what did you notice about what got in the way?
- If you did what we planned, what did you notice about how you felt and went about things in order to execute the plan?
- If we pause for a moment to seek – what is becoming clear to you?
- What is making sense for you?
- How are you progressing in your thinking?
- What do we need to consider in maintaining progress towards your goal?
- What do you know about yourself that might hinder progress? What could my role be, therefore? Where do we go next?
- What do you need to maintain focus and momentum?

Closing remarks

This chapter hopefully has equipped you to address the meta-question of what success is to your clients. The knowledge about how beliefs are formed and the latest research about the components of success are now in your toolbox and will enable you to have rich conversations with your clients. This, matched with staying client-centred and following the thread of what our clients are saying, is important for them and will allow you to cover the ground thoroughly. The tools and techniques we introduced in the later part of the chapter help you identify what is important for the client and then aid you to analyse how close they are to what success looks like for them. We have suggested several tools and techniques, so it is up to you to pick and choose the right tool for your clients. Whilst working towards success, some areas of your clients' lives may become neglected; therefore, the next chapter, which is about resilience, is crucial. When you find the components of success and life satisfaction with clients you will naturally uncover any work-life imbalance. As they see this imbalance within the perspective of their success and satisfaction, they will be motivated to do something about it. Then you can work on how they can empower themselves to achieve and lead more of the life they wish to be leading. We think this is the definition of good work, lucky work, privileged work.

QUESTIONS FOR REFLECTION

- In this chapter, what aspect has been most salient for you in your work?
- What actions do you most want to take away and how are you going to ensure you take them away?
- What are your beliefs about your success as a coach and mentor? How are they enabling or constraining you?

Additional reading and resources

Covey, S.R. (2013). *The 7 Habits of Highly Effective People: Powerful Lessons in Personal Change*. New York: Simon and Schuster.

Hofstede, G. (1984). The cultural relativity of the quality of life concept. *Academy of Management Review*, 9(3), pp. 389–398.

Kahneman, D. & Deaton, A. (2010). High income improves evaluation of life but not emotional well-being. *Proceedings of the National Academy of Sciences*, 107(38), pp. 16489–16493.

References

Covey, S.R. (2013). *The 7 Habits of Highly Effective People: Powerful Lessons in Personal Change*. New York: Simon and Schuster.

Deci, E. & Ryan, R.M. (1985). *Intrinsic Motivation and Self-Determination in Human Behavior*. Berlin: Springer Science & Business Media.

Deci, E.L. & Ryan, R.M. (1987). The support of autonomy and the control of behavior. *Journal of Personality and Social Psychology*, 53(6), p. 1024.

Diener, E.D., Emmons, R.A., Larsen, R.J. & Griffin, S. (1985). The satisfaction with life scale. *Journal of Personality Assessment*, 49(1), pp. 71–75.

Erikson, E. (1963). *Childhood and Society* (2nd ed.). New York: Norton.

Erikson, E.H. & Erikson, J.M. (1998). *The Life Cycle Completed* (extended version). New York: WW Norton & Company.

Grant, A.M. & Cavanagh, M.J. (2011). *Designing Positive Psychology: Taking Stock and Moving Forward*. Oxford, UK: Oxford University Press.

Hofstede, G. (1984). The cultural relativity of the quality of life concept. *Academy of Management Review*, 9(3), pp. 389–398.

Hu, T., Zhang, D. & Yang, Z. (2015). The relationship between attributional style for negative outcomes and depression: a meta-analysis. *Journal of Social and Clinical Psychology*, 34(4), pp. 304–321.

Kahneman, D. (2018). *Daniel Kahneman on Cutting Through the Noise* (Ep. 56—Live at Mason). Accessed on 21st January 2019 at: https://medium.com/conversations-with-tyler/tyler-cowen-daniel-kahneman-economics-bias-noise-167275de691f.

Kahneman, D. & Deaton, A. (2010). High income improves evaluation of life but not emotional well-being. *Proceedings of the National Academy of Sciences*, 107(38), pp. 16489–16493.

Layard, R., Clark, A.E., Cornaglia, F., Powdthavee, N. & Vernoit, J. (2014). What predicts a successful life? A life-course model of well-being. *The Economic Journal*, 124(580), pp. F720–F738.

Locke, E. & Latham, G. (1994). Goal-setting theory. In John B. Miner (Ed.), *Organizational Behavior 1: Essential Theories of Motivation and Leadership* (pp. 159–183). London and New York: Routledge.

Lyubomirsky, S., King, L. & Diener, E. (2005). The benefits of frequent positive affect: does happiness lead to success? *Psychological Bulletin*, 131(6), p. 803.

MacDonald, M., Phipps, S. & Lethbridge, L. (2005). Taking its toll: the influence of paid and unpaid work on women's well-being. *Feminist Economics*, 11(1), pp. 63–94.

Mahdavi, I., (2010). Comparing men's and women's perception of modality of teaching business ethics. *Journal of Instructional Pedagogies*, 2, pp. 1–7.

Maslow, A. & Lewis, K.J. (1987). *Maslow's Hierarchy of Needs* (p. 987), 14. Salenger Incorporated.

Maslow, A.H. (1943). A theory of human motivation. *Psychological Review*, 50(4), p. 370.

McClelland, D.C. & Johnson, E.W. (1984). *Learning to Achieve*. Glenview, IL: Scott, Foresman & Co.

Moynihan, D.P., DeLeire, T. & Enami, K. (2015). A life worth living: evidence on the relationship between prosocial values and happiness. *The American Review of Public Administration*, 45(3), pp. 311–326.

Peterson, C., Seligman, M.E. & Vaillant, G.E. (1988). Pessimistic explanatory style is a risk factor for physical illness: a thirty-five-year longitudinal study. *Journal of Personality and Social Psychology*, 55(1), p. 23.

Sandstrom, G.M. & Dunn, E.W. (2014). Social interactions and well-being: the surprising power of weak ties. *Personality and Social Psychology Bulletin*, 40(7), pp. 910–922.

Seligman, M.E. (1972). Learned helplessness. *Annual Review of Medicine*, 23(1), pp. 407–412.

Shin, D.C. & Johnson, D.M. (1978). Avowed happiness as an overall assessment of the quality of life. *Social Indicators Research*, 5(1–4), pp. 475–492.

Sirin, S.R. (2005). Socioeconomic status and academic achievement: a meta-analytic review of research. *Review of Educational Research*, 75(3), pp. 417–453.

The Telegraph. (2015). Just three in 10 people feel 'happy with their lives'. Accessed on 12th October 2018 at: https://www.telegraph.co.uk/news/uknews/11362246/Just-three-in-10-people-feel-happy-with-their-lives.html.

Vaillant, G.E. & Mukamal, K. (2001). Successful aging. *American Journal of Psychiatry*, 158(6), pp. 839–847.

Ware, B. (2012). *The Top Five Regrets of the Dying*. New York: Hay House, Inc.

Weiner, B. (1985). An attributional theory of achievement motivation and emotion. *Psychological Review*, 92(4), p. 548.

Wigfield, A. & Eccles, J.S. (2002). The development of competence beliefs, expectancies for success, and achievement values from childhood through adolescence. In *Development of Achievement Motivation* (pp. 91–120). San Diego, CA: Academic Press.

Wilkinson, R. & Pickett, K. (2010). *The Spirit Level: Why Equality is Better for Everyone*. London, UK: Penguin.

4 Stage 3

Resilience and coping with setbacks

Introduction

In the last 20 years, there has been a growing surge of research on resilience in different sectors and disciplines from both theoretical and empirical perspectives. Four distinct levels of exploration have emerged – individual, groups and teams, organisational, and community resilience. For this chapter and book, we are primarily interested in developing individual resilience – the resilience of your clients. The content of this chapter forms the basis of the third stage in our Four-Stage Model for Work-Life Balance, illustrated in Figure 4.1.

A plethora of resilience books, programmes, and short courses have emerged from the research in response to increased interest in the topic, the recognition of growing health concerns, the known consequences of poor resilience, and individuals' and organisations' willingness to invest time and money in this area. In the introduction and chapter 1, we explored the areas of attention in the lives of our clients which need continuous care to maintain a sense of work-life balance. The areas broadly encompass career, work, social, community, private/home life, finances, and health. We add that universal needs of self-fulfilment, happiness, autonomy, competence, and a sense of belonging also need to be present to enable work-life balance. For your clients, to make it through some events in life, they might choose to temporarily downplay some of these areas, but doing so for an extended period usually produces negative effects in other areas of life and can strain resilience. This has been documented as the case for people who concentrate most or all of their energies into work and career. When we have seen this occur in our own research and practice, in a variety of sectors, where the risk of burnout is magnified, sickness, work absence, and ultimately resignation are a common occurrence. Physical, emotional, and mental exhaustion can occur in challenging cultures and environments and can be triggered by multiple sources. The consequences of burnout are that people feel:

- Overwhelming exhaustion.
- Irritable and frequently exasperated.
- Forgetful, and have a harder time remembering things.
- Cynical and detached.

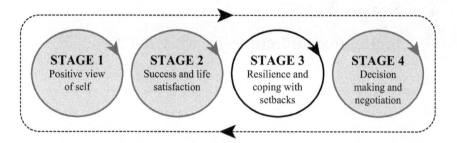

Figure 4.1 Four-Stage Model for Work-Life Balance

- Less happy and satisfied with career and with home life.
- Disillusioned with work and obsessively worrying about performance.
- A sense of ineffectiveness and lack of accomplishment.
- Low self-esteem.

Attending to all areas of our lives, and understanding which areas may need greater attention at different times, requires a high degree of self-insight, self-awareness, situational awareness, and an understanding of what we can and can't influence and control. We have already visited some of these areas in chapters 2 and 3 when we explored themes such as locus of control.

Your clients at some point in their lives (and often whilst they are in contact with you) will come up against a major setback, a life-changing event that changes the course of their lives. For some, it may be a divorce or redundancy; for others, a critical illness, or the death of a parent or child. These are pivotal moments that can lay a heavy toll on their ability to cope. Their work-life balance and energy supplies will determine their ability to manage and overcome the setbacks they encounter. This chapter is not intended to make you an expert in resilience but to instead support you to help your clients manage the risks from stressors, achieve greater self-insight, control and influence, increasing their capacity to cope, adapt, and thrive.

We begin the chapter with an overview of the origins of the term resilience and how it is defined in a variety of contexts, as well as the relationship between work-life balance and resilience. Then we explore the impact of stress on resilience levels and how stress can lead to burnout. Clients can think they are coping and coping until they suddenly aren't, and by learning the early-warning indications and the antecedents to burnout, you might help clients avert it. Next, we examine the relationship between coaching, mentoring, and resilience and look at how, through the process of dialogue, enquiry, and deliberate practice, you can help your clients achieve resilience. Your coaching or mentoring sessions provide a space where your clients' work-life balance issues can be addressed, helping them to be at their most effective, productive and positive. In turn, this will increase their capacity to cope and bounce back from change and pressures. In this way, they can adopt a flexible and adaptive approach to the challenges they face.

We propose that six masteries – mental, emotional, physical, social, spiritual, and environmental – all require tending to if your clients are to achieve work-life balance. We then describe each of the six masteries and illustrate how they can be applied in your coaching or mentoring practice. We refer to several case studies to illustrate how resilience features in practice; we demonstrate some of the tools and techniques so that you can see how developing resilience and coping with setbacks works in real situations.

At the end of each section, there will be a series of reflective questions to prompt your consideration of your coaching or mentoring practice and your clients' perspectives and behaviours. Should you wish to explore this area further, we have provided additional reading and resources.

What is resilience?

Theoretical and empirical studies into resilience can be traced back over 40 years to the work of Professor Norman Garmezy and later, his colleagues from the University of Minnesota and Arizona State University, USA (Masten, Best & Garmezy, 1990). Their studies found that resilience played a significant role in the mental health of children experiencing significant adversity. Over time, numerous studies have been published, and numerous definitions have emerged, such as:

- 'Resilience is the process, capacity or outcome of successful adaptation despite challenges or threatening circumstances ... good outcomes despite high risk status, sustained competence under threat and recovery from trauma' (Masten, Best & Garmezy, 1990, p. 426).
- 'Resilience ... individual ... refers to successful adaptation despite risk and adversity' (Masten, 1994, p. 3).
- 'Capacity to overcome personal vulnerabilities and environmental stressors, to be able to "bounce back" in the face of potential risks, and to maintain well-being' (Oswald, Johnson & Howard, 2003, p. 50).
- 'Capacity to continue to "bounce back", to recover strengths or spirit quickly and efficiently in face of adversity ... a dynamic construct subject to influence by environmental, work-specific and personal contexts' (Sammons et al., 2007, p. 694).
- 'Resilience is the capacity to bounce back from disruptions ... resilience is the capacity to continue making progress toward your current career goals with the resources and strategies you have already developed' (Seibert, Kraimer & Heslin, 2016, p. 245).

Defining resilience is problematic due to the different views about whether it is a skill, a process, a set of intelligences, a condition, or a group of outcomes. Determining its meaning is further complicated by the interaction between variables such as gender, education, culture, heritage, history, and local environmental issues. This problem is further compounded by the multitude of challenges or risk factors and the many protection factors which have been identified, in addition to the complex, dynamic relationship between them. However, the common thread amongst the various definitions is the degree to which we are able to withstand and recover from challenges, pressure, or stressors; and the extent to which we are adaptable and can retain our capacity to remain flexible in our thoughts, behaviours, and emotions when under stress. Typically, if your clients are being resilient, they will:

- Adapt to changing circumstances.
- Avoid negative self-talk and self-defeating behaviours.
- Be open to new experiences.
- Problem-solve.
- Reformulate their goals and/or strategies to adapt to changing circumstances.
- Self-reflect and ask penetrating questions of self.
- Stay focused and work towards a goal.
- Think flexibility, appreciate novelty, and show curiosity.
- Think creatively and use their imagination.
- Use humour to see the lighter side of a situation.

Research on resilience focuses on what are called risk and protective factors, alongside individual and internal resiliency factors, resiliency processes, and outcomes. Risk factors are associated with adverse conditions or challenging situations. Protective factors are often described as 'buffers'; they provide a cushion when we encounter difficult times; coaching and mentoring are regarded as a protection intervention, providing a buffer.

Depending on the context, risk and protection factors might be grouped as followed:

- Individual.
- Peer.
- Family.
- School.
- Sport.
- Work.
- Community.

In any context, risk factors might include, amongst others:

- Family and/or work conflict.
- Lack of positive role models.
- Lack of connected social relationships – alienation, isolation, and lack of social bonding.

- Relentless competition, ranking, and constant comparison.
- Access to education, development, information, and resources.
- Life transitions.

In any context, protective factors might include, amongst others:

- Connected social relationships – positive relationships that promote close bonds.
- Positive role models.
- Healthy beliefs and clear standards.
- Opportunities to participate in activities which promote connectedness.
- Opportunities to participate in activities which support physical health.

Professor Karol Kumpfer's research and work with the Strengthening Families Foundation suggests that the environmental context within which a child functions is very influential on risk and resilience processes: 'Aspects of the family, neighbourhood, school, and peer group impact the socialization process of the child. When acute or chronic stressors occur, this environmental context can buffer or exacerbate the negative impact on the child' (Kumpfer, 1999, p. 189). External influences can act as a buffer or exacerbate the impact of challenging and stressful situations. Considering resilience from a multilayered perspective has yielded rich findings. Research has shown the efficacy in understanding environmental risk factors, protective factors, resiliency factors, and the interaction between the internal characteristics of the person and the final outcome (Kumpfer, 2002; Rutter, 1987; Werner, 1993).

Reflecting on your own practice:

- To what extent do your clients experience challenging and stressful situations?
- How well have you been exploring how your clients' environment is softening or hardening the negative effects of stressors in their lives?

Clients are likely to experience a variety of stressors; some may come from a one-off event that may not be predictable, whilst others might involve being exposed to persistent demands over a sustained period. As a coach or mentor, our role is to assist our clients to focus on the aspects of their resilience that have been impacted, and our intention in this chapter is to help you build that capacity.

How to recognise and identify varying levels of resilience

As you learn to be more aware of the level of your clients' resilience through the use of the six masteries, your clients will better appreciate their choices and their rationale behind a number of their behaviours. You will also help them gauge their level of resilience, and this will help them identify what specific focus, decisions, and actions to take to build their resilience.

If your clients' resilience in under strain, you may find that it is due to:

- A lack of self-belief and self-confidence.
- Difficulty in making decisions or plans.
- Their outlook, beliefs, and mindset.
- Unhealthy habits.
- A tendency to be overly independent.
- A focus on work at the exclusion of social events.

You may notice that they:

- Exhibit anxiety during conversations about a particular issue.
- Avoid discussions about emotions.
- Avoid discussions about potential conflicts.
- Avoid discussions about challenges.

What is the relationship between work-life balance, resilience, and burnout?

When your clients encounter situations they find stressful, the mental and physical strain experienced may result in anxiety, tension, insomnia, and illness, and if these conditions are chronic, ultimately, burnout. The meaning and scope of the concept of burnout differ between countries and contexts. The term 'burnout' was first used by Freudenberger (1974) to describe the emotional and physical exhaustion of staff members of alternative healthcare institutions.

Some researchers and practitioners consider burnout to be a generic term which can apply in any context, even outside of the work environment (Kristensen, Borritz, Villadsen & Christensen, 2005); others have tended to associate burnout with occupations and the workplace (Maslach, Jackson & Leiter, 1996). Sweden and the Netherlands regard burnout as a psychiatric diagnosis; others simply regard burnout as a psychological state of exhaustion. However broadly, burnout is regarded as a common reaction to chronic stress, as is a state of physical, emotional, and mental exhaustion (Schaufeli, Leiter & Maslach, 2009).

A considerable amount of research has been devoted to the understanding of factors contributing to burnout and its consequences for individuals and their health. Burnout is prevalent in professions which are characterised by an intense pace compounded by numerous conflicting demands, high expectations, and the competitive environment common in many professions and industries today.

This is particularly the case in sports and elite athletes. In the context of sports, burnout has been defined as: 'a psychological, emotional, and physical withdrawal from a formerly pursued and enjoyable sport as a result of excessive stress that acts on an athlete over time' (Smith, 1986, cited in Lu et al., 2016, p. 202). The elite sports environment is typified by the combination of high expectations, relentless competition, ranking, comparison, and pressure to please others which results in high levels of burnout. Professor Daniel Gould and his colleagues carried out several mixed method studies to identify and psychologically describe junior tennis burnouts and compare these individuals to players who did not burn out of junior tennis. Their research found that there were distinct differences in demographic, psychological, personality, and coping skills between those players that experienced burnout and those that did not. In particular, tennis players who experienced burnout lacked the coping skills and were therefore less likely to use planning strategies and lacked the ability to reinterpret adversity (Gould et al., 1996).

Reflecting on your own practice:

• To what extent have you noticed any trends in relation to burnout in your clients?
• What connections are there with burnout in particular professions and industries in your coaching or mentoring practice?

Numerous studies, including special issues in the *Journal of Psychology and Health* and the *Journal of Work and Stress*, suggest that individual and internal resiliency factors can lower vulnerability and therefore reduce the risk of burnout. The key areas of importance are:

1. Awareness of and management of risk factors.
2. Awareness, management, and bolstering of protective factors.
3. Awareness of individual resiliency factors.
4. Developing positive self-talk and self-calming skills, and reframing/reinterpretation skills.
5. Views, attitude, and motivation towards the outcomes.
6. Goal-directed behaviour.
7. Absence of self-defeating thoughts and behaviours.
8. Developing coping skills.

In circumstances where individual areas of our lives are downplayed for extended periods, and your clients are not able to maintain a sense of work-life balance, a strain is often experienced. As stress levels increase, the capacity to cope is affected, individual resources such as self-efficacy and self-belief are reduced, and exhaustion creeps in. Therefore, working towards work-life balance, while tending to the individual resiliency factors and addressing the risk and protective factors, can enhance resilience and help prevent burnout.

Exploring the relationship between coaching, mentoring, and resilience

There are numerous empirical studies which demonstrate the impact of coaching or mentoring in supporting and enhancing an individual's resilience. In this section, we provide an outline of some of the most well-known studies from a range of sectors, in addition to our own research. The literature presented provides the backdrop for the sections which follow and support your clients to develop their six masteries: mental, physical, emotional, social, environmental and spiritual mastery.

Coaching as a protective factor in resilience

There have been a number of studies that illustrate how a range of coaching interventions are able to provide protection in situations of immense change, particularly in the organisational setting where restructuring and downsizing are commonplace.

Professor Anthony Grant and his colleagues at the Coaching Psychology Unit, University of Sydney, Australia, have conducted a series of empirical studies into the impact of coaching on metacognition, mental health, and goal attainment. Perhaps one of the most relevant studies was published in 2009 in the *Journal of Positive Psychology*. Their mixed method randomised control study of 41 executives in a public health agency assessed the impact of a number of interventions, including four individual coaching sessions over ten weeks (Grant, Curtayne & Burton, 2009). The public health sector agency was going through a period of significant change and organisational restructuring. A further environmental influence was the degree to which the agency experienced intense scrutiny and pressure both internally and externally. The professional executive coaching sessions were underpinned by a cognitive-behavioural, solution-focused framework previously published by Professor Grant in 2003.

The outcomes of the coaching were measured by an adapted version of a well-known Cognitive Hardiness Scale originally developed and first published by Dr Suzanne Kobasa (1979) and frequently used as the basis of studies by her colleagues (Kobasa, Maddi & Courington, 1981). The findings showed that coaching was effective at enhancing resilience, although the sample size was small. Through the coaching intervention, participants were able to address and overcome barriers and challenges, including, amongst others, negative self-talk and self-defeating behaviours. Combined with the coaches' support to stay focused and work towards a goal, the participants grew in self-confidence and increased their resilience levels, addressing both their mental and emotional needs.

A mixed method study conducted by Professor Gordon Spence and Professor Anthony Grant in 2005 replicated the earlier study by Professor Grant and colleagues in 2003, extending it to include one-to-one life coaching. This enabled the comparison between professional coaching and peer coaching, following research designs in clinical settings where the use of randomised control groups is commonplace. The purpose of the study was to investigate the impact of life coaching on four domains associated with well-being and quality of life – goal-striving, mental health, personality, and metacognition. The nature of the coaching was solution-focused and future-orientated. The study found that individually coached participants experienced a greater sense of environmental mastery and openness to experience.

The research into athletes and their responses to stress and resultant burnout have been the subject of numerous studies. One of the most recent studies published in the *Journal of Psychology of Sport and Exercise* explored the interaction of athletes' resilience and coaches' social support on the stress-burnout relationship. This study, by Professor Frank Lu from the Chinese Culture University, Taiwan, and his colleagues in Taiwan and the USA recommended that athletes be supported by interventions (Lu et al., 2016). They believed a combination of support interventions would reduce risk factors, reduce stressors, strengthen resilience, and promote protective factors. Amongst the many interventions to enhance protective factors was coaching, which would provide much-needed informational, emotional, tangible, and social support.

Reflecting on your own practice:

- To what extent do your clients view coaching as a buffer or protective factor in their lives?
- What other buffers or forms of protection do your clients have in place to support their needs?

Mentoring as a protective factor in resilience

A number of studies have found that mentoring can help build your clients' protective factor, a known buffer of stressors. This section illustrates the degree to which mentoring can act as a facilitator for the development of positive self-concept, self-regulation, and management of emotions, self-confidence, decision-making, empowerment, and relational and social skills.

Professor Kathy Lemon Osterling and colleagues at San Jose State University, USA, have spent many years focusing on how child welfare practices and policies influence child and family well-being, particularly amongst culturally diverse populations (Osterling & Hines, 2006). Typically, foster youth transitioning out of the child welfare system are at risk for low attainment, homelessness, employment and financial difficulties, and mental and physical health problems. Mentoring is considered to be one of the protective factors that can help to buffer at-risk youth from poor transitional outcomes. These include, amongst others, lack of positive self-concept, poor relational skills, and poor job and educational attainment (Grossman & Tierney, 1998; Turner & Scherman, 1996; Zippay, 1995). Mentoring enables mentees to develop soft and hard skills, including self-regulation, understanding and managing their own emotions, resulting in less anger in addition to broader living skills, finding a job, and completing their education.

An important study in this context is one that proved mentoring helps people make transitions in their career, providing a vital source of personal and professional support, particularly in difficult environments. Dr Robert Fantilli and his colleague, Professor Douglas McDougall at the University of Toronto, CA, conducted a mixed method study with graduates from a two-year Master pre-service programme and two teachers to understand the transition into teaching. Against the backdrop of high attrition rates – Ontario Teachers' Pension Plan reported a 22–33% attrition rate over the first three years for new teachers (McIntyre, 2004) – their study found that teachers benefitted from informal supports such as teacher colleagues, friends, and family; however, mentoring would provide a valuable source of personal and professional support (Fantilli, & McDougall, 2009). This is further supported by a number of studies undertaken by Professor Brad Olsen and his colleagues, who found that mentoring is vital in helping early-career urban teachers to remain in urban education (Olsen & Anderson, 2007). Overall, mentoring within the teaching profession has been shown to support self-reflection and problem-solving; enhance levels of self-esteem, positive attitude, and confidence; and reduced feelings of isolation.

Two recent large-scale mentoring impact evaluation studies, conducted over the last three years, supported the position that mentoring helps people adapt and act in empowered ways, bounce back from adversity, and cope with excessive challenges (Youth Business International, 2018). The first study was conducted in partnership with Youth Business International (YBI) and Middlesex University Business School. The research aimed to understand the impact of voluntary business mentoring on mentees, their businesses, and their mentors. Conducted over two years, across the globe, the research found that there was a significant increase in mentees' confidence, self-awareness, and decision-making between the first and second phases; with the support of their mentors, mentees were able to adapt and continue to make progress towards their goals.

The second project was commissioned by Médecins Sans Frontières (MSF) Norway Mentoring and Coaching Hub in 2017, to evaluate the impact of mentoring on MSF Field Managers, to specifically understand if mentoring positively impacts on Field Manager's personal and professional development. The interim findings demonstrated that mentoring positively impacted on mentees' ability to bounce back and cope with challenges. Mentees recognised the intense pace of their role, the challenges associated with their mission, and – in some cases – the high-risk, volatile, and violent environmental context. Mentors were able to provide a safe space for mentees to vent, reflect, gain perspective, and recognise their strengths and needs. As a result of the mentoring, the majority of mentees were able to shift from a constant state of panic to a stretch zone, where mentees felt a sense of empowerment, greater confidence, and self-esteem alongside an enhanced ability to see and understand their development areas and access resources to support their needs.

Overall, the empirical research backs up and gives credence to coaches or mentors adopting the use of a rounded approach like our six-mastery model to help their clients gain, maintain, and grow their resilience. It focuses our attention on understanding the different needs of individuals, individual psychological characteristics, how individuals interact within diverse environments, and how these different variables may influence resilience levels. Research also helps us to appreciate how coaching or mentoring can support clients to enhance their resilience through a combination of mental, emotional, social, physical, spiritual, and environmental mastery. We use the term *mastery*, as it denotes an ability to understand and learn new knowledge and skills, apply the learning, and develop expertise. We know that resilience can be developed through the process of dialogue, enquiry, and deliberate practice, and that your skills in creating a psychologically safe space where work–life balance issues can be addressed can help your clients adapt and thrive even in volatile, uncertain, difficult times. In the following sections, we explore each mastery in more detail, provide a series of case exemplars, and present a number of tools and techniques you can use with your clients.

Reflecting on your own practice:

- To what extent do your clients view mentoring as a buffer or protective factor in their lives?
- What other buffers or forms of protection do your clients have in place to support their needs?

The six masteries

Our clients live within an ecosystem which is often highly complex and always influenced by the interaction between the different layers and actors in the ecosystem. Our ecosystems require a high degree of navigation skills. It is no wonder our clients can feel overwhelmed. Our ecosystem is never static; it is continually changing, as we change, as those around us change, and as the nature of work, systems, processes, and structures change.

In this section, we take an ecological approach to resilience implicit in our model of 'six masteries of resilience'. It states that:

- An individual's development is influenced by their surrounding environment.
- As individuals change, they also influence their home, work, and broader environment.
- Individuals are connected with others in a community network.
- Strategies, tools, and techniques work together as an integrated approach to help build an effective system of resilience.

The six masteries of resilience include:

- *Mental mastery* relates to our ability to develop self-awareness, self-insight, and reflectivity skills.
- *Emotional mastery* relates to our ability to understand and manage our own emotions and understand and respond to the emotions of others.
- *Social mastery* relates to our ability to develop strong relationships and good support networks, at home, at work, and in our broader network.

- *Physical mastery* relates to our ability to manage our health and energy levels.
- *Spiritual mastery* relates to our ability to seek and express meaning and purpose and to understand the way we experience connectedness.
- *Environmental mastery* relates to our ability to analyse and manage our environment, appreciate potential resources, access resources, navigate complex external routes to help meet our needs, and address all aspects of our lives.

Our model – six masteries of resilience – can be viewed in Figure 4.2. The diagram shows a continuous loop between each of the six masteries. The masteries can be explored individually within the coaching and mentoring relationship and as a whole within our ecosystem. For example, supporting your clients with their social mastery – the development of strong relationships and good support networks – will require the exploration and development of emotional, spiritual, and environmental mastery. Often relationships and our support network can be neglected in times of pressure and stress, but supportive relationships have been proven to be one of the most significant protective factors in maintaining and enhancing our resilience. Developing positive and

Figure 4.2 Six masteries of resilience

strong relationships requires a high degree of emotional mastery and the ability to relate to other people and connect with them in a deep and meaningful way. It requires spiritual mastery, our ability to seek meaning and purpose and express ourselves and, environmental mastery to understand how and where we might seek sources of support, and who we can go to for support, advice, and friendship.

We explore each mastery and the theory and evidence underpinning each area as important building blocks in enhancing your clients' resilience and ability to respond to setbacks. We provide a number of case exemplars to illustrate some of the challenges your clients may face and provide tools and techniques to support the development of your clients' resilience.

Mental mastery

The term mental mastery refers to the ability to develop self-awareness, self-insight, and reflectivity skills. Mental mastery is regarded as one of the most significant determiners of resilience. Self-insight is the mental habit of asking penetrating questions of oneself and having the willingness to be vulnerable and the courage to provide honest answers.

In chapter 2 on 'self' we explored the development of self-insight, positive self-regard, challenging beliefs, cognitive bias, and thinking errors. Therefore, we do not need to focus on the literature or tools and techniques related to these topics in this chapter. Instead, we reinforce the power of mindfulness as a way of developing the right state of self-awareness and introduce you to a technique you can share with your clients. We also share some reflexivity exercises that you might like to do with your clients.

Through the technology now available, neuroscientists can explain how our brain works better than ever before. The brain uses more energy than any other human organ; it draws approximately 20% of our energy every day (Swaminathan, 2008). The brain is a complex organ with chemicals that are released and flow when we experience different feelings. Understanding some of the basics of neurohormones and neurotransmitters is helpful to the coach and mentor. The hormone oxytocin influences our behaviour and physiology; it originates in the brain, where it's produced by a structure called the hypothalamus, and then transfers to the pituitary gland which releases it into the bloodstream. Oxytocin receptors are found on cells throughout the body. Oxytocin typically flows when we feel trusted, connected with someone or something, and sense rapport. One of the brain's neurotransmitters, a chemical that transfers information between neurons is dopamine; this substance helps regulate movement, attention, learning, and emotional responses. When we feel innovative, creative, and motivated, dopamine is in our system. Serotonin is another important chemical and neurotransmitter in the human body. It regulates mood and social behaviour, appetite and digestion, sleep, memory, and sexual desire and function. We feel the effects of serotonin when we feel a sense of agency, belief, confidence, and self-efficacy. Typically, higher serotonin levels are related to a more positive mood and higher energy levels. Lower serotonin levels may be related to lower energy levels, negative moods, increased irritability, and depression.

In this section, we hope to highlight a number of ways in which you can help your clients to re-energise their brain, mood, and energy, and in doing so, help them become more aware of subtle clues from their body, breathing, and thought processes that will help them have more control over their emotions and actions. In later sections, we address the importance of sleep, healthy eating, and exercise, which are also ways of re-energising the brain. Should your clients be depleted and exhausted, they will lose access to their optimum brain functioning because the body is judicious in its use of fuel and diverts energy to basic functioning. Clients might lose concentration, higher-order thinking, be easily distracted, react impulsively, fail to see the long-term implications, and make poor decisions in this state. If you suspect your clients are in this state, you could explore mindfulness practices.

Mindfulness practices

Research shows that people spend nearly 47% of their waking hours thinking about something other than what they're doing (Bradt, 2010). This constant mind-wandering is a barrier to being fully present – in the here and now. Mindfulness is considered by many to be one of the ways that we can become connected to the moment – being present – at the same time as we are helping to take care of ourselves in the midst of our everyday busy lives. Mindfulness has been defined to include:

- 'Focusing one's attention in a non-judgmental or accepting way on the experience occurring in the present moment' (Baer, Smith & Allen, 2004. p. 192).
- 'The mind is trained to remain in the present, open, quiet and alert, contemplating the present moment. All judgments and interpretations have to be suspended, or if they occur, just registered and dropped' (Bodhi, 1984, pp. 75–76).
- 'Mindfulness is the quality of mind that notices what is present without judgment, without interference' (Goldstein, 2002, p. 89).
- 'Mindfulness is basically just a particular way of paying attention. It is a way of looking deeply into oneself in the spirit of self-inquiry and self-understanding' (Kabat-Zinn, 1990, p. 12).

The origins of mindfulness can be traced back to Eastern spiritual traditions, including Buddhism. Those who practise mindfulness develop greater awareness and compassion for self and others (Goldstein, 2002; Kabat-Zinn, 2000). In recent years, there has been a significant development of mindfulness practises and interventions, taught and practised independently from spiritual origins and traditional meditation. In medical and healthcare settings, mindfulness-based stress reduction and mindfulness-based cognitive therapy are commonplace.

We do not intend to make you an expert in mindfulness but rather help your clients to understand how connected they are to themselves and the degree to which this influences their connectedness with other parts of their lives. Through mindfulness we can help to nurture resilience.

A starting point might be to ask your clients to focus their attention on an ordinary activity, such as breathing, walking, or eating, and to observe it carefully. Then invite your clients to:

- Notice what is happening in that moment.
- Notice to what extent does their attention wander into thoughts or memories.
- Note when the mind has wandered and to gently resume attending to the target of observation.
- Note at any time the bodily sensations or emotions as they arise, to lean into them and observe them carefully.
- Bring an attitude of friendly curiosity, interest, and acceptance to all bodily and mental or emotional sensations whilst at the same time refraining from evaluation or self-criticism.

Professor Rasmus Houggard and Professor Jacqueline Carter (2016) recently published an article in the *Harvard Business Review's Emotional Intelligence* series explaining how to practice mindfulness through your working day. Their article suggests a number of techniques which help to focus our attention on self that you might like to set as 'prep' for your clients and ask them to come back with their reflections:

- When you wake up in the morning, spend two minutes in bed noticing your breath. As thoughts come into your mind, let them go and return to your breath and noticing your breathing.
- When you get to the office or work location, take 10 minutes to do the following before starting a work activity:
  - First notice how you are feeling (mood wise), how you are feeling (in your body), and how you are thinking – about someone or something.
  - Close your eyes, relax, and sit upright but not too stiffly erect.
  - Place your full focus on your breath.
  - Just notice your breath as you inhale, exhale, inhale, exhale.
  - Count silently, lengthening the breath to a count of 4 on the inhalation and exhalation.
  - Notice (without trying to change) how smooth or jagged the breath is.
  - Any time you find your mind distracted, gently return your focus to your breath without castigating yourself, just say, 'Thinking!' with humour and curiosity and return to focusing on your breath for a few more seconds.
  - Once you have finished this practice, notice how differently you feel and are thinking.

There are numerous ways to practice mindfulness. When trying mindfulness, encourage your clients to start by taking 10 minutes every day to engage in one of the ways to practice mindfulness, which might include:

• Mindful walking.
• Mindful eating.
• Mindful bathing: washing or swimming.
• Mindful listening.
• Mindful speaking.

Any of the above can become part of our mindful practices. The foundation of our mindfulness practices is the awareness of thoughts, feelings, and sensations – allowing thoughts, feelings, and sensations to come and go, without judgement or the need to do anything with them. For those of you who wish to explore more on mindfulness, we recommend a resource in the final section of the chapter – further reading and resources – in addition to the reference list at the end.

Reflexivity practices

By helping your clients reflect on their thoughts, feelings, motivations, decision points, and actions – you are helping them make the opportunity to learn from experience and develop a 'learning personality'. The work of Professor Donald Schon (1987) and subsequent studies on the subject of 'reflection' and the Reflective Practitioner say that the key is to develop a 'theory of practice' in real time. This involves reflecting on 'micro theories' – ideas about what works in the real world. One way to do this is to invite clients to keep a journal or diary throughout the day. We refer to the process and benefits of journaling in chapter 2. The journal or diary can include:

• What I perceived and observed in the situation.
• What I thought.
• How I felt.
• What I did, said, and chose not to do.
• What were my assumptions?
• The reaction.
• My reaction.
• What value judgments did I make?
• What beliefs did I act on?
• What strengths did I use?
• What strengths didn't I use?
• How did the situation/others affect me?
• What surprises were there?
• What have I learned?
• What will I do next time when I meet a similar stimulus?

Nancy Kline's (1999) book *Time to Think* explored the thinking environment over 15 years. Kline is the Founder and President of Time To Think, the thinking environment that is now a well-known approach to helping individuals, groups, teams, and organisations to develop their thinking. This is achieved through a combination of paying attention and listening, asking incisive questions, maintaining equality, and considering the role of thinking partners. The approach includes several dimensions, including appreciation balanced with critique, encouragement and removal of competition, emotional release and restorative time, and information and reality testing. We can consider each within the context of mindfulness and reflection.

Reflecting on your own practice:

- What other ways can you help your clients to become more connected with themselves?
- What mindful exercise might you do?
- How might your experience of reflexivity influence your coaching or mentoring?
- How might the activities inform your next coaching or mentoring session on mental mastery?

Emotional mastery

Emotional mastery as we define it as it relates to resilience is someone's ability to understand and manage their own emotions and understand and respond to the emotions of others. In 1998, in *Working with Emotional Intelligence*, Daniel Goleman set out a framework of emotional intelligence (EI) that reflects how an individual's potential for mastering the skills of self-awareness, self-management, social awareness, and relationship management translate into on-the-job success.

As developments in neuroscience have progressed, so too has our knowledge and understanding of the relationship between brain activity and emotional intelligence and cognitive intelligence. As Goleman (2001, p. 4) explains:

> Intellectual abilities like verbal fluency, spatial logic, and abstract reasoning – in other words, the components of IQ – are based primarily in specific areas of the neocortex. When these neocortical areas are damaged, the corresponding intellectual ability suffers. In contrast, emotional intelligence encompasses the behavioral manifestations of underlying neurological circuitry that primarily links the limbic areas for emotion, centering on the amygdala and its extended networks throughout the brain, to areas in the prefrontal cortex, the brain's executive center.

You can help your clients gain emotional intelligence, and that will help them provide a layer of protection in stressful circumstances that will help them access their resources. Those who are aware of their emotions and can perceive, appraise, and regulate them are better able to regulate their mental and physical state in stressful situations and when coping with setbacks (Firborg et al., 2005).

If your clients lack emotional mastery, you may find that they:

- Make assumptions quickly and defend them vehemently.
- Often feel misunderstood.
- Often don't know the things that trigger negative feelings or behaviour.
- Blame other people (particularly, for how they 'make' them feel).
- Exhibit anxiety during conversations about a difficult situation.
- Avoid discussions about emotions.
- Avoid discussions about others' perspectives.
- Lack empathy towards themselves and others.
- Avoid discussions about challenges.

There are a variety of ways you can help your clients to develop and enhance their emotional intelligence. Here are some examples:

1. **Developing greater self-awareness.** Self-awareness is necessary to understand ourselves and relate to others. Understanding our personality, values, motivations, and emotions are all necessary for developing emotional mastery. Self-awareness also enables clients to relate to other people by affecting how clients perceive people, their attitudes, and their behaviours, and how they respond to them in the moment. Self-awareness also encourages self-reflective questions that help clients to understand themselves and others, supporting the development of their emotional intelligence.
2. **Developing positive plans and steps to stay motivated.** Self-motivation refers to our inner drive to achieve goals, accomplish our aims, our readiness to act on opportunities, and our overall optimism. Personal and professional goals can provide long-term direction and short-term motivation, both of which are important in the context of emotional mastery and our clients' ability to stay positive in the face of adversity and to identify setbacks as opportunities to learn and change.
3. **Developing and practising empathising with yourself and others.** Empathy is about understanding how someone feels or behaves and communicating with them effectively. Encourage your clients to notice what they are thinking and how they are behaving, and to question their thinking and behaviour in order to understand impact and outcome.
4. **Developing and practising active listening skills.** This is a key aspect of effective two-way communication. In the previous section, we referred to the work of Nancy Kline and the 'thinking environment'. Communication skills and listening, in particular, are core skills that help to determine our ability to relate to ourselves and others.
5. **Developing and practising the management of negative emotions.** When you're able to manage and reduce your negative emotions, you're less likely to get overwhelmed. Identifying the negative emotions and using techniques from cognitive behavioural therapy explored in chapter 1 can assist.

CASE STUDY

Alice and Thomas had a young family and were keen to have a third child, both coming from large families themselves. Alice and Thomas both had long and stable careers in the education and teaching profession which worked well with their family commitments. They also had a good support network in place and felt that the time was right to try for a third child. Everything was going well with the pregnancy when Alice fell ill in the final trimester and was taken into hospital for rest and monitoring. The baby was born by caesarean section and was found to have cerebral palsy and was hard of hearing. For the 12 months that followed, Alice was in and out of hospital with the baby and found that she was not able to return to work as a primary school teacher. She quickly realised that it would not be possible for her to return to her full-time position as a teacher, as her child's needs required her to be flexible through the usual working week. The baby's needs were so great that this may always be the case. For the first two years of the baby's life, Alice felt consumed by her parental caring responsibilities and found that her emotions and thoughts were negative – she felt constantly on a short fuse and overwhelmed by her situation. Her relationship with her husband and friends had deteriorated, and she had difficulty tending to her needs, let alone the needs of her husband and friends.

Working with her mentor, she explored her current reality, what she was thinking and feeling, and how this translated to her behaviours. Alice realised that her sense of self and professional identity were eroded. She felt consumed as a parent and carer, which meant that she felt she had no space for herself. As a consequence, she was short and snappy with her husband and friends and had retreated from some of her most supportive family members and friends.

Working with her mentor, Alice recognised that she needed to regain a sense of self whilst fulfilling her parental responsibilities and maintaining a loving marriage. Alice considered an alternative career, a career which would make use of her knowledge and experience but also provide sufficient flexibility to ensure the needs of her baby and family were met. Alice quickly realised that in relation to her child's circumstances there was very little that she was able to influence and even less that she was able to control. She was, however, able to exert control and influence over her future professional identity and forge a new career which might work around her care commitments and provide sufficient work-life balance to work for her and her whole family. She also recognised the need to rebuild the relationships with her husband, family, and friends which had become strained.

The case study illustrates the degree to which a mentor can assist in developing a client's ability to understand and manage their own emotions as well as understand and respond to the emotions of others. In doing so, the rewards can be significant, helping clients to manage adversity and cope with setbacks.

Reflecting on your own practice:

- In what ways can you help your clients to become more connected with their emotions and the emotions of others?
- How might your knowledge and experience of developing emotional intelligence impact on your coaching or mentoring?
- How might the above inform your next coaching or mentoring session on emotional mastery?

Social mastery

Social mastery involves the ability to develop strong relationships and good support networks at home, work, and in one's broader network and to use them to provide stability, security, purpose, joy, and ultimately enhanced resilience. Professor Roy Baumeister and Professor Mark Leary (1995) published an empirical review based on the hypothesis of 'belonging'. The hypothesis holds that we all need to feel we belong, and that we relate to others and others relate to us ('social relatedness'). Their research found that humans are motivated by a strong desire to form and maintain enduring relationships. We seek frequent, affectively positive interactions; humans are intrinsically social and have a need to belong (Maslow, 1968), therefore making connections is an important aspect of our social experience both in and outside of the work environment. A constellation of development relationships can positively impact on work-life balance – people who we can turn to for support, and help in a crisis.

Developing an effective network of professional colleagues and friends can be one of the most powerful sources of career resilience and adaptability. The ability to connect in meaningful ways with others builds resilience because it helps cushion people from other adverse effects of shocks. Possession of an extensive professional network has been found to help people to be psychologically resilient against many types of shock, some of which might include an unexpected poor appraisal or annual review or the loss of one's job. For some, the notion of a network or networking may sound or feel artificial or contrived. However, research by Professor Jane E. Dutton and her colleagues has demonstrated that the existence of high-quality connections can induce a sense of vitality and a heightened sense of positive regard (Dutton, 2003).

Research into broader contexts than work, such as marriage and divorce, has shown that people benefit from social support from family and friends during a divorce (Spanier & Casto, 1979). Older people who have recently retired from work, or may have lost their spouse, find support and happiness in the development of close personal relationships (Kaufman, 1986).

Some clients might say that they do not want or care about or believe in work-life balance. Their purpose and focus are about work, about making money, or achieving something special. Many Olympic athletes forgo and neglect their relationships with family and friends. They may have an imbalanced life in order to aim for a gold medal, and it isn't the job of the coach or mentor to persuade them to live a balanced life. It could be argued that it is the coach or mentor's responsibility to explore the consequences of a narrowly focused existence, but the coach or mentor needs to respect the choices of clients.

For some of your clients, engaging with fewer people and focusing on tending to high-quality connections might feel more appropriate. Clients often feel they haven't time to grow their network or engage with their network. Encouraging clients to seek diversity within their networks can help to develop new and unique sources of learning and development for them. As we know, diversity comes in many forms and may include, amongst others, gender, culture, education, functional, and professional background. People with different knowledge and skill sets to your clients can help to provide a different perspective and challenge their thinking. Evidence demonstrates that a strong support network can have psychosocial, career, and work-life balance outcomes. A good starting point is to help your clients think about their support network. Knowing who we can go to for support acts a key protective factor in supporting clients' resilience.

The next activity (see Table 4.1, below) involves helping your clients to think about different aspects of their lives that are important to them and who in their network can support them with various aspects of their life, who they go to for support, and who they could go to that they don't yet go to for advice and friendship. The final step is then to think about who they support in each of the areas.

Table 4.1 Identifying your support network

Support needs	Who supports me?	Who could I go to that I don't yet go to?	Who do I support?
Work-related issues (person outside of work			
Work-related issues (person within work)			
Family-related issues			
Personal issues (e.g. health)			
Relationship issues			
For fun and laughter			
Exercise and fitness			
Spiritually			
In the community/charity			
In a crisis and can call at any time of day			
Add other areas of support			

The activity involves helping your clients to think about any gaps they might have, either with areas they may need support with or where they may support others. You can also help your clients analyse and reflect on the depth and breadth of their support network.

Ask your clients to think about what has been learnt from the activity, in particular:

- Where are the gaps in the support network?
- How might the gaps be filled?
- Who can you reach out to or will you ask for support and help when you need it?
- How often do you offer support to others?
- What is the quality of the support you offer?
- To what extent are you a key person in someone else's network?
- Thinking about some of the most important people in the network, how can you show your appreciation for their support?

Reflecting on your own practice:

- What other ways can you help your clients to identify and develop their support network?
- How might the activity inform your next coaching or mentoring session on support network development?
- Whom do you support and what patterns are in the kind of support you offer and don't offer?
- To whom do you go for support and what patterns are in the support you seek and don't seek?

Developing strong relationships

Developing strong relationships is not only about creating a good support network and extending networks but also about working to improve existing relationships. Strong relationships rely on effective communication, including mutual respect and rapport, in addition to self-insight and commitment to working towards developing the relationship. One of the greatest sources of stress can often come from difficult work relationships where communication breaks down and confrontation begins to creep in. How well do you understand your clients' line managers' work style, communication approach, strengths, pressures, and influences, and have you explored with them the levers they could use to make a proactive, significant first step towards improving a problematic working relationship?

The next activity involves helping your clients to think about a relationship that they would like to improve at work, although this activity can be adapted for any relationship. The purpose of the exercise is for clients to step into someone else's shoes and think through the needs, approach, strengths, development areas, and challenges that the person might experience. Once an individual has been identified, ask your clients to work through the questions in Table 4.2: Stepping into someone else's shoes. You may decide to do this activity together, or your clients might go away and bring the answers to the next session.

Ask your clients to think about what has been learnt from the activity. In particular:

- How easy was it to answer each question?
- Were there any gaps?
- Were there any surprises?
- How well do you really know the person?
- How different are you to the person?
- What are the common areas?
- To what extent did the exercise help to identify the challenges or issues in the relationship?
- How might you address the challenges or issues in the relationship?

Table 4.2 Stepping into someone else's shoes

What are their main work goals – what is the individual seeking to achieve? And why?
What are the biggest challenges, stressors, and demands?
What are their concerns or fears?
What's important to them? What motivates and drives them?
What is the most significant challenge?
What are their key strengths and development areas?
What are the key external issues or challenges that impact the style and approach?

CASE STUDY

Alan had worked for an experienced and senior Manager (Mihir) previously in an interim position for six months within his organisation and found himself back with Mihir in a permanent position 14 months later. He took on the interim position with a view to progressing and moving upwards within the organisation. Alan had what he described as 'a really yo-yo relationship' with Mihir. He felt that Mihir was the sort of chap who relished pressing people's buttons and deliberately being antagonistic just to get a reaction out of people. Alan felt that Mihir was all stick and no carrot and would often take his frustrations out on his direct reports; it felt like he got pleasure from putting people in uncomfortable positions and initiating confrontation and conflict. Alan felt woefully unprepared in his first interim position; he had not worked with a manager like Mihir previously, and it was a huge cultural shock. Alan felt that he was constantly criticised – unjustly – and Mihir rarely, if ever, gave Alan any positive feedback. When praise was given it was in the form of a backhanded compliment or given begrudgingly, e.g. saying things like 'Well done for not messing that up,' or 'Even a broken clock is right twice a day.' Alan very quickly felt emotionally fatigued and drained, depleted of his energy and drive. Alan survived the six-month interim position and moved into another internal position which was a sideways move. One year later a promotion opportunity was presented to Alan which would require him to work under Mihir again. Alan was keen to take on the new role and secure the promotion but was concerned that his relationship with Mihir would fall into the same unhealthy cycle of constant confrontation and resulting fatigue. Alan was determined to improve the relationship and understand what he might do differently next time around. His mentor helped him to work through a series of questions to help develop Alan's insight into not only Mihir's behaviour but also his own reaction to difficult situations.

Having worked through the questions with his mentor, Alan was able to understand the behaviours Mihir adopted more clearly and prepare himself for the new position with Mihir as his manager. Alan compiled a list of Mihir's key focus areas and trigger points that might result in confrontation and conflict. Alan sat down with Mihir to discuss his overall expectations and ways of working in the new role. Alan was able to express what he needed from Mihir to excel in the role, to be motivated, and to feel supported in his development in the role. During the following 12 months Alan and Mihir developed an improved working relationship which was less volatile and resulted in far fewer confrontations.

Table 4.3 Stepping into someone else's shoes (illustrated)

What are the main work goals – what is the individual seeking to achieve? And, why?
Mihir was numbers-focused and relentless in achieving his key performance indicators. Of crucial importance was the financial performance of the business.
What are the biggest challenges, stressors, and demands?
Mihir's line manager exerted a huge amount of pressure on him to outperform his key performance indicators and achieve results through any means necessary, often turning a blind eye to malpractice.
What are their biggest concerns or fears?
Mihir was always concerned about performance, numbers, figures, ultimately, the financial performance of the business.
What is important to them? What motivates them?
Mihir was motivated by financial reward. He has gone through a messy divorce and only saw his children every other weekend. He made significant maintenance payments and seemed to want to do extravagant activities when he had the children at weekends.
What is their most significant challenge?
Mihir found it incredibly difficult to manage his line manager, who he felt was unreasonable and placed incredible pressure on him to deliver, no matter what the cost.
What are their key strengths and development areas?
Mihir was extremely tenacious and had incredible organizational knowledge and insight. Every time Mihir moved roles in the organization it was to fix a problem; he had a reputation for being very pragmatic and getting results. He lacked empathy and compassion and the ability to adapt his leadership style to get the best out of different team members.
What are the key external issues or challenges that impact on the style and approach?
Mihir's home situation was very unhappy, having gone through a messy divorce and only seeing his children every other weekend. He had moved into temporary accommodation to be nearer to his children, but that extended his daily commute to a 160-mile round trip. He suffered ill health, with an ongoing heart complaint that slowed him down and made him breathless. Mihir came across as constantly miserable, irritable, and tired. This resulted in his having an extremely short fuse.

The case study illustrates the insight that can be developed through stepping into someone else's shoes and then developing a strategy to address difficult issues in the relationship.

Reflecting on your own practice:

- How would you have helped Alan to develop greater insight about a difficult relationship?
- How would this case inform your next coaching or mentoring session on managing a difficult relationship?

Physical mastery

Physical mastery relates to our ability to manage our health and energy levels; sleep, rest, a balanced diet, the absence of abuse/dependency or addiction, and exercise help to boost our immune system, increase our stamina, resist illness, and help to build our resilience. Exercise not only triggers the release of neurotransmitters and hormones that make us feel good and energised but it helps us burn off stress and combat anxiety and worries. We consider how you can help support your clients in building their resilience by taking care of themselves and making sure they are healthy, rested, and focused. For some, this may appear the most straightforward of all six masteries. However, clients can often find themselves caught in an unhealthy spiral – they are too busy with work, and as a consequence, they start to feel stressed. They know that they need to take care of themselves, but they keep putting off opportunities for 'me time' because they are too busy. In this section, we focus on sleep, healthy eating, and exercise.

Sleep

Sleep is incredibly important for our *health* – it is *just as* important as healthy eating and exercising. Sleep is essential for our long-term physical resistance against disease as well as our everyday resilience. Professor Mathew Walker, a leading neuroscientist and Director of the Center for Human Sleep Science at the University of California, Berkeley, USA, in his *New York Times* bestseller book *Why We Sleep* (Walker, 2018) explains that sleep enriches our ability to learn, memorise, and make logical decisions. It recalibrates our emotions, replenishes our immune system, supports our metabolism, and regulates our appetite. Taking a longer-term perspective, sleep deprivation is associated with dementia, most notably Alzheimer's disease. Walker's (2009) earlier article, published in the New York Academy of Sciences, reviewed the literature to look for the degree of convergence of themes associated with the brain functions that appear to be regulated by sleep. His findings suggest that the benefits of sleep are significant and should not be underestimated in the context of physical mastery. Together with impairments of attention, alertness, memory, and plasticity, sleep deprivation is commonly associated with increased subjective reports of irritability and affective volatility. Sleep allows us to regenerate both physically and mentally, yet most of us don't get nearly enough of it. Many of us are sleep deprived and fall into sleep disruptive habits. New research shows that in spite of some people thinking they can exist well on less than seven hours of sleep and some thinking they need nine or more, we all benefit from a time frame of seven to eight hours of sleep at night. There may be days when this total is fewer hours, but less sleep over a sustained period will have a detrimental effect on our health. Therefore, lack of sleep has a cumulative effect on our health; the damage can't be undone by catching up at the weekend.

There are three distinct areas where sleep has a significant impact on our resilience.

1. Sleep helps us to regulate our emotions. When we are sleep-deprived our rational decision-making ability is strained and we tend to act on impulses rather than thinking through issues and challenges in a structured and logical way.
2. Sleep is essential for learning. During the rest period, our brain processes new experiences, which helps with sense-making.
3. Sleep helps us to cope with setbacks, changes, and unexpected events that are often outside of our control.

CASE STUDY

Steve felt that he had suffered with poor-quality sleep for a long time. He would go to bed at a reasonable hour – between 10 p.m. and 11 p.m. – and would set his alarm for 7 a.m. every morning. But when he woke up, he felt absolutely shattered, like he had not slept during the night. He started to self-medicate, consuming three or four high-energy drinks daily in the hope that this would energise him, but he found that this compounded the situation. When the energy drink euphoria wore off, he felt ill and exhausted. His snoring at night had worsened, to the extent that his wife would go to bed earlier so that she was asleep when he went to bed. But over time, his snoring would wake her, and she was unable to go back to sleep. Within a short period, they started sleeping in separate bedrooms and this started to strain their relationship.

At work, Steve found that his energy levels were depleted, which resulted in his cutting corners, becoming less meticulous, and becoming apathetic towards mediocracy and low-quality work. His attitude shifted to 'that will do' and simply getting through the day. He began to fall asleep at his desk, and on one particular day driving home, Steve fell asleep at the wheel of his car on the motorway and woke up in a different lane. Having discussed the situation with his mentor, the mentor asked Steve if he had considered seeking medical advice. Steve did this and was later diagnosed with sleep apnoea. He was asked to attend a sleep clinic for an overnight stay where his sleep was monitored. Through this process, it was discovered that he was constantly waking up throughout the night, six times per hour. Steve needed to be issued with a continuous positive airway pressure (CPAP) ventilator. Within four weeks of using the CPAP ventilator, his sleep was radically improved, he began sharing a bedroom with his wife again, and felt that his energy levels had been restored.

The case study illustrates the detrimental impact prolonged absence of quality sleep can have both at home and work. Reflecting on your own practice:

• What others way can you help your clients to address the duration and quality of their sleep?
• How might the literature and case study inform your next coaching or mentoring session on physical mastery?

There are many sleep hygiene practices to support good night-time sleep quality and full daytime alertness. Organisations such as the National Sleep Foundation suggest:

• Avoiding caffeine, alcohol, nicotine, and other chemicals that interfere with sleep.
• Steering clear of food that can be disruptive right before sleep. Heavy or rich foods, fatty or fried meals, and spicy dishes can trigger indigestion for some people. When this occurs close to bedtime, it can lead to painful heartburn that disrupts sleep.
• Keeping your internal clock set with a consistent sleep schedule. Going to bed and waking up at the same time each day sets the body's 'internal clock' to expect sleep at a certain time night after night. Try to stick as closely as possible, even at weekends. Waking up at the same time each day is the very best way to set your clock, and even if you did not sleep well the night before, the extra sleep drive will help you consolidate sleep the following night.
• Establishing a regular relaxing bedtime routine. A regular nightly routine helps the body recognise that it is bedtime. This could include taking a warm shower or bath, reading a book, or doing light stretches. Avoiding screens – mobile phone, iPads, etc. at least 30 minutes before bedtime.
• Making sure that the sleep environment is conducive to sleep. The bedroom should be cool for optimal sleep. Bright light from lamps, cell phone, and TV screens can make it difficult to fall asleep; consider using blackout curtains, eye shades, or earplugs.

When working with someone in your coaching or mentoring practice who exhibits sleep issues, you might ask them:

• What is your sleep pattern?
• What is your sleep hygiene?
• How would you rate the quality of your sleep?
• What impact does the quality of your sleep have on your behaviours?
• What sorts of things get in the way of a good night's sleep?
• What can you do to change your sleep routine?

Diet and exercise

In addition to sleep, a balanced diet and regular exercise are both determinants on our health and well-being. Increasing our energy levels is one of the ways to enhance resilience to expand and grow, reduce the risk of stress, and increase the capacity to cope with change, pressure, and setbacks. Physical energy is improved with regular eating and drinking – the right foods and liquids – and avoiding skipping meals and spikes in blood sugar levels.

When exploring your clients' energy levels, you might ask your clients to look at any given day or week:

- How often do you eat?
- What is the gap between meals or snacks?
- What do you eat at different times?
- How often do you have caffeine or sugary drinks?
- How much and how often do you drink water?
- How often and how much alcohol do you have?
- Do you take drugs?
- What do you eat or drink before sleeping?
- What patterns do you notice?

A simple set of questions can help your clients to start to think about their habits and notice good or bad routines, and days of the week that might be particularly prone to imbalance.

Exercise is one of the most effective ways your clients can enhance and maintain their resilience, and so it is an important area of questioning. When we exercise, we trigger the release of neurotransmitters and hormones that make us feel energised and help reduce stress levels and anxiety. Building exercise into their daily routine can be one of the ways to see fast results. Some clients really have such a big to-do list that they believe they can't cram any visit to the gym into their diary, nor might they care to. But deciding to use the stairs rather than the lift; walking rather than taking a bus, train, or car; and parking at the far end of the car park can be small changes that add up to a basic exercise routine. They might use the gym before they start work or during their lunch break, go and see people face-to-face rather than email all the time, take a lunchtime walk. There are so many different ways of introducing exercise into their life without the need to feel that they have to run eight miles on a treadmill! It helps to explore what they do enjoy; their exercise adherence will be greater if they enjoy it.

CASE STUDY

A 2016 study published in Talent Development at Work documented a case study (Haddock-Millar & Clutterbuck, 2016) highlighting the relationship between exercise and conversation. The case study below further illustrates this.

Terry and his team worked in a busy, noisy, open plan office which was not always conducive to holding high-quality conversations. Finding time in the working day to talk to one another was difficult. With the agreement of the team, Terry introduced a team lunchtime walk, during which all members completed an outdoor circuit of two miles. This allowed for up to 30 minutes of uninterrupted conversation. The group included all six team colleagues of varying ability, both in terms of performance and productivity and also relative to their well-being and level of fitness. Initially, the team would walk as a large group, but they quickly realised this wasn't productive, as some team members moved on ahead whilst other struggled to keep up with the pace and the conversation! So, the team decided to walk in pairs, and alternate pairs so everyone had a chance to talk to each other. The benefits were felt by all the team – the value-add of networking with one another but also a more energised team, both in body and mind.

- Thinking about your coaching or mentoring practice, how might you engage your clients in creative ways to increase their exercise levels whilst also increasing their social mastery?

When exploring your clients' energy levels, you might ask your clients to consider their exercise regime (if they have one at all, that is). A good starting point might be:

- What exercise activities are you currently doing?
- Are the activities alone or with family, friends, and colleagues?
- To what extent would you like to take part in exercise with family, friends, and colleagues?
- How might you do this?
- How might you engage in different or more activities during the week or at weekends?
- Cast your mind back to a time when you did take up a new hobby or sport that you enjoyed – what was it that you enjoyed?
- How do you find enjoyment from exercise?
- What can you start doing tomorrow that is different or new?
- What can you start doing next month that is different or new?

Reflecting on your own practice:

- What tools and techniques do you currently use to support your clients' physical mastery?
- How can the insight into diet and exercise inform your next coaching or mentoring session on physical mastery?
- Coaching and mentoring is a sedentary task, as is doing continuing professional development (CPD) or research. A lot of coaches and mentors work from home where the biscuit tin is around the corner. What are you doing to install a healthy physical mastery in your daily routine?

Spiritual mastery

Spiritual mastery relates to our ability to seek and express meaning and purpose and to understand the way we experience connectedness. Spirituality is a broad concept with many different perspectives and interpretations. When engaging in spiritual coaching and mentoring, coaches or mentors may support clients as they explore and discover their true motivation and aim in life and how they experience connectedness. For some, a sense of connectedness can occur through a variety of mediums, connectedness to the moment, to self, to others, to nature, to the community, to the significant or sacred, or, to religion. As we explained previously, one of the authors has been engaged in a large-scale global longitudinal mentoring impact evaluation research project for the last two years. Some mentees and mentors who were interviewed described their role within the humanitarian aid organisation as their 'life purpose', and many saw it as their destiny to go to the field and provide humanitarian aid to those in need. Mentees and mentors gave their whole selves to the mission; they gained strength, satisfaction, and fulfilment from going to the field to support others. Spirituality may change throughout our lives, shifting as we adapt to our own experiences and relationships. Studies have found that an individual who experiences traumatic events often has to rebuild their assumptions of the world, especially those related to the purpose of life. Research suggests that the quality of life of cancer survivors partly rests on the outcome of the meaning-making process. Survivors who are still struggling to find meaning in life have a poorer quality of life, and those who have a sense of purpose display less psychological distress and better emotional and social functioning.

In previous chapters we addressed topics such as values and life satisfaction, gaining a sense of meaning and purpose. In relation to mental mastery, we also addressed the importance to connect to self and the application of mindfulness and reflexivity as techniques to re-energise or calm the brain to induce self-awareness and self-insight. In this section, we build on those chapters and focus on the ways you can help your clients discover what fuels their soul and spirit, what gives them inner strength, with a view to enhancing their resilience.

A sense of meaning and a sense of peace has been found to be the essence of spirituality. Professor Cecilia Chan and her colleagues in Hong Kong have spent many years studying the relationship between mind, body, and spirit, particularly with regard to health and negative health outcomes. Professor Chan and her colleagues suggest that 'the search for new meanings in life and a sense of peace is the essence of spirituality' and emphasise body-mind-spirit interconnectedness (2006, pp. 22–23). One of their studies applied an approach called the Strength-focused and Meaning-oriented Approach to Resilience and Transformation (SMART). Through time-limited contacts (ranging from one whole-day training to six weekly meetings) in a group setting, the SMART intervention attempts to foster growth in people undergoing a crisis. The purpose of the SMART intervention is the attainment of resilience and transformation. The goals were as follows:

- Resilience: Resistance against the disruptions of normal functioning in the face of a crisis (Bonanno, 2004).
- Transformation: The ability to grow in the aftermath of a crisis (Tedeschi & Calhoun, 1995).

Their study showed positive results from the SMART intervention. For the adolescents at junior high school, it was found that 'the sense of social commitment, mastery of life, and learning and growth among the participants increased significantly after the intervention, and that their sense of social disintegration and loss of security decreased significantly' (Chan, Chan & Ng, 2006, p. 27). Taking these and previous research findings, we outline an approach in Table 4.4 that suggests a number of questions you may wish to consider using with your clients in your coaching or mentoring practice.

Table 4.4 Assessing spirituality

Theme	*Coaching or mentoring questions*
Exploring the mind-body-spirit connection	• How do your clients perceive the relationship between their spiritual well-being, mood, and body? • How does taking care of their physical needs support their spiritual strength?
Developing an appreciation of nature	• What is your clients' relationship with nature? • How can your clients connect more closely to nature?
Promoting the compassionate helper principle	• How can your clients develop self-compassion? • How can your clients develop compassion for others?
A sense of peace	• When are your clients most at peace? • When are your clients most at peace with others?

Reflecting on your own practice:

- What questions can you add to explore your clients' spiritual mastery?
- How might the activity inform your next coaching or mentoring session on spiritual mastery?
- What tools and techniques do you currently use to support your clients' spiritual mastery?
- What other ways can you help your clients to identify and develop their spiritual mastery?

Environmental mastery

Environmental mastery relates to our ability to analyse and manage our environment, appreciate potential resources, access resources, navigate complex external routes to help meet our needs, and address all aspects of our lives. We recognise that we all live within an ecosystem, so understanding and appreciating our clients' context can help to support and develop their mastery and resilience. Assisting your clients in continuing to build their knowledge and strategies to successfully navigate their ecosystem and access resources to support their needs is a vital protective factor in developing their resilience.

In this section, we focus on helping your clients concentrate their energies on understanding their environment and what is affecting and changing in the world that will influence their ability to thrive and adapt in the future.

There are a variety of tools that you can use with your clients, drawn from a number of different disciplines. Three strategic management techniques commonly used to identify and evaluate the impact of the environment are PESTLE, SWOT, and Gap Analysis. The tools are often used together to provide a comprehensive picture. This picture includes not only the environment but also your clients' internal strengths and weaknesses and external opportunities and threats in relation to each of the environmental influences. It provokes the question, given where your clients are presently, what do they need to think about?

The PESTLE technique is a strategic framework for understanding external influences on any individual, team, organisation, or community. PESTLE stands for:

- Political – The extent to which government and government policy may impact on an individual, team, community, organisation, or a specific industry.
- Economic – The degree to which interest rates, employment, or unemployment rates, raw material costs, exchange rates, or BREXIT may impact on an individual, team, community, organisation, or a specific industry.

- Social – The degree to which the social environment, including changing family demographics, education levels, cultural trends, and changes in lifestyles may impact on an individual, team, community, organisation, or a specific industry.
- Technological – The rate of technological innovation and development that could affect an individual, team, community, organisation, or a specific industry.
- Legal – Changes in legislation and the impact this may have on an individual, team, community, organisation or a specific industry.
- Environmental – Changes in corporate social responsibility and sustainability practices, climate change, recycling, carbon footprint, and the impact these may have on an individual, team, community, organisation or a specific industry.

A SWOT analysis is a way of looking at your clients' situation by identifying:

- Strengths – Knowledge, skills, experiences, and resources that are available; a unique aspect of your clients' repertoire.
- Weaknesses – Are your clients confident in their knowledge, education, skills, and experiences? If not, what are the areas they need to develop?
- Opportunities – External possibilities that your clients can take advantage of to help them achieve their goals and ambitions.
- Threats – External issues or events that might be worrying your clients and that your clients might feel potentially prevent them from achieving their goals or taking advantage of the opportunities.

A SWOT analysis can be useful to help your clients to focus on a specific goal or problem. Gap Analysis can then be used to focus on where your clients are now, where they wish to be in the future, and the gap between the current and future positions, including resources which might encompass knowledge, skills, experience, finances, and systems. By doing a Gap Analysis, clients can bridge the gap between their current reality and future objective or plan. Tables 4.5 and 4.6 pull together the main elements of PESTLE, SWOT, and Gap Analysis that can assist your clients in developing their knowledge of the environment, identifying the resources they currently have and the resources they may wish to access to turn their future plans into a reality.

First, ask your clients to consider each domain (PESTLE) and list all questions that might be relevant to their future objective or plan (Table 4.5). Next, ask your clients to consider what they already know the answers to, where the gaps might be, and where they can find out the answers to their questions (Table 4.6).

In the context of work-life balance, we will illustrate the application of the PESTLE and SWOT tools in a specific case study.

Table 4.5 Environmental evaluation, internal and external

Domain	Questions
Political	
Economic	
Social	
Technological	
Legal	
Environmental	

Table 4.6 Environmental knowledge, bridging the gap

What do I currently know?	What don't I know?	How do I bridge the gap?

CASE STUDY

David had developed a very successful interior blinds and curtain business based within Greater London. He felt that he was a victim of his own success, working seven days, ninety hours a week, transforming a small business into a medium-scale growing business. In the early days, 75% of his business customers were based in London – walk-ins, people coming through the door to order and purchase their blinds and curtains. However, in the last two years, David noticed that his business had transitioned to almost fully online – 90% of his customers ordered either online or over the phone. At the same time, his property rates had increased substantially and he needed to look for a larger business unit to manufacture and hold inventory. He imported stock from Europe and made the blinds and curtains in his manufacturing unit. David worked with his mentor to understand the implications of his current situation and develop a five-year business plan. David was keen to look to expand his online business across Europe, increasing his market presence and share. He was keen to explore a move to a different location in the UK which might provide him with the space he needed for a larger business unit, lower business rates, and favourable labour market conditions. This would enable David to recruit a Business Unit Manager to take on the day-to-day running of the business and allow David to transition into a three-day work week. David's health had taken a turn for the worse over the last five years, having been in and out of hospital on two separate occasions with a suspected heart attack which the Doctors described as 'stress, exercise and diet related'. David and his wife were keen to use the business relocation as an opportunity to purchase a home close to work which would reduce the number of hours commuting from two hours a day to a 30-minute round trip. That change would help him regain a greater sense of work-life balance which had been missing from their lives for several years.

With his mentor, David considered the different aspects of the PESTLE model in relation to his current and future business. He recognised that the change required a change in his business model, structure, and culture, in addition to a relocation for work and home. You can see some of the questions David identified in Table 4.7.

David realised that there were many different aspects to consider in relation to the remodelling and relocation of his business. The next stage involved David identifying what questions he already knew the answers to, where the gaps might be, and where he could find out the answers to his questions.

Table 4.7 Environmental evaluation, internal and external (illustrated)

Domain	Questions
Political	• What is the Government manifesto in relation to import and export relations across Europe? • What is the impact of the changing political climate, e.g. BREXIT?
Economic	• What are employment rates, salary rates, and business rates in different areas of the UK? • What are the trade taxes in Europe?
Social	• Access to the internet (which can differ between countries and people of lower levels of income)? • What are the consumer buying behaviour patterns in Europe?
Technological	• What are multichannel shopping options? • What are the opportunities to utilise social media channels, e.g. Facebook and Twitter?
Legal	• What are the regulatory issues I need to consider? • What are the implications for staff redundancies and the legal requirements regarding notice and payment?
Environmental	• What are the opportunities for carbon footprint reductions? • What are the workplace efficiency regulations? • What are the local Council environment-related regulations?

The tools enable you to work with your clients to develop their knowledge of their ecosystem, enabling them to support their journey in developing strategies and responses that can help them successfully navigate their environment.

Control and influence

As discussed in chapter 2 in the locus of control section, it is helpful to assist your clients in focusing their energies on the issues and situations they can control or influence. We have previously pointed out that it is easy to waste energy with negative thinking and dwelling on things we have little or no control over. There are few things we can control and there are some situations and issues which we have absolutely no control over. Therefore, we explore how you can support your clients in their focusing only on issues and situations upon which they can have some control. This will enable them to be less fatigued and exhausted, avoiding wasting time and energy on issues they can't control.

One way to help address this is to identify what is causing any concerns and establish whether or not they are in control, able to influence, or should let go of those concerns. This can be achieved by using the tools and techniques in chapter 2 which involved a three-stage process:

1. Listing all concerns currently in their mind and ranking each concern.
2. Identifying the degree of control and influence and what to let go.
3. Creating an action plan with specific next steps, taking into account any practicalities such as timescale.

In the section on emotional mastery, we described the case of Alice. We revisit the case of Alice below, focusing on her situation and the stages she worked through with her mentor to create an action plan based on her future goal.

CASE STUDY

Working with her mentor, Alice explored her current reality, what she was thinking and feeling, and how this translated to her behaviours. Alice quickly realised that in relation to her child's circumstances there was very little that she was able to influence and even less that she was able to control. She was, however, able to exert control and influence over her future professional identity and forge a new career which might work around her care commitments and provide sufficient work-life balance to work for her and her whole family. Over the next two years, Alice worked with her mentor to create a business plan which would balance her needs and the needs of her youngest child with those of her family, her husband, and her desire to create a successful and thriving business which utilised her many years of teaching and education knowledge and experience.

The case study illustrates the degree to which a mentor can assist in developing clients' environmental mastery and help them to successfully create and achieve their plans and goals.

Reflecting on your own practice:

- What tools and techniques do you currently use to support your clients' environmental mastery?
- How are you dealing with the PESTLE (or other) aspects of your environment? What are you avoiding? What do you need to find out about? What might affect your ability to adapt to changing conditions in the future?
- How can the insight into aspects of control and influence inform your next coaching or mentoring session on physical mastery?

Closing remarks

This chapter is not intended to make you an expert in resilience but instead to help you to help your clients to enhance their resilience. Reducing the risk of stress and increasing their capacity to cope will allow your clients to achieve greater self-insight and control, and will assist them in achieving greater work-life balance. The coach or mentor plays a critical role in helping clients work towards optimum physical and mental health, cope with life's stressors, and learn and adapt so that they are fit for the future. The six masteries – mental, emotional, physical, social, environmental, and spiritual – all require tending to if our clients are to achieve work-life balance.

Maintaining work-life balance is a high priority for some clients; for others, it is an absolute imperative. For those with childcare responsibilities, elderly caring responsibilities, and single-parent families, the constant juggling of home, work, and wider commitments is commonplace. In situations where access to care is difficult, the workplace culture is orientated towards 24/7 working practises, organisational structures, and processes which are not sufficiently supportive and inhibit flexibility. Thus, the road to achieving work-life balance is paved with challenges. The impacts of low resilience are well documented. The evidence shows that when stressful circumstances arise, physical and mental strain increases. If the strain is sufficiently intense and prolonged, performance declines, ill health occurs, and in some extreme circumstances, individuals need medical support to overcome the period of ill health.

Viewing each of the six masteries as enablers of resilience and malleable to different degrees, it is possible for our clients to become more resilient. Arguably, some personality traits are more stable than others, and clients may not be able to change certain environmental conditions, but we can work with clients to maximise their resilience within their own ecosystem and their internal and external context.

QUESTIONS FOR REFLECTION

- To what extent do conversations around building a resilient mind and body currently feature in your coaching or mentoring practice?
- How much more do you think you need to cover the six resilience masteries in your coaching or mentoring sessions?
- How do your clients view their resilience, e.g. physical energy, strength of support networks, and quality of relationships?
- What 'buffers' do your clients have in place to protect their resilience?
- How comfortable have you been with helping your clients to enhance their resilience, and how much better will you feel when helping your clients in the future?
- What further support do you need and who can you reach out to in order to ensure that you are comfortable in talking about your clients' resilience with them in sessions?

Additional reading and resources

Burch, V. & Penman, D. (2013). *Mindfulness for Health: A Practical Guide to Relieving Pain, Reducing Stress and Restoring Well-Being.* London, UK: Hachette.

Garmezy, N. (1992). *Risk and Protective Factors in the Development of Psychopathology.* Cambridge University Press.

Joseph, I. (2012). The Skill of Self-Confidence. TEDxRyersonU. https://www.youtube.com/watch?v=w-HYZv6HzAs

Morin, A. (2015). The Secret of Becoming Mentally Strong. TEDxOcala. https://www.youtube.com/watch?v=TFbv757kup4

Walker, M. (2018). *Why We Sleep: The New Science of Sleep and Dreams.* New York: Scribner.

References

Baer, R.A., Smith, G.T. & Allen, K.B. (2004). Assessment of mindfulness by self-report: the Kentucky inventory of mindfulness skills. *Assessment,* 11(3), pp. 191–206.

Baumeister, R.F. & Leary, M.R. (1995). The need to belong: desire for interpersonal attachments as a fundamental human motivation. *Psychological Bulletin,* 117, pp. 497–529.

Bodhi, B. (1984). *The Noble Eightfold Path* (p. 63). Kandy, Sri Lanka: Buddhist Publication Society.

Bonanno, G.A. (2004). Loss, trauma, and human resilience: Have we underestimated the human capacity to thrive after extremely aversive events? *American Psychologist,* 59(1), pp. 20–28.

Bradt, S. (2010). Wandering mind not a happy mind. *Harvard Gazette,* 11 November, p. 11.

Chan, C.L., Chan, T.H. & Ng, S.M. (2006). The Strength-focused and Meaning-oriented Approach to Resilience and Transformation (SMART) a body-mind-spirit approach to trauma management. *Social Work in Health Care,* 43(2–3), pp. 9–36.

Dutton, J.E. (2003). *Energize Your Workplace: Building and Sustaining HQC Connections at Work*. San Francisco, CA: Jossey-Bass.

Fantilli, R.D. & McDougall, D.E. (2009). A study of novice teachers: challenges and supports in the first years. *Teaching and Teacher Education*, 25(6), pp. 814–825.

Freudenberger, H.J. (1974). Staff burn-out. *Journal of Social Issues*, 30(1), pp. 159–165.

Garmezy, N. (1992). *Risk and Protective Factors in the Development of Psychopathology*. Cambridge University Press.

Goldstein, J. (2002). *One Dharma: The Emerging Western Buddhism*. San Francisco, CA: Harper Collins.

Goleman, D. (1998). *Working With Emotional Intelligence*. New York: Bantam Books.

Goleman, D. (2001). An EI-based theory of performance. In D. Goleman & C. Cherniss (Eds), *The Emotionally Intelligent Workplace: How to Select for, Measure, and Improve Emotional Intelligence in Individuals, Groups, and Organizations* (pp. 27–44). San Francisco, CA: Jossey-Bass.

Gould, D., Tuffey, S., Udry, E. & Loehr, J. (1996). Burnout in competitive junior tennis players: II. Qualitative analysis. *The Sport Psychologist*, 10(4), pp. 341–366.

Grant, A.M. (2003). The impact of life coaching on goal attainment, metacognition and mental health. *Social Behavior and Personality: An International Journal*, 31(3), pp. 253–263.

Grant, A.M., Curtayne, L. and Burton, G., 2009. Executive coaching enhances goal attainment, resilience and workplace well-being: A randomised controlled study. *The journal of positive psychology*, 4(5), pp. 396–407.

Grossman, J.B. & Tierney, J.P. (1998). Does mentoring work? An impact study of the Big Brothers Big Sisters program. *Evaluation Review*, 22(3), pp. 403–426.

Haddock-Millar, J. & Clutterbuck, D. (2016). *5 Critical Conversations to Talent Development*. 33 (1607), pp. 1–17. American Society for Training & Development.

Hougaard, R. & Carter, J. (2016). How to practice mindfulness throughout your work day. *Harvard Business Review*, 7 March, pp. 2–5.

Joseph, I. (2012). The Skill of Self-Confidence. TEDxRyersonU. Accessed on 12th September 2018 at: https://www.youtube.com/watch?v=w-HYZv6HzAs.

Kabat-Zinn, J. (1990). *Full Catastrophe Living: Using the Wisdom of Your Body and Mind to Face Stress, Pain, and Illness*. New York: Delacorte.

Kaufman, S.R. (1986). *The Ageless Self: Sources of Meaning in Late Life*. New York: Meridian.

Kobasa, S.C. (1979). Stressful life events, personality, and health: an inquiry into hardiness. *Journal of Personality and Social Psychology*, 37(1), p. 1.

Kobasa, S.C., Maddi, S.R. & Courington, S. (1981). Personality and constitution as mediators in the stress-illness relationship. *Journal of Health and Social Behavior*, 22(4), pp. 368–378.

Kline, N. (1999). *Time to Think: Listening to Ignite the Human Mind*. London, UK: Hachette.

Kristensen, T.S., Borritz, M., Villadsen, E. & Christensen, K.B. (2005). The Copenhagen Burnout Inventory: a new tool for the assessment of burnout. *Work & Stress*, 19(3), pp. 192–207.

Kumpfer, K.L. (2002). Factors and processes contributing to resilience. In M.D. Glantz & J.L. Johnson (Eds), *Resilience and Development* (pp. 179–224). Boston, MA: Springer.

Lu, F.J., Lee, W.P., Chang, Y.K., Chou, C.C., Hsu, Y.W., Lin, J.H. & Gill, D.L. (2016). Interaction of athletes' resilience and coaches' social support on the stress-burnout relationship: a conjunctive moderation perspective. *Psychology of Sport and Exercise*, 22, pp. 202–209.

Maslach, C., Jackson, S.E. & Leiter, M.P. (1996). *MBI: The Maslach Burnout Inventory: Manual*. Palo Alto, CA: Consulting Psychologists Press.

Maslow, A. (1968). *Toward a Psychology of Being* (2nd ed.). Princeton, NJ: Van Nostrand.

Masten, A.S. (1994). Resilience in individual development: Successful adaptation despite risk and adversity. In M. Wang & E. Gordon (Eds.), *Risk and resilience in inner city America: Challenges and prospects* (3–25). Hillsdale, NJ: Erlbaum.

Masten, A.S., Best, K.M. and Garmezy, N., 1990. Resilience and development: Contributions from the study of children who overcome adversity. *Development and psychopathology*, 2(4), pp. 425–444.

McIntyre, F. (2004). New teachers thriving by third year. *Professionally Speaking: The Magazine of the Ontario College of Teachers*, pp. 41–46.

Morin, A. (2015). The Secret of Becoming Mentally Strong. TEDxOcala. Accessed on 1st October 2018 at: https://www.youtube.com/watch?v=TFbv757kup4 (accessed on 7.01.2019).

Olsen, B. & Anderson, L. (2007). Courses of action: a qualitative investigation into urban teacher retention and career development. *Urban Education*, 42(1), pp. 5–29.

Osterling, K.L. & Hines, A.M. (2006). Mentoring adolescent foster youth: promoting resilience during developmental transitions. *Child & Family Social Work*, 11(3), pp. 242–253.

Oswald, M., Johnson, B. & Howard, S. (2003). Quantifying and evaluating resilience-promoting factors: teachers' beliefs and perceived roles. *Research in Education*, 70(1), pp. 50–64.

Rutter, M. (1987). Psychosocial resilience and protective mechanisms. *American Journal of Orthopsychiatry*, 57(3), pp. 316–331.

Sammons, P., Day, C., Kington, A., Gu, Q., Stobart, G. & Smees, R. (2007). Exploring variations in teachers' work, lives and their effects on pupils: key findings and implications from a longitudinal mixed-method study. *British Educational Research Journal*, 33(5), pp. 681–701.

Schaufeli, W.B., Leiter, M.P. & Maslach, C. (2009). Burnout: 35 years of research and practice. *Career Development International*, 14(3), pp. 204–220.

Schon, D.A. (1987). *Educating the Reflective Practitioner. Toward a New Design for Teaching and Learning in the Professions*. The Jossey-Bass Higher Education Series. San Francisco, CA: Jossey-Bass Publishers.

Seibert, S.E., Kraimer, M.L. & Heslin, P.A. (2016). Developing career resilience and adaptability. *Organizational Dynamics*, 45(3), pp. 245–257.

Smith, R.E. (1986). Toward a cognitive-affective model of athletic burnout. *Journal of Sport Psychology*, 8(1), pp. 36–50.

Spanier, G.B. & Casto, R.F. (1979). Adjustment to separation and divorce: a qualitative analysis. In G. Levinger & O.C. Moles (Eds), *Divorce and Separation: Context, Causes, and Consequences* (pp. 211–227). New York: Basic Books.

Swaminathan, N. (2008). Scientific America. Accessed on 13th January 2019 at: https://www.scientificamerican.com/article/why-does-the-brain-need-s/.

Tedeschi, R.G. & Calhoun, L.G. (1995). *Trauma and Transformation: Growing in the Aftermath of Suffering*. Thousand Oaks, CA: Sage Publications.

Turner, S. & Scherman, A. (1996). Big brothers: impact on little brothers' self-concepts and behaviors. *Adolescence*, 31(124), p. 875.

Walker, M. (2018). *Why We Sleep: The New Science of Sleep and Dreams*. New York: Scribner.

Werner, E.E. (1993). Risk, resilience, and recovery: perspectives from the Kauai Longitudinal Study. *Development and Psychopathology*, 5(4), pp. 503–515.

Youth Business International. (2018). Exploring the Impact of Volunteer Business Mentoring on Young Adults. London, UK: YBI. Accessed on 1st September 2018 at: https://www.youthbusiness.org/file_uploads/YBI-Report-Exploring-the-impact-of-voluntary-business-mentoring-on-young-entrepreneurs-Digital.pdf.

Zippay, A. (1995). Expanding employment skills and social networks among teen mothers: case study of a mentor program. *Child and Adolescent Social Work Journal*, 12(1), pp. 51–69.

5   Stage 4

Decision–making and negotiation

Introduction

For many seeking to address their work-life balance, often their primary reason for engaging with a coach or mentor is to provide a reflective space to help problem-solve, reach a decision, and take action. People are frequently faced with a number of different choices which present wide-ranging extremes: Appealing or unappealing, low impact or high impact, simple and straight-forward or complex and far-reaching. In other scenarios, the choices present subtle or unknown consequences. Faced with any of these situations, people can feel overwhelmed – a common anxiety symptom – and paralysed. As a coach or mentor, our role, amongst others, is to assist people with major changes in life, work, and context. In reaching decisions, we help our clients think through the options available, consider alternatives, understand the consequences of action or inaction, and move forward in achieving the clients' short-, medium-, and long-term aims.

The coach or mentor can help clients gain a deeper understanding of their internal and external context. To gain an understanding of context, it is critical for clients to have purposeful, critical conversations with a wide range of stakeholders, often referred to as our developmental network. If we look at our immediate stakeholders – for example, when a potential job move is going to affect a partner or children – we might have a number of conversations with our partner and children. More broadly, it is often necessary to have conversations with our line managers, colleagues, and personal and professional confidants – for example, to discuss career progression scenarios, motivations, and aspirations. As a coach or mentor, a significant part of our role is to help our clients identify what types of conversations need to take place, with whom (their stakeholders), and when. That is not forgetting, of course, the conversation clients need to have with themselves! In turn, this will involve helping the client prepare for the conversations that need to take place to move forward.

Another crucial role of the coach or mentor is helping clients develop the ability to address their work-life balance by effectively negotiating and influencing. Negotiation and influencing are a critical part of our clients' personal and professional lives; indeed, negotiation happens in all aspects of life:

- Between parents and children.
- Between spouses and partners.
- Between friends.
- Between individuals and their line managers.
- Between team members.

Evidence shows that effective negotiations can lead to better working relationships and to personal and professional success.

Therefore, this chapter consists of two related themes of our Four-Stage Model for Work-Life Balance, as illustrated in Figure 5.1.

The first section focuses on decision-making, conversation, and developmental networks, helping your clients develop knowledge and expertise to have the conversations needed, with the right people at the right time, to achieve the change they wish. In previous chapters, we explored how the coach or mentor can prepare their clients to have these conversations through the discussions and work on self-identity, sense of meaning, values, confidence, and self-esteem. In our experience, helping clients gain confidence to navigate conversations is essential in addressing work-life balance. This involves identifying their key stakeholders, their influence and impact, the conversations they need to have, and the questions they need to ask. We refer to this section as critical conversations because they enable and facilitate the decision-making process and ultimately taking action. We consider the following questions:

- Why is it important to have conversations with others (and with yourself!)?
- What types of conversations need to take place?
- Who is within the developmental network (and outside of the network) that might provide valuable insight?

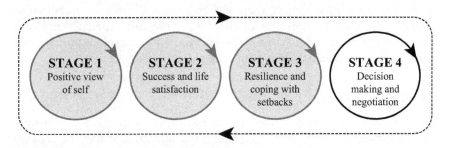

Figure 5.1 Four-Stage Model for Work-Life Balance

The second related theme focuses on negotiation and influence and considers how you are able to develop your clients' confidence and expertise to address the balance of power, maximise their impact, and secure a positive outcome for all. We consider the following questions:

- When is it important to be able to negotiate with others (and with yourself!)?
- What prevents us from negotiating successfully?
- What are the key skills and how can we develop these?

We present a number of techniques and approaches which can be used in different contexts and settings. We also provide a number of case studies which illustrate real examples where colleagues, associates, and friends share their experiences of addressing their work-life balance by drawing on a number of the techniques and approaches discussed.

Decision-making and critical conversations

This section identifies the crucial role critical conversations and developmental networks play in achieving work-life balance. In chapters 2 and 3 we examined theory and tools to help you assist your clients in uncovering what really matters, their priorities, their deepest interests, needs, and values. Therefore, we do not intend to address these aspects in this chapter. Instead, we focus on helping clients to identify the kinds of conversations that need to take place and with whom they need to take place. Consider the range of options available that can enhance their capacity to find new and better solutions to problems through the optimum use of their developmental networks and key stakeholders. We identify some of the barriers to choice and decision-making and look at how barriers can negatively influence work-life balance outcomes, and conversely, how the impact of actively-choosing can impact positively on work-life outcomes.

We refer to one in-depth case study to illustrate some of the conversations and dynamics your clients may encounter; we include a number of reflective questions to enable you consider your practice and how you might approach particular situations and scenarios with your clients. We illustrate some of the tools and techniques so that you can see how they work in a real situation.

At the end of each section, there will be a series of reflective questions to prompt your consideration of your coaching or mentoring practice and your clients' perspectives and behaviours. Should you wish to explore this area further, we have provided additional reading and resources.

Deciding and choosing

Most decisions will involve your clients identifying their goal(s), evaluating the importance of each goal, recognising the options available (or creating new options), weighing up each of the options, deciding on which option to take, and taking action. This all sounds very straightforward and rational, but how many of our clients use a process for thinking through important decisions? Dan Ariely's (2008) *Predictably Irrational* text suggests that in conventional economics the assumption that we are all rational implies that we compute the value of all the options we face and then follow the best possible path of action. But in an environment which is increasingly described as volatile, uncertain, complex, and ambiguous (VUCA), where we are constantly bombarded with information, we can feel overwhelmed, stressed, and paralysed, unable to focus, plan, and solve problems. Our ability to see and think through options can be significantly hindered by the environment and our own mental state.

Short-term emotions can tempt us away from making the 'right' choice. We see this all the time in everyday choices. At the beginning of each New Year, friends and relatives – as do we! – often decide to go on a health kick, improve their well-being, and shed excess weight, but within the first few weeks, days, or hours, we choose to have that one additional chocolate or glass of wine, or decide to stay home rather than go to the gym. Experiencing shifts in short-term emotions is not the only thing that can get in the way of our ability to decide and take action.

We might choose the path of least resistance because we lack the energy and capacity to choose a road which requires greater effort and application. Chip and Dan Heath (2013) in their book *Decisive* claim that psychologists have identified two contrasting mindsets that influence our motivation and our receptiveness to new opportunities:

- A prevention focus: An orientation towards negative outcomes and a spotlight on what might go wrong, what you might lose.
- A promotion focus: An orientation towards pursuing positive outcomes and a spotlight on new ideas and experiences.

In cognitive psychology and decision theory, numerous studies have found that people tend to prefer avoiding *losses* to acquiring equivalent gains; referred to as loss aversion (Tom et al., 2007). Loss aversion can result in inertia, the tendency to stick to the status quo; procrastination can result in missed opportunities. Ruth Chang (2014) in her well-known TED Talk about 'Hard Choices', describes her choice to pursue a career as a lawyer rather than a philosopher because of 'fear of being an unemployed philosopher' led her to take the safe option, the known route of a lawyer. Social pressures and fear of failure and the unknown can lead us to adopt the safe option, the known option, and the socially acceptable option, influenced by the cultural, political, and economic context. Later Chang switched careers to become a philosopher, realising the role of lawyer was not the right fit for her. Her research now focuses on 'hard choices'. Chang claims that hard choices are perceived as hard because sometimes there is no best option – there are equally good options. Often we adopt a narrow frame, described by the Heath brothers as one of the villains of decision-making. Narrow framing can result in clients only seeing binary choices: This or that; leave or stay; yes or no. The Heath brothers encourage us to look inside and outside to identify and explore options and solutions. They suggest that we should consider our own *'bright spots'*, those moments that can act as a source of inspiration. When we look outside and take an external perspective, we might find someone who has faced a similar problem or situation that can provide a different perspective and draw our attention towards different options, thereby widening the potential options available.

In Barry Schwartz's (2005) Global TED Talk, he refers to choice providing freedom and improving welfare in relation to health and happiness: 'the more choice people have, the more freedom they have, the more freedom they have the more welfare they have'. But in affluent Western society, instead of increased choice acting as a liberator, it can induce paralysis because too much choice overwhelms us.

When we find ourselves in a situation we are unhappy with, there are four options: Change the situation; move out of the situation; change ourselves; or put up with the situation and maintain the status quo. The power of choice lies in its ability to discover the best option possible out of all of those available. Schwartz, in his text, *The Paradox of Choice* (2004), distinguishes between what he calls 'choosers' and 'pickers'. A chooser is someone who:

- Actively thinks about the possibility before making a decision.
- Reflects on what's important in life.
- Reflects on what's important about this particular decision.
- Understands what the short- and long-range consequences of the decision will be.
- Has an awareness of what the choice means to him/her as a person.
- Understands that the available alternatives might not be satisfactory and that another alternative might need to be created.

In contrast, a *picker* does none of the above; instead a picker will grab this or that and hope for the best. Richard Talker and Cass Sunstein (2009), authors of *Nudge, Improving Decisions about Health, Wealth and Happiness*, refer to this approach as mindless choosing, signalling a real lack of attention and insight.

Reflecting on your own practice:

- How well have you been exploring how your clients approach choice?
- What is your clients' degree of mindfulness when choosing?
- What skills do your clients draw on when choosing?
- To what extent do you explore your clients' skill in choosing?

As identified in the previous section, the latter scenario – being a picker – can occur when we feel overwhelmed and stressed. As a coach or mentor, you can help create a space to provide perspective, calm, and clarity. William Ury (2007), co-author of *Getting to Yes*, in his more recent text *The Power of a Positive No*, uses the metaphor of 'Going to the Balcony' which is described as a 'detached state of mind you can access any time you choose ... picture yourself up on a balcony overlooking the stage, a place where you can see the scene clearly from above' (p.30–31). Ury talks about this in the context of influence, self-regulation, and managing emotions. We suggest that this is a useful analogy for the role of the coach or mentor; clients visit the balcony to help survey the landscape, gain a clearer picture of what is happening around them, experience a sense of calm and clarity, and in those moments can adopt the role of the *chooser*. Taking this holistic view – surveying the landscape – we focus on three aspects that may make a significant difference to your client's perspective:

1. What are the critical conversations that need to take place?
2. To whom do I need to talk?
3. What questions do I need to ask them?

Critical conversations

What is a critical conversation?

Critical conversations 'have the power to create change, including shifts in perspective, knowledge, and understanding' (Haddock-Millar & Clutterbuck, 2016), all of which are vital in the context of work-life balance. Critical conversation in itself is not decision-making but a process for getting all relevant information and insight in order to make an informed decision; having critical conversations ensures that your clients adopt the role of *chooser* and by doing so:

•   Actively think about the possibility before making a decision.
•   Reflect on what's important in life.
•   Reflect on family values, needs, and practical issues.
•   Reflect on what's important about this particular decision.
•   Understand what the short- and long-range consequences of the decision will be.
•   Have an awareness of what the choice means as a person.
•   Reflect on what is going on around them and how to relate to it.
•   Consider different scenarios and their implications.
•   Understand how to harness their developmental network to develop new and alternative options.

We want to avoid confirmation bias, which might lead your clients to gather self-serving information, narrowing their options and choices. Helping your clients to identify the type of conversations that need to take place is the first stage in gaining a wider perspective. Broadly, the critical conversations can be grouped into four themes:

1. Internal dialogue.
2. Systemic dialogue with immediate stakeholders.
3. Colleague/organizational dialogue.
4. Social networking dialogue.

Internal dialogue

Here, your clients ask questions of themselves, and in doing so reflect on their identity and values, self-belief, and motivation. We addressed the internal dialogue in chapters 2 and 3; to summarise briefly, the areas you may address include:

- Self-awareness: Reflecting on identity and values, self-belief, and motivation.
- Environmental awareness: What is going on around me, and how do I relate to it?
- Purpose: What do I want to achieve for myself and others? Whom do I want to become?
- Strengths and development areas: What do I do well? What don't I do well? What new strengths am I developing?

Systemic dialogue with immediate stakeholders

Systemic dialogue is important because it helps clients to develop a picture of how different aspects of the situation influence each other and connect in such a way that facilitates greater clarity of understanding. Often it is helpful to seek others' guidance or just have someone listen to where your head is. At other times, it is critical to have conversations with immediate stakeholders – for example, when a job move is going to affect a partner or children. These are examples of the types of conversations:

- Reflecting with family about values, needs, and practical issues.
- Asking how family members can articulate their needs in relation to the situation.
- Identifying people with expertise and experience that will enable learning and insight.

Colleague/career dialogue

These conversations will help to shine a light on your clients' career. Some stakeholders may be more invested than others. A career sponsor may have a vested interest in helping your clients achieve internal upwards promotion; informal career mentors tend to help individuals think more objectively about their careers. Examples of conversations include:

- Conversations to develop scenarios for career development and discussions with informal mentors.
- Conversations with line managers to help to identify interesting assignments and moves either within or outside of the organisation.
- Conversations with colleagues to understand the wider work context.

Social networking dialogue

Social networking takes a variety of forms, including informal networks such as events organised by professional and development associations to share ideas with others and provide opportunities to meet others with similar or different interests. Parent and toddler groups, parent and school social evenings – the list is endless! Furthermore, internet-based social networking has become a widespread phenomenon; Statista (2018), an Internet-based statistics company, reported that in 2017, 81% of Americans had a social media profile. Social media usage is highest in suburban America, amongst those earning over $75,000 a year, and amongst those with the highest degree of education. Similarly, in the UK, social media usage was at an all-time high at the beginning of 2018, with 83% of the adult population using at least one online social media platform (Flint, 2018). Globally, as of January 2016, Facebook has some 1.5 billion accounts and is followed by WhatsApp and Tencent QQ (QQ) with 900 million and 860 million users, respectively. Knowing that so many of us are engaged in social networking, how can your clients harness their informal and formal networks to support developmental conversation? Specific examples of social networking include:

- Within the profession or current organisation.
- Peers in other professions.
- Identifying and developing new opportunities through connections.

Wendy Murphy and Kathy Kram (2014) in their text *Strategic Relationships at Work* explain that developmental relationships provide three main types of support:

1. Career support – Instrumental aspects of development that support career advancement impacting on current and future growth.
2. Psychosocial support – Develop aspects of competence, clarity, and professional identity, and self-worth impacting on areas such as confidence and self-esteem.
3. Role-modelling – Encompass those aspects of the other person that are admired and that offer a source of inspiration, providing a vision of what the person wants to become, and impact on trajectory and advancement.

Here we see that critical conversations with key stakeholders have the potential to support developmental growth in knowledge, including technical and behavioural competence; enabling levers, including learning resources and a wider network of opportunities; career needs, including goals, aspirations, and growth; emotional needs, including increased confidence, altruistic satisfaction, status, and intellectual challenge.

In chapter 4, we examined the hypothesis that a network of development relationships impacts positively on work-life balance. As we know, the evidence demonstrates that quality constellation developmental networks do have positive psychosocial, career, and work-life balance outcomes. Therefore, we do not intend to revisit this area. However, a necessary step is to help your clients to identify who is within – or outside – their current developmental network that can assist in their decision-making process. The case study below provides a real example of the process in action. We described John's (the client) experience, the conversations he had, with whom he spoke, and the longer-term outcome. We also describe how his coach helped him to work through the process of identifying his key stakeholders, analysing their relationship and understanding the types of conversations that he needed to have to help assist in this thought process.

CASE STUDY

John had worked for his current and only employer in the retail sector for 23 years. He had always worked in a retail store environment, involving long hours, including weekends, evenings, and overnight shifts. This wasn't a problem before having children, as it was all he knew and had come to accept that this was typical of the retail environment. John found it increasingly difficult to maintain a healthy balance between meeting the demands of his job and the demands of having a young family (twins aged 2). His wife was unhappy with his working pattern; she felt that their time together as a family was very limited and as a consequence, she felt that they were beginning to lead 'separate lives'. John found himself somewhat unexpectedly with an opportunity to take a job moving to the company's head office in a role that would stretch him in different ways and potentially allow him to develop his leadership and managerial skills, his networking skills, and his relationship building skills, as well as experience a different working environment. John could see there was a chance to grow in his career and have a healthier work-life balance. Nonetheless, he was hesitant.

Working with his coach, John explored a number of themes which enabled him to identify his thoughts (mind talk) and explore his concerns:

- **Comfort zone/Institutionalisation** – John recognised that he had become institutionalised in the sense that he had come to accept and abide by the cultural and organisational norms of the environment and felt secure with an abundance of tacit knowledge. He felt that he would be moving away from a role he could do on 'auto pilot', leaving a role he knew he could deliver exceptionally well and was consistently a high performer. His questions included:
    - What if I couldn't adapt to a different way of working, a different culture, and new people?
    - Would this hinder my ability to progress in the business?
    - Would there be a route back into stores or would I have to leave the business if it didn't work out?

- **Income and financial implications** – In the store, John worked both Saturday and Sunday with Monday and Tuesday as his days off and was responsible for the childcare on those two days. Working weekends, early morning and evenings, had the added benefit of a premium payment. Moving to a Monday to Friday job role would mean a net loss of 40% income due to additional childcare costs and increased travel costs, with no additional salary to cover the shortfall. John would also lose the option of working overtime to cover holidays, etc. His questions included:
    1. Could I/my family afford to absorb these costs with both children needing to move to a full-time nursery arrangement?
    2. How could the financial shortfall be mitigated, if at all?
    3. Would the financial impact be in the long term?
- **Flexibility** – John was keen to understand if he would still be able to have a degree of flexible working if he worked 50 miles away versus two miles from home. His journey involved the notorious M25 motorway; what would he do if he was stuck on a day where he had to pick up the twins from the nursery?
- **Career ambitions** – John wanted to understand what he wanted to do in the longer-term. Until now, he had not taken responsibility for his own career; internal moves had been offered rather than John seeking them out. The new opportunity would potentially take John in a different direction. This would be more of a strategic role than an operational role. Is this something John wanted?

John worked with his coach to identify who he needed to have conversations with and what those conversations looked like in practice. They did this by creating a visual map and then connecting relationships with the four themes he discussed with his coach.

John felt that it was important to talk through the situation with a number of people he valued and trusted, people who would help him to reflect more fully on his needs and those of his family. With his coach, he identified the following people:

- Wife.
- Father.
- Current line manager.
- New line manager.
- Informal mentor.
- Close colleague.
- Family friend.

Key stakeholder mapping

Figure 5.2 provides a visual representation of the mapping exercise. This can be a useful tool to help your clients not only identify their key stakeholders but the proximity, power and influence of the stakeholders. Proximity refers to nearness in space, time or relationship and can be defined by a number of different dimensions such as proximity to you, proximity to the situation, and/or proximity to the outcome. Taking this one step further, you can assist your clients in analysing their degree of power and influence on the situation. Therefore, there are three dimensions in focus. Table 5.1 shows how John chose to identify the proximity of his stakeholders.

Once John had identified his key stakeholders, he was then able to work with his Coach to identify the types of conversations he needed to have. Let's now return to the case study.

Reflecting on your own practice:

• How might you use this tool with your clients to explore a particular scenario?
• What additional elements might you add?
• How might this process inform your next coaching or mentoring session?

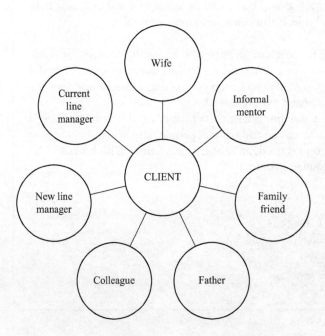

Figure 5.2 Visual mapping

Table 5.1 Key stakeholder mapping: interest, power, and proximity

Key Stakeholder	INTEREST	POWER	PROXIMITY		
			Proximity to You	Proximity to Situation	Proximity to Outcome
Wife	High	High	High	High	High
Colleague	Low	Low	Low	Medium	Low
Family friend	Low	Low	Medium	Low	Low
Father	Medium	Medium	High	Medium	Medium
Informal mentor	Low	Low	Medium	Low	Low
New line manager	Medium	High	Low	Medium	Medium
Current line manager	Medium	Medium	High	Low	Low

CASE STUDY

Once John completed the stakeholder mapping exercise with his coach, they were then able to explore the nature of the conversations – what did John need to find out and why?

Wife – The decision didn't just affect John – moving to the head office would have a big impact on his family, so the most important stakeholder was his wife. He was keen to explore how he could make a move into the office work, both from home life and career perspective. He was fortunate that his wife had experience of working in both a front-facing retail and office environment and could understand the pros and cons of the move; therefore, she was able to empathise with his hesitancy.

The conversation predominantly focused on finances, and specifically their ability to absorb the additional childcare and travel costs, and how they could make it work. They also talked about the impact a change to their routine would have on their home life – it would be a huge benefit to be able to play a bigger part in the twins' upbringing and to spend quality time as a family at weekends and evenings. John and his wife agreed that he should try and find out as much about moving to the office as possible, so he sought guidance from the following people.

Father – John was rather fortunate (or unfortunate depending on your perspective!) that his father loved to give career advice. He had a very similar career to John in terms of being somewhat institutionalised and having to make a decision on moving away from operations and into a strategic role while juggling a young family. To reinforce a poignant point, he would often say to John: 'we're travelling the same road, just think of it as I'm further along it and can help you navigate the bumpy bits and choose which forks to take'. John was interested to get his point of view, as he could see the similarities. John found his father's insight into how his decisions impacted on his family life the most helpful, as this was the one element of this decision that weighed heaviest on his mind.

Current line manager – John had a good relationship with his line manager and was comfortable discussing his thoughts and feelings with him. High on his agenda was achieving a better work/life balance at the same time as gaining a more holistic view of his organisation and the retail business. His line manager advised that it was a great opportunity; he got him to think about his brand and marketability. Moving to the office would enable him to broaden his thinking and become more strategic by understanding the wider business, and it would improve his marketability for other jobs within or outside of the organisation in the future. John would be exposed to senior managers within the business, which would provide a platform to showcase his brand and gain sponsorship from senior figures across the business.

New line manager – These conversations were mainly functional and centred around John's expectations and the differences in working practices when in the office rather than stores. John wanted to know the likelihood of his being able to meet the demands of having a young family and new job, and he was concerned about whether he would be given the flexibility he might require. He also wanted to understand the line manager's career path; John wanted to know if the line manager had plans to move on, how frequently job roles and structures changed, and how the line manager viewed both his own progress in the organisation and his approach to supporting and developing his team. If he was going to leap from stores it had to be for the right role and the right manager – in 23 years he had definitely learned that people usually don't leave the job – they leave their boss.

Informal mentor – John had worked hard in store to develop a relationship over time and a number of shops with his retail director to a point where he was his business sponsor. He was concerned he would lose that relationship by moving to the office. John got in contact with a previous store manager he used to work for who made the transition into the office as a director to see if he would be okay with John working with him as a mentor and helping John identify a sponsor in the office. In John's organisation, sponsorship was a prerequisite to promotion.

Colleague – John talked at length to a colleague who had made the transition from stores to the office; she also had a young family. John was keen to understand her take on the differences in culture and how she adapted to this, and whether there was anything he could take away from her. Conversation was fairly functional, such as good e-learning courses and short skill sessions to take to get started in the office, some etiquette (stores can be quite blunt and intolerable environments to work in!) to observe, as well as insider tips on traffic, parking arrangements, etc. John had also come to learn that restructuring and redundancies were fairly common and frequent in the office and so was understandably anxious. He had never been through anything like that and wanted to find out as much as he could about it.

Family friend – John spoke to his best friend's father a few times. John found this really helpful; as the man was far enough removed from the day-to-day intricacies of this decision, he often injected some welcomed clarity. John felt that he had a good mix of all the attributes all the other stakeholders had without any of their vested interest; it was easy to have balanced, impartial conversations.

At the beginning of this section, we explained that most decisions will involve your clients identifying their goal(s), evaluating the importance of each goal, recognising the options available (or creating new options), weighing up each of the options, deciding on which option to take, and taking action. Once John had the conversations he felt were necessary to have the level of insight necessary to make a decision, he was ready to take the next step – taking action. Taking action can sometimes be the toughest part of any decision-making process – there are consequences! Let's now return to the case study.

Reflecting on your own coaching and mentoring practice:

- When working with your clients, how often do stakeholder conversations occur in your coaching or mentoring sessions?
- How widely do your clients explore their stakeholder network?
- How might this information inform your next coaching or mentoring session?

CASE STUDY

After careful consideration, John decided it was too good an opportunity to pass up and took the position. It is true to say he hasn't looked back since. John has improved his work-life balance; the quality of his work has improved, and he feels that he has a more fulfilling home life. His wife is happier, and she has been able to make a shift in her career, developing a professional portfolio as she has yearned to do over the last 10 years. She and John make the most of their time with the children over the week-end, and football and swimming have become a key staple! Since moving to the new role, John's pay has increased to more than cover the cost of the childcare and travel – the 40% net loss was short-lived – this has been a direct result of achieving his objectives in the job and 'over perform-ing' during the last two years. John was able to bring a sense of pace and urgency to an environment which was characterised by bureaucracy and regimentality. This added a degree of dynamism to a team which needed to respond urgently to store issues. Overall, the organisation has benefit-ted as John has navigated his way constructively through a significant period of change. John feels that he has landed on his feet with his line manager – it was prudent to understand the character of his new manager before committing to taking the role. The line manager challenges John's thinking and allows him the room to take risks and learn from experi-ences. John has also been actively encouraged to take a wider perspective and look outside of his immediate environment to broaden his career opportunities.

The case study illustrates the multiple benefits of positive change. Reflecting on your own practice:

- How would you have helped John to identify the types of conversa-tions he needed to have and with whom he needed to talk?
- How would this case inform your next coaching or mentoring ses-sion on decision-making and choice?

Negotiation

This section identifies the crucial role negotiation plays in achieving work-life balance. It explores the degree to which your clients are both willing and able to negotiate effectively. We identify some of the impacts of poor negotia-tion and how this can negatively influence work-life balance outcomes and conversely, how good negotiation attitudes and skills can impact positively on work-life outcomes. Pay, career trajectory, promotion, and employment conditions are the serious outcomes of work-related negotiation. We examine some of the consequences of the absence of negotiation or ineffective negotiation and uncover common barriers to effective negotiation. Next, we identify the skills required to negotiate effectively and how you can support your clients to recognise their strengths and areas for development, creating a supportive dialogue to facilitate change. Throughout this section, we consider how you as coach or mentor can assist your clients in identifying the root cause of any resistance to negotiation, which is often unconscious. We show you techniques for overcoming these barriers and explore how you can develop your clients' skills to enable them to feel comfortable and confident in negotiation situations. Case studies will illustrate some of the issues your clients may encounter; we illustrate some of the tools and techniques so that you can see how they work in a variety of situations. At the end of the section, there will be a series of reflective questions to prompt your consideration of your coaching or mentoring practice and your clients' perspectives and behaviours. Should you wish to explore this area further, we have provided additional reading and resources.

So what is negotiation?

At its simplest level, negotiation is the discussion that takes place between two or more parties to reach an understanding, resolve differences, or gain advantage through coming up with a workable solution. Numerous definitions have emerged in recent years, such as:

- 'Negotiation is a basic means of getting what you want from others. It is back-and-forth communication designed to reach an agreement when you and the other side have some interests that are shared and others that are opposed (as well as some that may be different)' (Fisher, Ury & Patton, 2012, p. xxv).
- 'A negotiation is – a situation in which two parties with potentially competing incentives and goals come together to create a solution that satisfies everyone' (Weiss, 2016, p.12).
- 'Negotiation is a collaborative problem solving process which considers the other as well as self' (Neil and Lys, 2015, p.1).
- 'Negotiation is a process by which a joint decision is made by two or more parties' (Pruitt, 2013, p.1).
- 'Bargaining (give and take) process between two or more parties (each with its own aims, needs, and viewpoints) seeking to discover a common ground and reach an agreement to settle a matter of mutual concern or resolve a conflict' (Business Dictionary, 2017).

We negotiate all the time

Your clients might not like the thought of negotiating, to them it might be game-playing or placing themselves in a situation where they might lose something. You might have clients who enjoy it – but for the wrong reasons – they might like a fight, like a chance to 'win' over others. They might have old-fashioned views of negotiating, not fit for purpose in today's more collaborative working environment. Regardless of your clients' attitudes, beliefs, assumptions, and behaviour, we all negotiate unconsciously in our day-to-day lives. Indeed, opportunities to negotiate present themselves in so many aspects of business and life; we negotiate in various capacities and in different roles. We often negotiate with our work colleagues to address accountabilities, responsibilities, goals, and tasks. In the context of work-life balance, here are some examples:

- Negotiating a new employment contract.
- Negotiating a pay rise.
- Agreeing to a change of work pattern to enable greater flexibility, including addressing long hours, weekends, and travel.
- Agreeing with your spouse how you will manage childcare responsibilities.
- Deciding on whether or not to apply for voluntary redundancy.
- Deciding to move house to address a long work commute.
- Deciding how to best support an elderly parent.

As the world of work transforms to become more global, agile, digital, connected, and collaborative, negotiation is a skill that your clients increasingly need to have in order to successfully navigate dynamic career models and become agents of their own career and life destinies, applying autonomous control over their personal *and* professional development. Negotiation is a skill and business competence that one can easily find today in books, guides, self-help tools, short courses, long courses, and qualifications such as master's programmes in Negotiation and Conflict Resolution. For the last 30 years or so, academics and practitioners have been studying what makes for effective negotiation, addressing the way we make decisions with our families, organisations, and society. Numerous books, guides, and tools have emerged to assist organisations and individuals in developing their understanding and skills in negotiation. By understanding some theoretically based negotiating principles and tactics, you will be better placed to ask the right questions of your clients as they go into critical discussions with their stakeholders. As we saw in the previous section, critical conversations with key stakeholders help to elucidate and resolve issues such as pay, role, responsibilities, work conditions, alignment between the individual and the line manager, and organisational expectations.

In the third edition of the popular text, *Getting to YES*, authors Roger Fisher, William Ury, and Bruce Patton (2012) acknowledge the following:

> A generation ago, the prevailing view of decision-making in most places was hierarchical. The people at the top of the pyramids of power – at work, in the family, in politics – were supposed to make the decisions and the people at the bottom of the pyramids to follow the orders ... in today's world, characterized by flatter organisations, faster innovation, and

the explosion of the Internet, it is clearer than ever that to accomplish our work and meet our needs ... we are compelled to negotiate (p. ix).

One of the most common forms of negotiation, particularly in the workplace, is positional negotiation. This involves clarifying position and defending against it. Fisher, Ury, and Patton (2012) suggest that positional negotiating is to be avoided because it encourages ego, damages relationships, and makes people stubborn and short-sighted. Business is high stakes, and no one likes to lose, but their research suggested that it is possible for people to reach an agreement and negotiate in a way that is wise and efficient and that improves relationships. They created the Principled Approach (Fisher, Ury & Patton, 2012) to overcome previous problems caused by positional negotiating, an approach that would be deemed by all parties to be fair and have more chance of achieving a lasting outcome.

The Principled Negotiation, or Negotiation on the Merits, attempts to create a deal that's good for both parties – the goal is not to get a greater portion of the benefit than your counterpart, to beat the counterpart, or to take away any of the counterpart's power or influence; it aims for a win–win. The goal is to create an agreement in which both parties feel as if they walked away with a good deal and that they secured not only everything they wanted but perhaps even more than they wanted.

The Principled Approach encompasses four pillars and can be adopted in almost all circumstances. As you read them, have a client in mind, someone who is trying or has recently failed or is about to negotiate better work-life balance with their employer. You might like to consider role-playing the conversation with them and listen out for the four pillars. They are:

1. Separate the people from the problem – What you would want to hear from your client is that they are avoiding any blame or personal attack. They are inviting you in role play to express how you feel; they listen well, without reacting. They avoid 'reading your mind' and making presumptions about how you feel or what you are thinking or what you want or need. They own their own feelings and wishes with 'I' statements that disclose their thoughts and feelings succinctly. If you roleplay with them, ask yourself how well you feel you have been heard and understood.
2. Focus on interests and values, not positions – We all share fundamental human needs like security, connection, competence, and autonomy; by uncovering each participant's fundamental needs, it is likely that your client will find some common ground with the person they are negotiating with. This requires openness, articulation of what is really important to them, and clearly communicating what it is they are asking for. You may need to help your client cope with the other side adopting tactics such as emotional blackmail and giving veiled or outright threats, bribes, or other types of pressure.

3. Widening the options where mutual gain can be found – Just as in coaching, you know the benefit of widening the client's views of their options; help your client constantly search for opportunities to widen the options whereby they could find mutual benefit for both parties. As you probably know, research by Chip Heath and Dan Heath (2013), and by Daniel Kahnemann (2011), shows that the human tendency is to go for 'binary thinking' – we stop when we find two options, the 'either/or' solution. Your client needs to be encouraging their counterpart to brainstorm and generate as many options as possible and then evaluate them together against the criteria of success they both hold.
4. Be careful to only use objective data – Do what it takes to ensure that your client goes into negotiations with the attitude and skills to co-manage a joint search for objective criteria and data.

Another model might suit situations where your clients just do not believe in the optimistic outcomes of the Principled Approach. They may insist that they are in a 'dog-eat-dog' negotiation and that there simply will be a winner and a loser. In such cases, the Four Choice Mode – introduced by Peter Stark and Jane Flaherty (2003) – might appeal to them more. In the Four Choice negotiation model, individuals start off acknowledging that there are four possible outcomes: win-win, win-lose, lose-lose, or no outcome at all. The concept of win-win in this model means both parties get a large enough portion of what they wanted. The goal is to be satisfied that everyone leaves the negotiation feeling that they attained their fair share of the bargain. The win-win approach in this model typically involves both parties giving up a little of what they had hoped to achieve but not so much that they feel that they've lost. Regardless of the approach taken, it is important to focus on the issue(s) at hand, on solutions that address the issue(s), and where possible achieve mutual gain and benefit. A win-lose approach rarely has long-lasting benefits because the 'loser' feels dissatisfied and as research shows either withdraws or becomes aggressive and uncompromising at a later date.

The relationship between negotiation and work-life balance

Helping clients to develop their ability to negotiate can influence both short-term and long-term outcomes in many different aspects of life. Numerous studies have found that in the education profession, an inability to balance academic and family responsibilities was a critical factor influencing women's departure from academia (Moen & Sweet, 2004). More recently, there has been a surge in studies examining fathers' experiences in the home and work. Research by Harrington et al. (2012) found that fathers who had high levels of involvement with their children experienced positive benefits. A mixed method empirical study by Reddick et al. (2012) of junior male professors with young families found that the balance between their tenure-track work situation and raising children placed a strain on their relationships. One participant explained: 'It took a toll on my marriage. My wife was really upset with how little time I had for us. She would say, "I don't want to live like this"' (p. 5). Furthermore, participants claimed that 'they would cut their salaries by one fourth if they could have more family and personal time' (p. 2). In doing so, this would involve navigating and negotiating the demands and expectations of the organisation and management team alongside the personal desire to be more involved in home life, well-trodden territory for the experienced coach or mentor.

What prevents us from negotiating successfully?

Another area of research that has received a lot of attention is the interplay between gender (women), behaviour, negotiation, and outcomes. Linda Babcock and colleagues' (2003; 2009) research delves into the impact of avoiding negotiation. They undertook a variety of studies which examined the relationship between gender, negotiation behaviour, and starting salaries (of Carnegie Mellon University MBA graduates); gender differences in a lab; the extent to which men and women placed themselves in negotiation situations; and the ways in which women regard interactions as potential negotiations. In the first study, the findings were stark:

- Starting salaries of men were 7.6%, or almost $4,000, higher than those of women.
- Only 7% of the women, but 57% of the men, had asked for more money (i.e. negotiated on salary).
- Of those students who negotiated (most of whom were men), they were able to increase their starting salaries by 7.4% on average – or $4,053 – almost exactly the difference between men's and women's starting salaries.

Interestingly, graduating students at Carnegie Mellon University were strongly advised by the school's Career Services Department to negotiate their job offers. Regardless of the advice given, very few women had followed this advice, while the men did, resulting in a significant financial divergence between women and men. In another study, 20% of the women polled said that they never negotiate at all. It is worth understanding why many women avoid negotiating, even in situations in which they know that negotiation is appropriate and expected. Due to social conditioning, women, more than men, become victims by their need to be 'likeable': they see negotiating as causing conflict, problems, and rocking the boat. Research at Stanford's Clayman Institute found that women's need to be likeable does not stem from a neurotic need but rather is the result of conditioning and their evaluation of facts: Women who are likeable are promoted over those who are not likeable. Women have had to use indirect power to get what they want, and negotiating is very 'in your face'. It is a particular conundrum for women. Female modesty is valued in most cultures, and modesty plays down the self and doesn't seek rewards for self (Wade, 2001). Women have been socialised to think that they will not advance if they are seen to be aggressive or competitive (Daubman & Sigall, 1997). This tendency debilitates their willingness to negotiate. Any coach or mentor needs to be acutely aware of this tendency in women and help them work through their will and skill in negotiating so that they reach their goals. As the author of the book *Nice Girls Don't Get the Corner Office*, Dr Lois Frankel (2014), says, you might have to help your clients explore their concepts around 'being nice' and negotiating.

CASE STUDY

We provide an example of a client's unwillingness to negotiate due to social conditioning and the perceived tension between individual and organisational cultural origins and practices. Jane was a very successful engineer. She had a PhD, had led and delivered three critical projects. Her team, consisting of mostly professional men, hugely respected her. Her boss thought she could 'go all the way'. But she felt she didn't fit in. She was dismayed to see other people being paid more and being promoted above her. In a very macho environment, she was easy to underestimate and ignore. She was very quiet, very polite. Her coach explored her early life and found out that her mother and grandmother had been ballerinas. Her upbringing had almost centred on being gracious, 'nice', aesthetic. The cut and thrust of pay and project negotiation felt rather ugly to her, and she backed away from it. The consequence was that this remarkably able, steely, creative young woman was being overlooked. She didn't even want to play the game and negotiate.

- Give some time now to think through how you would best approach this client if you were coaching or mentoring her?

Women are losing out on earning more because they are not negotiating. In the book *Get Paid What You're Worth* by Robin Pinkley and Gregory Northcraft (2014), the authors estimate that a woman who routinely negotiates her salary increases will earn over $1 million more, by the time she retires, than a woman who accepts what she's offered every time without asking for more. Think about that. The cumulative effects of the gender gap in asking (negotiating) for more pay creates an enormous gap in what could have been their potential power. According to Linda Babcock and Sara Laschever, in their book *Women Don't Ask, Negotiation and the Gender Divide* (2009), in the territory of social equity, small inequalities between men and women, between racial groups, or between heterosexuals and homosexuals have been shown to accumulate rapidly and dramatically to one group's advantage and the other's disadvantage.

How to recognise and identify negotiation avoidance?

As a coach or mentor, as you learn to be more aware of the extent to which your clients avoid negotiation, understanding their behaviour in this area will help you address barriers and explore what is getting in the way of your clients' willingness to negotiate.

If your clients avoid negotiation, you may find that they:

- Frequently talk about postponing an issue until a 'better time'.
- Make lots of statements about what they are *not* good at, where they have made mistakes, and what they *don't* know and *can't do*.
- Don't like asking for things because they are afraid of how they may be perceived. Frequently for women this might be in the area of pay, bonuses, and their perceived ability to be assertive.
- Talk about not having enough time to deal with issues.
- Express concern about the impact actions will have on relationships.
- Have had feedback from others that they are unable to deal with conflict.
- Frequently talk about the protection of personal connections.
- Appear reluctant to take on experiments and rehearsals in the sessions.
- Exhibit anxiety during conversations about entering a negotiation scenario.
- Avoid discussions about emotions.
- Avoid discussions about potential conflict.
- Have closed body language.

In relation to work–life balance, failing to negotiate comes at a high cost; if your clients are reluctant to negotiate, they will be far less likely to obtain what they want, at work and at home. It is your responsibility as a coach or mentor to address this. Changes in workplace culture, where individuals are increasingly being expected to take charge of their own learning and career trajectory, are making it essential for people to exercise more control over their career development and employability (Sullivan & Baruch, 2010). If you and your clients are not engaged in these discussions, you are failing to equip them to succeed. In what has been described as the boundaryless career (Arthur & Rousseau, 1996), successful individuals are now wedded to their career and personal stakeholders, not the organisation. Therefore, negotiation is no longer an option but an essential skill in your clients' toolkit.

What are the key skills for effective negotiation and how can we develop them?

A coach or mentor working with clients to develop their skills to support effective negotiation will, in turn, enhance their confidence in entering a negotiation. There are many skills needed to ensure effective negotiation. Key skills include:

- Building trust and rapport: Establishing a bond or connection; making the communication process easier and more effective.

- Active listening: Listening with all the senses; mindfully hearing and attempting to comprehend the meaning of what is and is not being said.
- Effective questioning: Selecting the right questions at the right moment; asking questions that are powerful and thought-provoking.
- Dealing with conflict: Identifying the root causes and engaging different strategies to resolve differences.
- Persuasion: Communicating an idea or suggestion to another person(s) and obtaining the acceptance of the idea or suggestion.
- Regulating emotions: The ability to respond appropriately in a measured way to the situation at hand.
- Knowing the difference between being assertive but not aggressive or passive: Being able to assert views whilst still being respectful of others rather than attacking or ignoring others' perspectives or failing to state a view.
- Alert to our assumptions: Self-aware of the truths we determine with or without evidence; attentive to other's intentions, reasons for actions, or understanding of the situation.
- Being persistent: Maintaining a mindset that there is a workable solution; uncovering the reasons for a 'no'; knowing when to keep going even after being told 'no' by the other person(s).
- Creative thinking: The ability to look at problems and situations from a fresh perspective; developing novel solutions.

There are a number of tools you can use to help your clients understand their level of competence and confidence in negotiation scenarios. Using the tools, you will be able to assist your clients to identify their strengths and areas for development, which in turn may help to identify any resistance to negotiation.

Skills assessment

Initially, to help your clients assess their current level of competence and confidence in each of the skill areas, you might ask them to complete a skill self-assessment inventory. This is illustrated in Table 5.2.

Next, ask your clients to:

- Identify what they perceive to be their strongest and weakest areas.
- Describe and reflect on situations where they believe they performed well in a negotiation situation.
- Describe and reflect on situations where they did not perform well in a negotiation situation.

This is illustrated in Table 5.3.

Following this, ask your clients to identify any common themes in the situations where they feel they performed well and not so well.

Next, you will need to explore your clients' level of confidence in each of the skill areas in a negotiation scenario. Ask your clients to reflect back on

Table 5.2 Negotiation skills self-assessment inventory – competence

Negotiation skills	Level of competence (1 low – 10 high)									
	1	2	3	4	5	6	7	8	9	10
Building trust and rapport										
Active listening										
Effective questioning										
Dealing with conflict										
Persuasion										
Being assertive and knowing the difference between assertive, aggressive, and passive										
Ability to regulate emotions										
Being alert to our assumptions										
Being persistent										
Creative thinking										

Table 5.3 Negotiation scenario – performance and outcome

Negotiation scenario – reflection
Please provide an example of a recent negotiation where you believe you **performed well**.
Can you describe the situation; what you saw and heard; what was the outcome?
Please provide an example of a recent negotiation where you believe you **did not perform well**.
Can you describe the situation; what you saw and heard; what was the outcome?

Table 5.4 Negotiation skills self-assessment inventory – confidence

	Level of confidence (1 low – 10 high)									
Negotiation skills	*1*	*2*	*3*	*4*	*5*	*6*	*7*	*8*	*9*	*10*
Building trust and rapport										
Active listening										
Effective questioning										
Dealing with conflict										
Persuasion										
Being assertive and knowing the different between assertive, aggressive, and passive										
Ability to regulate emotions										
Being alert to our assumptions										
Being persistent										
Creative thinking										

one of the previous scenarios, or think more broadly about how they feel in negotiation scenarios. Ask your clients to give themselves a grade of 1–10 for each skill as listed on the inventory based on their current level of confidence (see Table 5.4).

You can use the results to compare your clients' view of their level of competence and confidence in each area. This can provide the basis for the development of strategies your clients might adopt to address specific negotiation skills.

The next stages involve helping your clients gain a 360-degree perspective of their negotiation skills – how others perceive their expertise and behaviours – and assisting them to reflect on the extent to which colleagues and/or friends see negotiation skills in action (see Table 5.5).

Table 5.5 Negotiation skills – summary of 360-degree feedback

Negotiation skills	Perception and experience of ... in a recent negotiation scenario (1 low extent – 10 high extent)									
	1	2	3	4	5	6	7	8	9	10
To what extent is ... able to build trust and rapport?										
To what extent does ... show active listening skills?										
To what extent does ... ask effective questioning?										
To what extent is ... able to deal effectively with conflict?										
To what extent is ... able to persuasion others?										
To what extent is ... able to be assertive without being aggressive?										
To what extent is ... able to regulate their emotions?										
To what extent does ... make assumptions about others or situations?										
To what extent is ... persistent?										
To what extent is ... able to think and act creatively?										

Table 5.6 Negotiation scenario – stakeholder reflection

Negotiation scenario – reflection
Please provide an example of a recent negotiation where you believe ... **performed well**. Can you describe the situation; what you saw and heard; what was the outcome?
Please provide an example of a recent negotiation where you believe ... **did not perform well**. Can you describe the situation; what you saw and heard; what was the outcome?

Use the following process with your clients:

1. Ask your clients to give the 'Negotiation skills – summary of 360-degree feedback' to between 8 and 10 trusted colleagues, friends, and/or family members who will be prepared to give honest feedback.
2. Ask each individual to rate your clients 1–10 for each skill as listed on the inventory based on their experience of your clients in a recent negotiation scenario.
3. Next, ask the individuals to describe and reflect on a recent situation where they believe your clients performed well in a negotiation situation.
4. Next, ask the individuals to describe and reflect on a recent situation where they believe your clients did not perform well in a negotiation situation.
5. Then ask the individuals to identify what they perceive to be your clients' strongest areas and areas for greatest development.

Next, you will want your clients to compare their 360-degree results with their own view of self. Ask your clients to identify any common themes in the situations where their colleagues and/or friends and family felt they had performed well and not so well.

CASE STUDY

A group of mature MBA students studying at the International University of Monaco was invited to complete the individual and 360-degree feedback exercises. The cohort had been working together for three months and had recently completed a group assessment which required the team to reach a consensus. The group of 10 students were split into two groups, consisting of individuals from different cultural backgrounds, experiences, education, and gender. In the majority of cases, women assessed themselves at the low to mid-point scale for competence and confidence in all areas. Conversely, their colleagues (male and female) tended to regard the women's ability to negotiate as significantly higher. In the majority of cases, men assessed themselves at the top end of the scale for competence *and* confidence in all areas, which was supported by colleagues. Consistently, the areas that were regarded as needing most development and attention were being alert to assumptions and how they influence behaviour in negotiation scenarios, and the ability to regulate emotions.

Reflecting on your own practice:

- To what extent do you notice gender differences in the way in which your clients perceive their competence and confidence in negotiation scenarios?
- In what ways do you encourage your clients to seek feedback from others to raise their awareness about their negotiation behaviours?
- How might the case study inform your next coaching or mentoring sessions?

Developing your clients' skills

Following the negotiation skills inventory and 360-degree feedback, your clients will have a clearer picture of where they need help and where to focus their attention. Having raised your clients' awareness and understanding of recent scenarios and having had them consider the external lens, you are in a position to help your clients consider what strategies might be adopted to address specific negotiation skills. We suggest a number of strategies below to help address their needs.

Building trust and rapport

The reciprocal nature of trust reinforces the value of taking time to get to know the other party and build rapport before your clients begin to negotiate. Forging personal connections is important in any situation in order to build rapport that will help smooth the discussion. In Janice Nadler's (2004) empirical study of the impact of small talk, she found that where law students each negotiated a commercial transaction with another law student at a different university using e-mail as the mode of communication, they were four times more likely to reach an impasse, feeling resentful and angry about the negotiation. Conversely, negotiators who engaged in a brief getting-to-know-you phone conversation built substantial rapport that resulted in positive social and economic benefits for both parties. This initial small talk by telephone made subsequent e-mail interaction proceed more smoothly because the early creation of rapport helped the negotiators approach the negotiation with a more cooperative mental model, thereby trusting in each other's good intentions. This, in turn, led to a successful negotiation that concluded with a contract and engendered positive feelings about one another along with expectations of successful dealings in the future. Your clients may not always be able to negotiate in person, but finding opportunities to have even the briefest conversation with the other party/parties has been shown to positively influence the chances of a successful negotiation outcome for all concerned. Furthermore, knowing how to build trust with colleagues from different cultures and backgrounds is important, because a trusting relationship allows for a meaningful and robust assessment of options.

Listening

Active listening requires your clients to give their full attention to what other people are saying *and* not saying, taking time to understand the points being made. Encourage your clients to tune in to body language, tone of voice, and choice of words. There are some common pitfalls in any situation: People tend to over-prepare what they are going to say and use their listening time waiting for their next turn to speak. They miss out on vital information and do not hear and appreciate what is being said, verbally and non-verbally. Also, our emotional filters and blind spots often prevent us from hearing what we do not want to hear. How can you help clients to be alert to their own emotions and reactions within any negotiation situation so they can regulate their own behaviours and actively engage in effective negotiation?

Effective questioning

Paramount amongst the skills for effective negotiation is your clients' ability to ask the right kinds of questions at the right time. Skilled negotiators ask significantly more questions than average negotiators. Thinking about our listening skills, when verbal and nonverbal cues don't match up, ask questions. For example, 'You are telling me you like this outcome, but you seem uneasy. Is something making you uncomfortable?' Asking pointed questions based on your perceptions of the other party's emotional expressions will make it easier for you to understand the other person's perspective. The types of questions asked and the timing of questions is important in a negotiation because the questions steer the discussion and help focus on the crucial issues. It is important to ask a range of question types to explore options but then narrow them down. That is, further along in the conversation, questions may need to be specific and targeted.

- *Open-ended questions*
  These are the kinds of questions that require a detailed answer in a negotiation and cannot be simply replied to with a 'yes' or 'no' response. They consist of using the words who, what, where, when, why, and how. The respondent has no alternative but to provide some detail. Examples: 'What else do you need to know?'; 'Why is that point or provision important?'
- *Open opportunity questions*
  This form of question invites the person to participate and offer their views. Example: 'What do you think of this option as a solution?'

- *Leading questions*
  Just like it sounds, you try to guide the person to your point of view in a persuasive manner. Example: 'And after we provide those documents that you just mentioned, you will … ?'

- *Probing deeper questions*
  When you need to gain a better insight into a person's thought process to further illuminate their rationale or position. Example: 'Could you provide us with more detail about how you analysed the data that you just described and how you reached your conclusion?'

- *Reflective questions*
  A reflective question repeats or rephrases what the other person's statements seem to imply. Their usual purpose is to clarify understanding of what a person really means or feels.

- *Directive or structured questions*
  Directive, or closed, questions require a specific answer, such as an actual date or time. They require expansion on a particular point and help maintain two-way communication. Usually, the directive question is used in conjunction with open or reflective questions to get more specific information. Example: 'How long do you think it would take to agree to the move?'

Dealing with conflict

Conflict can be commonplace in negotiation scenarios, caused by multiple factors, some of which include the employment relationship, different interests and values, ambiguity over responsibility or authority, distrust, misperceptions, and poor communication. Typically, there are two types of conflict:

1. *Personality clash*: Relational or emotional conflict, as when two people do not like each other.
2. *Substantive conflict*: People have different perspectives and ideas about the work they are involved in and how it is to be accomplished.

Organisational behaviourists have found that conflict can result in positive outcomes, as it can stimulate creativity, aid problem-solving, improve quality decision-making, and create a culture of self-evaluation and change (Cross & Carberry, 2016; Mullins, 2017). However, in our experience, very few clients are comfortable in dealing effectively with conflict. In the previous case study, the area all students felt least comfortable with in any negotiation scenario was facing conflict and knowing how to effectively manage the unfolding situation. Unsurprisingly, this was for a variety of reasons, including lack of experience, cultural orientation, socialisation, and gender differences. Researchers acknowledge that our cultural backgrounds often influence the negotiation approach we adopt, including communication styles, persuasion strategies, and protocols used (David, Francis & Walls, 1994). Helping your clients to identify the root cause of conflict and knowing how and when to use different conflict resolution strategies can help prevent a disagreement escalating and causing a breakdown in relationships.

Five conflict resolution strategies are commonplace:

- Compromising: Both parties of a conflict give up elements of their position in order to establish an acceptable, if not agreeable, solution.
- Obliging: Clients give the other parties what they want. The use of accommodation often occurs when clients wish to keep the peace or perceive the issue as minor.
- Avoiding: Clients seek to put off conflict indefinitely. By delaying or ignoring the conflict, clients hope the problem resolves itself without a confrontation.
- Collaborating: This works by integrating ideas set out by multiple parties. The object is to find a creative solution acceptable to everyone.
- Competing: Competition operates as a zero-sum game, in which one side wins and other loses.

There are a number of tools you can use to help your clients understand their preferred negotiation approach. Exploring the characteristics of each approach and the extent to which your clients adopt each approach can then give you and your clients insights to inform their ongoing development. We provide a self-assessment questionnaire you can use with your clients (see Table 5.7).

On completion of this exercise, ask your clients to total the scores and complete the following summary form (see Table 5.8).

The self-assessment summary will help to identify your clients' dominant negotiation style(s) and the style(s) least preferred. Helping your clients to understand their preferred or dominant negotiation style can shift the conversation to consider to what degree their negotiation style works effectively in achieving their desired outcome(s). The Harvard Law School Programme on Negotiation suggests that the most effective form of conflict resolution involves identifying shared interests, appreciating differences in preferences and priorities, acknowledging risk and potential future opportunities, and addressing potential problems up front. We accept that the programme focuses primarily on litigation avoidance; however, the advice is applicable to all negotiation scenarios. Assisting your clients to adopt a flexible approach in switching their negotiating style can pay dividends in achieving greater work-life balance. Consider the case studies below.

Table 5.7 Approaches to conflict resolution – self-assessment questionnaire

	Question: *To what extent do you feel you adopted the following approach in negotiation scenarios?*	Not at all (0)	A little (1)	To some extent (2)	A lot (3)	A great deal (4)
1	I frequently give up things that are important to me.					
2	I ignore issues that I know I need to resolve.					
3	I try to build strong relationships to overcome difference.					
4	I try to keep the peace, to the detriment of what I need.					
5	I find myself asking lots of different questions in negotiation scenarios.					
6	I frequently give others what they want.					
7	I often behave aggressively towards others when negotiating.					
8	I take time to understand what is important to others.					
9	I tend to put things off if I know dealing with them might result in disagreement.					
10	I work to find innovative solutions to solve problems.					
11	It is important to me that I win.					
12	I consider a wide range of outcomes and options in a negotiation scenario.					
13	I look for common ground when I negotiate.					
14	I tend to think will issues will get sorted without discussion.					
15	I do not probe into misunderstandings.					
16	I often find myself considering options which are not what I really want.					
17	I focus on maintaining harmonious relationships.					
18	I regard my interests as more important than others.					
19	I focus on short-term needs.					
20	I often make concessions to reach an agreement that everyone will accept.					

Table 5.8 Approaches to conflict resolution – self-assessment questionnaire summary

Negotiation Approach	Question Number	Score	Total Score
Compromising: Both parties of a conflict to give up elements of their position in order to establish an acceptable, if not agreeable, solution.	12		
	13		
	16		
	20		
Obliging: Clients give the other parties what they want. The use of accommodation often occurs when clients wish to keep the peace or perceive the issue as minor.	1		
	4		
	6		
	17		
Avoiding: Clients seek to put off conflict indefinitely. By delaying or ignoring the conflict, clients hope the problem resolves itself without a confrontation.	2		
	9		
	15		
	14		
Collaborating: This works by integrating ideas set out by multiple parties. The object is to find a creative solution acceptable to everyone.	3		
	5		
	8		
	10		
Competing: Competition operates as a zero-sum game in which one side wins and the other loses.	7		
	11		
	18		
	19		
Dominant style:			

CASE STUDY

Derek joined a humanitarian Non-Governmental Agency (NGO) as a Field Coordinator on a two-year, low-security, medical support mission in Congo. As this was his first appointment, he was provided with an experienced mentor who had worked in the field for many years. Derek was responsible for operational, financial, and human resources management, as well as communication with and representation of the organisation toward local, national, and international actors. Derek's role was key in the design, implementation, and evaluation of the project activities. He had many years of previous leadership and management experience – in the private sector in a different context. Derek's approach to getting things done was dictatorial; if people didn't comply, he would be aggressive to the point where the team were in dispute with one another and one colleague wanted to leave the mission. Derek's mentor encouraged him to seek feedback from others about his leadership style, which in turn, provided feedback on his style of management and negotiation. A number of team members felt that Derek put his interests first, that he was not interested in their needs, that he seemed to take a short-term view focused only on the here and now rather than thinking about the mission and team's longer-term needs. Talking it through with his mentor, Derek realised that his behaviours were a by-product of his previous experience and context; he was formerly in a highly competitive, toxic environment where people focused on self-serving interests. Derek's mentor encouraged him to reflect on two core aspects of his management and negotiation style:

- Look for an identity or goal that is shared amongst the team and himself: this encouraged the discussion of points of similarity rather than differences.
- Look beyond the immediate issue to look for deeper underlying concerns: this encouraged the opening up of new interests and creative ways to solve short- *and* long-term issues.

Over time, Derek worked with his mentor and his colleagues to adopt a more collaborative approach, creating more harmonious and productive working relationships whereby conflict was reduced significantly.

CASE STUDY

Joan was a high-flying Operations Director of a leading American supermarket. The coach was called in by Joan herself to help her cope with a colleague 'who was out to get her'. The coach found Joan very affable – charming, in fact – obviously intelligent and seemingly highly admired by her boss. Joan agreed for the coach to undertake 360-degree internal feedback, and a very different story unfolded. Her direct reports and her colleagues found her underhanded, unsupportive, overly competitive, and aggressive. Joan was very upset by the feedback and couldn't understand it. It could have been a time for more investigation face to face by the coach with the team – team coaching, perhaps – but Joan was against the coach speaking to her team anymore. The coach tried to encourage Joan to have the conversations with the team herself, but she really didn't want to. So the coach held some role-plays, using a hired-in actor, so that the coach could observe rather than be the one role-playing. Immediately, Joan's problems were obvious. The moment the actor crossed her, her tone changed and she became sarcastic and patronising, putting down the person. In the debrief, she reflected on her thought process: 'He was obviously out to trip me up so I had to put him in his place'. The actor was doing no such thing. He was merely making an inquiry, merely not understanding and asking a question. Joan was oversensitive to people challenging her and had developed an almost constantly 'on' negotiation style – a win-lose style – that was losing her followers. As soon as the coach gave her interpretation, Joan was able to see that the pattern was created in her childhood from exposure to her highly competitive siblings who tried to gain the attention of neglectful parents. Armed with her realisation, she was open to investigate her beliefs, attitudes, and style. Within a very short time, her negotiation style transformed to one of curiosity, openness, equanimity, and non-defensiveness. She's now all about seeking win-wins.

Reflecting on your own practice:

- To what extent do you notice the degree to which your clients recognise their negotiation style?
- To what extent do clients recognise the factors that influence their negotiation style?
- How might the case study inform your next coaching or mentoring sessions?

Persuasion

In most negotiation scenarios, your clients are aiming to create a shift or a change in circumstance or situation. This requires a degree of persuasion in the negotiation process; that is, the ability of your clients to help their counterpart see their perspective and move towards the shift or change. People who are particularly persuasive tend to have high self-esteem and strong emotional intelligence, as they can build rapport quickly, empathise, and listen effectively. Lyle Sussman's (1999) work on the art of persuasion and negotiation suggests that we should properly articulate our message; doing so focuses the other person's attention on the crucial issue and prevents the issue from getting side-tracked by unimportant or less central issues. Working with your clients to role-play different scenarios can help to explore the effectiveness of your clients' skills in this area.

Knowing the difference between being assertive but not aggressive or passive

There is a fine line between being able to assert your views whilst still being respectful of others and attacking or ignoring others' perspectives. Your clients' behaviours will indicate the approach they take in negotiation scenarios. Table 5.9 gives some examples of behaviours associated with passive, assertive, and aggressive behaviours in negotiation situations. Encouraging your clients to reflect on their behaviours in recent negotiation situations will raise their level of self-awareness and help them to understand the degree to which they are able to distinguish between different approaches and their impact. If your clients have previously adopted a passive or aggressive style, helping your clients to shift their behaviours towards an assertive approach is likely to achieve better negotiation outcomes, such as keeping the discussion going; facilitating mutually beneficial outcomes; adopting a strong, steady tone of voice; using evidence-based data; and giving factual responses rather than emotional or critical ones.

Table 5.9 Passive, assertive, aggressive

Passive	*Assertive*	*Aggressive*
Is afraid to speak up	Speaks openly	Interrupts and 'talks over' others
Avoids looking at people	Maintains eye contact	Stares intensely at others
Makes themselves small and inconspicuous	Relaxed, open stance	Makes themselves big, occupies the space of others
Values others more than self	Values self and others equally	Values self more than others
Speaks quietly, softly	Speaks in a conversational tone	Speaks loudly, quickly
Shows signs of withdrawal	Engaged in the discussion at all times	Shows signs of irritation, restlessness

Ability to regulate our emotions

This new branch of research is proving extremely useful. We can all regulate how we experience emotions, and specific strategies can help us improve tremendously in that regard. We also have some control over the extent to which we express our feelings – and again, there are specific ways to conceal or to emphasise expression of emotion when doing so may be advantageous. For instance, research shows that feeling or looking anxious results in suboptimal negotiation outcomes. Individuals who are prone to anxiety when brokering a deal can take certain steps both to limit their nervousness and to make it less obvious to their negotiation opponent. The same is true for other emotions.

Alison Wood Brooks from the Organizations and Markets Unit at Harvard Business School explored how emotion influences the art of negotiation. Alongside her colleague Maurice Schweitzer, she researched the effect of anxiety on negotiations; specifically the degree to which anxiety influences negotiations (2011). They surveyed 185 professionals about the emotions they expected to feel before negotiating in a number of different scenarios: with a stranger, negotiating to buy a car, and negotiating to increase their salary. When negotiating with a stranger or asking for a higher salary, anxiety was the dominant emotional expectation; when negotiating for the car, anxiety was second only to excitement. The impact of anxiety in a negotiation can have negative consequences in relation to the behaviours of your clients during a negotiation, and the outcome of the negotiation. For example, it is not untypical for clients experiencing anxiety to make weaker first offers, respond more quickly to each move a colleague makes, and can very often exit negotiations early. Brooks and Schweitzer's (2011) research shows that anxious negotiators make deals that were up to 12% less financially attractive. People who gave themselves high ratings in a survey on negotiating aptitude were less affected by anxiety than others.

Reflecting on your own practice:

- To what extent is anxiety an issue for your clients?
- To what extent does anxiety get in the way of your clients' ability to negotiate effectively?
- How can you help your clients to reduce their anxiety in negotiation situations?

Having asked your clients to reflect on previous scenarios, you can explore what they felt and the impact it had on themselves, others, and the negotiation outcome. You can help your clients to practice and role-play different negotiation scenarios, which will help to raise their level of comfort and hone their skills. Anxiety is often a response to novel stimuli, so the more familiar the stimuli, the more comfortable and the less anxious your clients will feel.

Being alert to our assumptions

We frequently make assumptions, and other people are making assumptions about us. It happens all time. Being alert to our assumptions can help to identify the beliefs we hold and the way in which we view a negotiation scenario and its parties. Going into negotiation scenarios, we frequently make assumptions about how others will behave and what they are thinking. We often unconsciously stereotype others, adopt a halo effect, and generalise about others. We selectively perceive and project, and we create distortions of the anticipated negotiation scenario by assuming certain attributes and qualities of our counterpart. In each case, this distorts our view and can be harmful to your clients' ability to keep the communication channels open.

Being persistent

Maintaining a mindset that there is a workable solution can be tricky for some clients, particularly if they feel they have experienced setbacks previously or work with a team or boss that are unresponsive or often in a deadlock position. Revisiting a point that may have received a negative response in the past may feel uncomfortable for your clients, but it may be necessary in order to move on in the current situation. Additional information and discussion may change a no to a yes.

CASE STUDY

Hans worked for an investment bank in the city. He had a 'striving' personality: He called the coach to help him achieve Managing Director (MD) status. He was very keen as a coachee to do work in between sessions, wanting feedback from the coach all the time. He had been refused MD promotion already and was very annoyed, shamed, and frustrated about it. His sole goal from coaching was to get promoted. Knowing that happiness is often thwarted if you chase it, the coach wondered if his focus on the outcome was equally misguided, and whether the goal of the coaching ought to be more about his attitude and behaviour than the outcome. But Hans was insistent. He wanted the coach to speak to his boss to 'find out if he was going to put him forward and if he had any doubts, what they were'. The coach duly spoke with the boss. She found him very open and willing to tell her what he had told Hans already. He added, however, that he thought Hans's biggest problem was that people talked about him as being overly concerned about his pay and promotion, over and above passion for the work itself. The boss was fed up with having conversations about his promotion, all year, every year. The coach found out that Hans had come from a 'striving' family culture: Full of competition and 'rewards' for achievement.

Reflecting on your own practice:

- How would you coach or mentor Hans?
- How might you support Hans to develop his awareness of the impact of his behaviour on others?

Creative thinking

Bringing creative solutions to a negotiation scenario can help clients to consider different perspectives and options, or to consider new possibilities or new alternatives. It is a skill that is often underestimated in negotiation scenarios. An extensive literature review of empirical studies conducted by Elizabeth Ruth Wilson and Leigh Thompson for the *International Journal of Conflict Management* (2014) shows that some of the best practices espoused by creativity scholars seem to be consistent with the prescriptive advice offered to negotiators. For example, negotiators who engage in problem-solving and consider multiple perspectives and opportunities tend to make more integrative agreements. The process of making and receiving offers, including exploring the 'right fit' and the suitability and feasibility of the different options on the table, can facilitate the joint satisfaction of all. Helping your clients to see, hear, and appreciate the range of options available, even those currently unexplored, can stimulate the negotiation and lead to more effective outcomes.

Helping clients to prepare for a negotiation

The role of preparation in a negotiation is underestimated. Think about your forthcoming coaching or mentoring sessions with your clients – what negotiations are coming up for your clients? How well have you helped them prepare? Questions to help your clients to think through what they want to achieve might include that following:

- What do you want from the negotiation?
- What is your intention and how will you relate that to them?
- What would a terrific outcome look like for you?
- What will it mean to you if it goes well or if it goes wrong?
- How do you want to feel when you've left the negotiation?
- What is your 'walk away' point; that is, what won't you agree to?
- What is your strategy if you do not get what you want?
- What do you know about their challenges and point of view?
- What can you ask to gain more understanding of their situation and needs?
- What do you think they might fear?
- What do you fear?
- What facts do you have?
- What are you assuming?
- What might they be assuming?
- What facts do they have or could they have that you do not have?
- What do you think their core interest/value/priority is, and if you don't know, what are you specifically going to ask to find out?
- What might be a win–win?
- What would be a lose–lose?
- What would be a win–lose? And what might be the consequences?

- What will you do if … ?
- What are you going to say to encourage them to generate more options?
- How will you persevere? What words will you use to stay with your plan?
- How will others see your needs and their needs?
- How might others see your solutions?
- What values do you have – and how, explicitly, are you going to be sure that you live them: What will you say, not say, do, and not do?
- What sort of relationship do you want with this person and how will your behaviour show that?

Defining success

Regardless of the method used by your clients to negotiate, Fisher, Ury, and Patton (2012) suggest that when preparing, planning, and participating in a negotiation, we should consider three criteria:

1. To what extent does the negotiation result in a wise agreement – one that meets the legitimate interests between the parties, resolves conflicting interests fairly, is durable – if indeed agreement is possible?
2. To what extent was the negotiation efficient?
3. To what extent does the negotiation improve or at least not damage the relationships between the parties?

Researchers have uncovered a number of useful approaches and perspectives you can consider when helping your clients define success from negotiation. Weiss (2016) would encourage you to help your clients very carefully define the measures of success, aiming for an agreement that:

1. Satisfies everyone's core interests (yours and theirs) – Underlying needs, aims, fears, and concerns that shape what you want.
2. Is the best of many options –The solutions you generate that could meet your and your counterpart's interests.
3. Meets legitimate, fair standards – External, objective measures that can be applied to an agreement to assess its fairness.
4. Is better than your alternatives – An alternative is something you would do to fulfil your interests if you couldn't reach an agreement with your counterpart, something that would not require the other party's consent.
5. Is comprised of clear, realistic commitments – These promises – to alter an employment contract, adapt working conditions, provide resources – need to be operational, sufficiently detailed, and realistic.
6. Is the result of effective communication – Many negotiators make the mistake of focusing only on the substance of the negotiation (interests, options, standards, and so on). How clients communicate about that substance, however, can make all the difference.

7. Helps build the kind of relationship you want – Clients may want to establish a new connection or repair a damaged one; in any case, clients want to build a strong working relationship built on mutual respect, well-established trust, and a side-by-side problem-solving approach.

Some elements have more to do with the process, or the *how* of negotiation (1–4), and some are more relevant to the substance, or the *what* (5–7). The seven elements can be used as a framework to raise the questions with clients.

In addition to this, thinking more broadly ahead of the negotiation, questions might include:

- What are your assumptions about the negotiation, about the other party, and about how the negotiation will go?
- To what extent are you able to say that the assumptions are true, false, or that you don't know?
- What is your best alternative, and why?
- What might the other party want from the negotiation, and why?
- What specific criteria will help guide your preparation?
- What measures will you use to evaluate the agreement when it's complete?

CASE STUDY

Louella was a Distribution Manager for a drinks company. The coach was called in to coach her for just one session and then attend a meeting with a major supermarket. Apparently 'the relationship was broken' with the supermarket. One debriefing session with the coach would take place after the meeting with the supermarket. During the pre-meeting session, the coach found Louella to be highly motivated, previously successful with good intentions of bending as much as she could to the needs of the supermarket without totally relinquishing her company's objectives. She started the coaching session by stating her intention to 'work for a win-win, where the relationship was central'. At the meeting with the supermarket, the coach was staggered to hear the supermarket representative say, 'I don't give a ★★★★ about the relationship. You might be a nice person but to be frank, I don't give a ★★★★ about you. I'm just here to tell you that your product is not going on the top shelf'. As coaches or mentors, we need to be mindful that our clients are going to meet people who don't have the same intentions, manners, or willingness to flex. We need to prepare them to all eventualities.

- Thinking of this case, how would you have debriefed Louella (constructively!) and how would this case inform how you next coaching or mentoring session on negotiation?

Closing remarks

This chapter is intended to give you an insight into some of the challenges associated with decision-making and choosing. Within the day-to-day coaching or mentoring practice, you will be aware of many of the challenges identified in this chapter. Shifting the focus to build your clients' knowledge and expertise so that they can utilise their developmental networks effectively and make the best use of their key stakeholders is an important aspect in not only improving their well-being but helping to provide key information and support in making decisions to improve work-life balance.

We cannot overestimate the critical importance of negotiation as a core skill in achieving work-life balance. Supporting clients to successfully negotiate, whereby all parties' interests are considered and relationships are preserved, is a key role of the coach or mentor. The impacts of poor negotiation or at the extreme, avoidance and absence of negotiation, can be extreme and long-term. The evidence shows that pay, career trajectory, promotion, and employment conditions are serious outcomes of work-related negotiation; in family life, negotiation influences approaches to co-parenting, financial responsibilities, raising children, and sharing of domestic responsibilities.

We hope that by working with your clients to help develop their self-awareness, knowledge, and skills in this area, they will increase their willingness, confidence, and ability to have the critical conversations necessary to assist in choice and decision-making. At the same time, we hope your clients will feel confident and able to negotiate effectively.

QUESTIONS FOR REFLECTION

- How do your clients view decision-making, e.g. liberating, paralysing, confusing?
- In what scenarios, if any, do your clients adopt the role of chooser?
- To what extent do conversations around development networks within the context of decision-making and choice feature in your coaching or mentoring practice?
- How much more do you think you need to cover negotiation strategy and skills in your coaching sessions?
- How do your clients view negotiation, e.g. a battle; winning; collaborative problem-solving?
- How comfortable have you been with helping your clients negotiate, and how much better will you feel when helping your clients in the future?
- Do you see gender and/or cultural differences in how your clients approach negotiation? If so, how will you help your clients overcome any obstacles?

Additional reading and resources

Chang, R. (2014). *How to Make Hard Choices.* TEDSalonNY. Accessed on 27th December 2018 at: https://www.ted.com/talks/ruth_chang_how_to_make_hard_choices#t-217561

Heath, C. & Heath, D. (2014). *Decisive: How to Make Better Choices in Life and Work.* New York: Random House.

Fisher, R., Ury, W. & Patton, B. (1987). *Getting to Yes: Negotiating Agreement Without Giving In.* New York: Simon & Schuster Sound Ideas.

Schwartz, B. (2004). *The Paradox of Choice.* New York: Harper Perennial.

Schwartz. B. (2005). *The Paradox of Choice.* July 2005 at TEDGlobal. Accessed on 27th December 2018 at: https://www.ted.com/talks/barry_schwartz_on_the_paradox_of_choice#t-68277.

References

Arthur, M.B. & Rousseau, D.M. (1996). *The Boundaryless Career as a New Employment Principle. The Boundaryless Career.* New York: Oxford University Press.

Babcock, L. & Laschever, S. (2009). *Women Don't Ask: Negotiation and the Gender Divide.* Princeton University Press.

Babcock, L., Laschever, S., Gelfand, M. & Small, D. (2003). Nice girls don't ask. *Harvard Business Review*, 81(10), 14–16.

Brooks, A.W. (2015). Emotion and the art of negotiation. *Harvard Business Review*, 93(12), pp. 57–64.

Brooks, A.W. and Schweitzer, M.E., 2011. Can Nervous Nelly negotiate? How anxiety causes negotiators to make low first offers, exit early, and earn less profit. *Organizational Behavior and Human Decision Processes*, 115(1), pp. 43–54.

Business Dictionary. (2017). Accessed on 8th August 2017 at: http://www.Business dictionary.com/definition/negotiation.html.

Chang, R. (2014). *How to Make Hard Choices.* TEDSalonNY. Accessed on 27th December 2018 at: https://www.ted.com/talks/ruth_chang_how:to_make_hard_choices#t-217561.

Cross, D.C. and Carbery, D.R. eds., 2016. *Organisational Behaviour: An Introduction.* Palgrave Macmillan.

Daubman, K.A. & Sigall, H. (1997). Gender differences in perceptions of how others are affected by self-disclosure of achievement. *Sex Roles*, 37(1–2), pp. 73–89.

David, K.T., Francis, J. & Walls, J. (1994). Cultural differences in conducting intra-and inter-cultural negotiations: a Sino-Canadian comparison. *Journal of International Business Studies*, 25(3), pp. 537–555.

Fisher, R., Ury, W. and Patton, B., 2012. *Getting to Yes: Negotiating Agreement Without Giving In.* New York: Simon & Schuster Sound Ideas.

Flint. (2018). *Social Media Habits and Trends in the UK and US.* Accessed on 14th January 2019 at: https://weareflint.co.uk/press-release-social-media-demographics-2018/.

Frankel, L.P. (2014). *Nice Girls Don't Get the Corner Office: Unconscious Mistakes Women Make that Sabotage Their Careers.* London, UK: Hachette.

Haddock-Millar, J. & Clutterbuck, D.A. (2016). 5 Critical Conversations to Talent Development, *TD at Work*, Issue 1607. Accessed on 10th September 2018 at: https://www.td.org/Publications/TD-at-Work/2016/5-Critical-Conversations-to-Talent-Development.

Harrington, B., Van Deusen, F. and Humberd, B., 2011. *The New Dad: Caring, Committed and Conflicted*. Boston, MA: Boston College Center for Work & Family.

Harryuing, Van Deusen and Humberd Mullins, L.J., 2007. *Management and Organisational Behaviour*. Pearson Education.

Heath, C. & Heath, D. (2013). *Decisive: How to Make Better Choices in Life and Work*. Random House.

Kahneman, D. (2011). *Thinking, Fast and Slow*. London, UK: Macmillan.

Moen, P. & Sweet, S. (2004). From 'work–family' to 'flexible careers' – A life course reframing. *Community, Work & Family*, 7(2), pp. 209–226.

Mullins, L.J. (2007). *Management and Organisational Behaviour*. Pearson Education.

Murphy, W., & Kram, K. (2014). *Strategic Relationships at Work: Creating Your Circle of Mentors, Sponsors, and Peers for Success in Business and Life*. McGraw Hill Professional.

Nadler, J. (2004). Rapport in legal negotiation: How small talk can facilitate e-mail dealmaking. *Harvard Negotiation Law Review*, 9, p. 223.

Neale, M.A. & Lys, T.Z. (2015) *Getting More of What You Want*. New York: Basic Books.

Pinkley, R.L. & Northcraft, G.B. (2014). *Get Paid What You're Worth: The Expert Negotiators' Guide to Salary and Compensation*. St. Martin's Press.

Pruitt, D.G. (2013). *Negotiation Behavior*. New York: Academic Press.

Reddick, R.J., Rochlen, A.B., Grasso, J.R., Reilly, E.D. & Spikes, D.D. (2012). Academic fathers pursuing tenure: a qualitative study of work-family conflict, coping strategies, and departmental culture. *Psychology of Men & Masculinity*, 13(1), p. 1.

Schwartz, B. (2004). *The Paradox of Choice*. New York: Harper Perennial.

Schwartz, B. (2005). *The Paradox of Choice*. July 2005 at TEDGlobal. Accessed on 27th December 2018 at: https://www.ted.com/talks/barry_schwartz_on_the_paradox_of_choice#t-68277.

Stark, P.B & Flaherty, J. (2003). *The Only Negotiating Guide You'll Ever Need*. New York: Broadway Books.

Statista. (2018). Percentage of U.S. population with a social media profile from 2008 to 2018. Accessed on 8th January 2018 at: https://www.statista.com/statistics/273476/percentage-of-us-population-with-a-social-network-profile/.

Sussman, L. (1999). How to frame a message: the art of persuasion and negotiation. *Business Horizons*, 42(4), pp. 2–6.

Talker, R.H. & Sunstein, C.R. (2009). *Nudge: Improving Decisions About Health, Wealth, and Happiness*. London, UK: Yale University Press.

Tom, S.M., Fox, C.R., Trepel, C. & Poldrack, R.A. (2007). The neural basis of loss aversion in decision-making under risk. *Science*, 315(5811), pp. 515–518.

Ury, W. (2007). *The Power of a Positive No: How to Say No and Still Get to Yes*. London, UK: Hodder & Stroughton.

Wade, M.E. (2001). Women and salary negotiation: the costs of self-advocacy. *Psychology of Women Quarterly*, 25(1), pp. 5–76.

Weiss, J. (2016). *HBR Guide to Negotiating (HBR Guide Series)*. Harvard Business Review Press.

6 Self-care for coaches or mentors

Introduction

We are going to share with you the psychological concepts involved in the work we do as well as the research and tools of self-care. Self-care is the practice of taking an active role in protecting one's own well-being; we aim to provide you with a preventative practice to mitigate the known negative stressors embedded in the work of a coach or mentor. That work often brings us joy, energy, and purpose; it is interesting and satisfying work, but coaching and mentoring are complex roles. The accomplished coach or mentor acts as a fellow traveller on their client's life path. As a coach or mentor, you are with them and yet you need to be strong enough to be separate from them to maintain the objectivity that will allow you to best partner with them. You will respect their choices and yet at the same time you need to recognise your own (and not expect them to even know yours). You will understand and communicate your understanding of their feelings, wishes, and thoughts, and yet your feelings, wishes, and thoughts will probably not be shared. You need to be so strong that you will not become depressed by their depression or anxious by their anxiety or as consumed as they are by their worries.

The sophisticated and mature coach or mentor handles a session very differently to someone just trotting someone through the GROW model (Alexander, 2006) until they get an action or solution. The coach or mentor needs to be a mature, stable person, and that often involves work on self and ongoing self-care. The coach or mentor shares some of the burdens of the psychotherapist: Clients often bring heavy or difficult decisions, their frustrations, and their problems to the sessions. There is an intensity in the relationship in which we hold the space for clients to explore their emotions, and this work, called emotional labour, can be draining. Emotional labour is a concept developed by sociologist Arlie Hochschild (1983) that explains what a professional has to do to manage their emotions and only display emotions congruent with their role. This emotional regulation requires psycho-physical effort, and therefore has a psycho-physical cost. In coaching and mentoring, we hear about our clients' distress all the time, and we hold the space for them to expose their vulnerability. You may listen to clients saying they have been unhappy for years or reveal that now that they are coming to the end of their working life, they feel a failure and believe their accomplishments are poor compared to what they hoped they would have achieved. These are big disclosures, and the coach or mentor is vested with the onerous responsibility of helping clients gain insight and create strategies to improve their work-life balance.

To add to the challenges of the coach or mentor role, the work is usually done in isolation, and the necessity to hold the confidentiality of that relationship and conversation can feel like shouldering a huge responsibility alone. Furthermore, unlike the psychotherapist, the coach or mentor is often measured on the results achieved in a short intervention. The desired outcomes of the clients and the clients' organisation can feel like pressure on us to deliver results through their actions. Client are often put first. The urgency, importance, and demands of specific situations can result in coaches and mentors neglecting their own need for rest, exercise, recreation, and social time as they change their schedules to cater for the needs of their clients. Caring for oneself is something that can fall to the bottom of the list of priorities for coaches or mentors. Developing self-awareness around the toll that the work typically brings and practising self-care is critical to bringing our best selves to each session, being a role model for our clients, and having a happy, fulfilled, and balanced life and continuing to enjoy and sustain our work.

In this chapter, we will explain in more detail why self-care is of importance to our profession and the consequences of not engaging in self-care. We will also look at the common pitfalls in self-care, and you will prioritise your own self-care focus. Self-care is multidimensional and multifaceted; no single intervention will cater for all the aspects that need attention. At the end of the chapter, we offer you a range of tools and techniques that you can put in your self-care plan and try out, reflect upon, and see what suits your preferences, needs, and priorities. Use these tools and techniques to shape your self-care practice into something that will become sustainable. This will allow you to flourish while caring for others. The aim is to create a personalised living self-care practice that will enable you to cope with the high demands of the role and flourish at the same time.

Why self-care is important

There are real and frequent perils to your emotional, mental, and physical well-being inherent in the role of being a coach or mentor. We all need to manage our well-being and work-life balance, and it rarely happens by serendipity; it happens through purposeful planning and adherence to the plan. The more emotional our character is or the more emotional the client's story, the harder it is for us to maintain our professional objectivity. We make an emotional investment as we extend empathy and understand their pain, and unless we engage in self-care practices, we are in danger of carrying over that concern into our private lives as worry, anxiety, sadness, and even depression. Norcross and Guy (2007) found that psychotherapists can easily become over-involved in the lives of their clients, and the result of being in such emotionally intense relationships can be negative consequences in both their professional and private lives. Of course, we can take issues to supervision, but sometimes the weight and breadth of problems to bring to supervision might not match the hours of supervision we have, so we need to engage in self-care.

The risks associated with not doing self-care

If coaches or mentors don't engage in self-care, they could experience stress-related illnesses. It is now well accepted that 'stress' is a contributing factor in illnesses, anything from regular colds, herpes, and skin conditions to severe conditions like depression, anxiety, autoimmune diseases, rheumatoid arthritis, heart attacks, strokes, and cancer (Rabkin & Struening, 1976). Stressors might not be the sole factor or cause of illness, but it alters an individual's perceptibility to illness. A genuine and pertinent condition called compassion fatigue can affect those in the helping professions. Compassion fatigue can be seen in the coach or mentor who has become preoccupied with the suffering of their clients to the extent that they become traumatically stressed themselves. Simbula & Guglielmi (2010) found that the early-warning signs of compassion fatigue from emotional labour are feeling emotionally and mentally drained. If the strain continues without self-care intervention, the coach or mentor can experience mental and emotional distancing, either by developing negative attitudes or impersonal or cold responses to clients. Ultimately, if the stressors continue and the coach or mentor does not engage in purposeful self-care, they can suffer burnout, experience overwhelming exhaustion, lose optimism/ hope, and not see their work as having meaning or efficacy. The problem with burnout is that people cope and cope – and then they burn out – but they looked like they were coping! If you are experiencing warning signs of exhaustion, irritability, feelings of loneliness, feeling cynical or detached, having sleep issues, wondering if what you are doing is making any difference, coaching supervision is a safe place to discuss this. You might need to take a break, ease off the working hours and gain some skills/mindset to generate distance from the emotional load of your clients. If symptoms persist or they become severe, it is essential to talk to your doctor.

Our ethical responsibility

Self-care is not only key for our work-life balance and our continued personal and professional development but it is also a critical prerequisite for meeting professional responsibilities. This care can be done through our self-monitoring and self-management, through supervision, through peer groups, or through having your own coach, mentor, or therapist. Sometimes the stress from one client produces generalised anxiety and interferes with our ability to work with other clients. Sometimes, our work interferes with our personal lives, and sometimes our personal lives interfere with our ability to do our work. We all go through difficult times in our lives, and because of the nature of our work, it is essential to consider if we should be working when grieving, facing serious health issues, when dealing with divorce or in the midst of other struggles that change our attitudes and make it hard to focus on clients. The International Coaching Federation's (ICF) Code of Ethics (ICF, 2015) state that individuals must:

> strive at all times to recognise [their] personal issues that may impair, conflict with or interfere with [their] coaching performance or [their] professional coaching relationships. [They] will promptly seek the relevant professional assistance and determine the action to be taken, including whether it is appropriate to suspend or terminate [their] coaching relationship(s) whenever the facts and circumstances necessitate.

Therefore, it is your ethical responsibility to be aware of any symptoms, be proactive, and seek therapy if you are suffering from mental health issues before starting or continuing to coach or mentor.

Common pitfalls of coaches or mentors concerning self-care

Let's take a look at common pressure points, pitfalls, and antecedents of stress-related illnesses and burnout within our profession. As you go through each point, pause to consider how it relates to your character and situation. We have provided a basic template (see Table 6.7 below) that you may wish to start to populate as you go through the rest of this chapter. You might like to start by your view of the purpose of your plan and your intention with it. As you go through the analysis and develop some ideas around strategies, you will be prompted to pause and add to your plan the things that have become salient for you. At the end of this chapter, you can go on to build a robust self-care plan. You will be asked to reflect on the plan itself, your adherence to it, and changes you make to it over several months before you settle on a plan that is fit for purpose.

   Thinking back to chapter 1 when we were discussing the importance of clients knowing themselves, developing self-awareness is crucial for us as well. We need to be aware and monitor our own needs as carefully as we care about our clients. Self-awareness and self-monitoring have shown to be the top-ranked contributors to optimal functioning amongst psychologists (Schwebel & Coster, 1998). To deliver self-care to ourselves, we need to examine our beliefs, avoid bias, and live our values (Dorociak et al., 2017). The techniques to explore these aspects within you are the same techniques which we spoke of in the first and second chapter.

Burnout in leaders often results from the avoidance of a deep, honest conversation with oneself, as well as a too narrow a sense of personal identity, one that is derived from work and career as opposed to a broader concept of identity as a social, family, creative, community member (Casserley & Megginson, 2008). It is easy to become complacent and put off the essential core components of our self-care, yet Dorociak et al. (2017) found life balance to be one of the five factors that contribute to self-care. The other four are professional support, professional development, cognitive awareness, and daily balance, which we cover later in the chapter. Allow yourself some space now to reflect as you go through these questions. As you look through the prompts and reflect on your answers, check that you haven't fallen into too narrow a sense of personal identity derived from your work, as that might be driving you to give too much to your work at the expense of your health and enjoyment of the broader aspects of life. You might like to ask a fellow coach to ask you the questions, as this might provoke deeper thinking.

Experiencing empathic over-arousal

Empathy is a critical skill in coaching and mentoring, and enables you to see the world from the clients' perspective. It can be defined as 'an understanding of the inner experiences and perspectives of the client combined with a capability to communicate this understanding to the client' (Hojat & LaNoue, 2014). We need to be aware that if we allow our empathy to overrun, a condition called empathic over-arousal, we derail our ability to be professional and could be starting on the slippery slope to compassion fatigue and burnout (Decety, Yang & Cheng, 2010). The helping professions are particularly susceptible to 'catching' emotions from our clients (Young, 2016), and this emotional contagion results in bringing the emotions into the personal lives of the helper; for example, feeling sad after a session with a client who is sad. Empathic over-arousal creates an over-involvement and over-identification with the clients' problem. While we want to identify with the clients' issue – to relate to the issue – we don't want to over-identify.

Sometimes the clients' issue touches on current problems and pain of experiences that the coach or mentor is currently dealing with, or the clients' problem taps into past unresolved problems of the coach or mentor. When this happens, we have to be careful not to act from the place of a 'wounded healer' and instead to maintain our boundaries and self-management. Operating from the 'wounded healer' drives the helping professional to be overprotective of clients and makes boundaries blurred. If the coach self-discloses too much, loses emotional equilibrium, jumps to conclusions, becomes stuck in their thinking, or might be overly keen on a course of action – they can harm their ability to help clients in the moment. The coach or mentor may offer free sessions, think, worry, or contact clients outside of organised sessions to offer support and advice. The coach or mentor has to learn to notice when their memories and schemas are activated, to become aware of what emotions are generated, and to reflect upon the situation, perhaps with a co-coach or supervisor. If you identify with a client's issue, it is difficult to be real and congruent and at the same time express the right level of empathy in a way that doesn't impose on clients; it requires maturity, discipline, and training, and self-care practices to not to let your life erupt into their life and vice versa.

Preckel, Kanske & Singer (2018) found, using brain scans, that similar areas of the brain are activated both in the person who is suffering (the client) and the one who feels empathy (the coach or mentor). Coaches or mentors can 'catch' an emotion from their clients, at an unconscious level, and this emotional contagion can cause empathic distress and suffering, a maladaptive empathic resonance (Solon, 2012). The task is to be empathic without actually feeling what they feel. It is preferable to understand what clients are feeling and to communicate that understanding to clients without actually trying or allowing yourself to feel what they are feeling. If you allow yourself to feel what they are feeling, you are a short step away from slipping into over-identification, empathic over-arousal, and empathic suffering, which leads to the coach or mentor wanting to rescue, to alleviate, or relieve the clients' suffering (Omoto, Malsch & Barraza, 2009). Compassion, feeling what they are feeling, leads ironically, to a state of 'compassion fatigue', where the coach or mentor is drained of giving compassion and becomes cynical of clients and coaching or mentoring itself (Newell, Nelson-Gardell & MacNeil, 2016). Medical doctors are trained to be empathic and trained to avoid trying to feel what their patients feel lest they fall victim to compassion fatigue and over-identification and burnout.

A self-reflection exercise on the balance of your empathy

Think about a current or past client and consider to what extent you fully understood your client's inner experiences and perspectives and to what extent, if any, you overemphasised or over-identified and experienced empathic suffering.

Consider now, a few more clients:

- To what extent were you able to understand your clients' inner experiences and perspectives?
- Did they stir in you an emotional response that in any way inhibited your professional objectivity and equilibrium?
- Are any of your clients' issues akin to your issues, and how is that affecting what you feel or think? How is it affecting what you ask about and how you respond to them?
- When your clients have been emotional, how has it affected you outside of the session?

Managing our empathic response is vital for professional neutrality. What are you experimenting with? What more work do you need to do in your self-development? What are you monitoring? What is working for you? What more do you need to do to ensure you maintain 'warm acceptance' and 'neutral benevolence'? How workable are your emotional regulation strategies?

This might be a good time to pause and consider what might need to go into your self-care plan.

The aim is to show empathic concern *and* due professional detachment. If you let your empathy/compassion overrun, you will end up exhausted from the emotional drain and will be in danger of losing your professional neutrality. Engaging in emotional regulation training could help you to be able to show empathy, be genuine, and yet also be calm and serene (Zammuner, Lotto & Galli, 2003). One of the critical factors in preventing emotional burnout involves learning to distinguish and keep some distance between the feelings of clients and yourself (Young, 2016). As you think about your clients, ask yourself, what is it like to care just enough? In the last part of this chapter, you can find our suggested tools and techniques to develop these skills further.

Carl Rogers (Rogers, 1951) firmly believed that the success of the therapy depended on the relationship between the client and the therapist. The governing bodies of coaching and mentoring state the importance of building a trust-based relationship with the client in their competency frameworks. Rogers highlighted that the relationship was of a specific kind: A therapeutic relationship wherein the therapist or coach or mentor must cultivate what he called *a neutral benevolence,* show unconditional positive regard, and a warm acceptance – regardless of what the client says or does (Rogers, 1951). In his contribution to the famous Gloria Films, he can be found saying 'From my years of therapeutic experience, I have come to feel that if I can create the proper climate, the proper relationship, the proper conditions, a process of therapeutic movement will almost inevitably occur in my client. You may ask, "What is this climate? What are these conditions?"' (Shoshrom, 1965). We paraphrase his answers: Can I be real, genuine, congruent, transparent in the relationship and maintain a warm acceptance and neutral benevolence?

An exercise to analyse your 'warm acceptance and neutral benevolence'

Pause for a moment to reflect or listen to an audio recording of you working with one of your clients with the following questions in mind:

Do you tend to be very enthusiastic? Expressive? Do you speak in a rushed voice? Does your character show your feelings in your non-verbal expressions? Are you keen to share your experiences and knowledge? Do you find yourself lured to offer reassurance to those in distress? Do you notice that you want to rescue people who are in need? Do you tend to cross the boundaries of work relationships into friendships? If so, you may have strayed off 'warm' to 'too hot' in your responses. Coming across 'too hot' rather than giving a warm acceptance and neutral benevolence can lead to clients becoming too attached or dependent on us and our approval, as well as us growing attached to clients becoming happier and more successful. We can fall into worrying about clients in our spare time, being anxious for them, and being sad for them. Much of what they disclose and download to us can engulf us, and we can take the weight of their problem onto our shoulders and carry it with us that evening, that weekend, that month.

If you suspect that your tendency is to be on the 'hot' rather than 'warm' continuum, your self-care development might range from learning/discussing the philosophy of coaching with teachers, developing calming techniques like meditation and mindfulness, working with a voice coach, taking therapy or supervision on your need to rescue, or taking emotional regulation training. We discuss these strategies in the next part of the chapter. What else might work for you?

- What does it take from you in terms of emotional labour to show you 'prize' your clients, understand them, accept them?
- How does your neutral benevolence affect clients and then, in turn, you?
- What results do you achieve when you find the right notes of neutral benevolence and warm acceptance of the whole?
- What works for you and your clients that help them 'listen to themselves, listen to what is going on within their own experience, listen to some of the meanings they haven't been able to catch before' and move to a greater acceptance of themselves?
- How do you appear when you are empathic or when in the grip of empathic over-arousal?
- How do you appear and what effect does it have when you fall into compassion over-arousal and start to feel emotionally and mentally drained?
- How good are you at genuinely caring? Caring, but not caring too much?

Rogers showed time and again how, by maintaining this neutral benevolence and warm acceptance of the whole of his client, it released the client into:

- Exploring some of their feelings and attitudes more deeply.
- Discovering some hidden aspects of themselves that they were not aware of previously.
- Prizing themselves more as they felt prized by him.
- Moving toward more tentative ways of construing their experience after construing their life in somewhat rigid black and white patterns.
- Being more willing to 'listen to themselves, listen to what is going on within their own experience, listen to some of the meanings they haven't

been able to catch before' as they feel some of their meanings are understood. Their recognition of the understanding would then move them to a greater acceptance of themselves.

When we gain an equilibrium that is consistent and exemplifies non-possessive care, the effects on clients are massive but so too for the coach and mentor. Another way of talking about neutral equilibrium is compassionate detachment; we don't need to feel the pain for others literally: What we need is to be able to stand in the shoes of our clients yet still maintain professional objectivity. As you think back over your warm acceptance and neutral benevolence, your 'compassionate detachment' with all your clients, consider if there is anything you would like to take to supervision or put in your draft self-care plan.

Taking on the role of the rescuer

It is worth checking our impulse, intention, or wishes to 'rescue' clients. Psychologist Dr Karpman (1968) created a social model of human interaction regarding the rescuer, victim, and persecutor. He was a student of Eric Berne, who developed Transactional Analysis. In Karpman's model, called the Drama Triangle, he describes how people tend to adopt roles in social conflict. The Victim plays the role of the oppressed, helpless, hopeless, powerless, ashamed. Unwittingly, they unconsciously seek out a Persecutor! They are often rescued by someone playing the role of the Rescuer (who, ironically, perpetuates the Victim's negative feelings about themselves).

Many of our clients unconsciously play the Victim in the coaching or mentoring situation (but they might be seen as Persecutors in their working life by others). Their playing of the Victim role can lure the coach or mentor into playing out the Rescuer role. The coach or mentor as a Rescuer can set the scene for lack of professional objectivity: The coach or mentor will be concerned about clients outside of working hours, may take calls/emails/ad-hoc sessions at the will of clients, and the coach or mentor can find themselves emotionally and physically drained. Manfred F.R. Kets de Vries (2013) takes a harsh view of coaches who are motivated by the role of rescuer. He believes that rescuers are those with unfinished business, wounded healers, who haven't done the development work they need to do on themselves before they seek to help others. Needing to help can be a self-serving addiction that makes it difficult to distinguish between one's own needs and the needs of clients. The coach or mentor's desire to achieve a solution to the clients' problems is about the coach or mentor's needs, not the clients'. Rescuers tend to build unhealthy, dependent relationships with their clients. Rescuers may end up giving more extended sessions than is useful for clients, never challenging clients for fear of losing love, giving unnecessary advice out of the need to be authoritative, or overvaluing the clients' progress for their success (Williams, 2014). A common issue in supervision is performance anxiety on the part of the coach or mentor.

An exercise to reflect upon your need to rescue:

- Do you have clients who are a victim or who unconsciously play the victim? How do you respond?
- What is drawing you to help your clients?
- What are your hopes and aspirations? How do these fit the coaching competencies?
- What in your past is unfinished business that you need to deal with as a matter of importance?
- How can you set up an early-warning system for yourself that you are straying into a rescuer role?

Pause now to add to your draft plan anything that might be relevant for you right now.

Caving into demands on your time and allowing boundaries to blur

Clients are becoming more demanding about having coaching sessions outside of typical working hours – for instance at the weekends or very early morning or evening, as changing workforce dynamics have led to a global workforce working unusual or long hours. Such a situation is becoming the norm. Coaches or mentors with little experience, trying to add to their coaching hours may be too willing to adapt to clients' needs and so allow their encroachment on their private time by bending their working hours to the clients' requests. Novice coaches or mentors may be particularly susceptible to moderate-to-high levels of stress and burnout. Simionato & Simpson (2018) found psychotherapists with little experience were susceptible. So novice coaches and mentors might want to be particularly careful to manage their stressors.

Experienced coaches who might be coaching or mentoring very senior people whose schedules are crammed may give in to requests by clients to fit into their schedule even if it means working out of normal hours. Have you a thought-through plan of how many hours, when, and where you want to work? You will need to consider how flexible you are prepared to be and the consequences of doing so. Then you need to assert your choices and not give in to the demands of clients. If you do give in, you might well find yourself drained, and you won't be able to work in the way that you can work when you manage your time optimally.

We want to minimise the number of coaching sessions held outside of our pre-planned hours. There are three good reasons for doing this. Firstly, you are colluding with their busy-ness and their inability to manage their time when as a coach and mentor you are aiming to improve their well-being, performance, and development. Secondly, the dynamics between you and your clients may change, and thirdly, you may find you annoy your loved ones who want to spend time with you outside of your working week.

CASE STUDY

The coach in this case study was relatively new to coaching and was eager to gain experience and income. She began coaching a woman in a public services organisation. In the introductory emails, the client asked if she could hold the first call at 8 p.m. The coach wanted to have sessions between 9.00 a.m. and 4.00 p.m. but wanted to be obliging and caring, so agreed and took the first session at 8.00 p.m. to 9.00 p.m. In the contract discussion, the coach explained her office hours and her suggestions for the ways of working between them. The client said, 'I can only do a session at 7.00 am or after 7.00 pm or at the weekend, as I'm just too busy at work to take a coaching session in the middle of the day'. The coach felt obliged to schedule the first session at 7.00 p.m. on a weekday. The coach then brought this up in her supervision to ask whether this is a normal expectation within this industry. The supervisor informed her that this wasn't the norm and advised her to push back to her client. The coach went back to her client and re-contracted and informed her client of her work hours, stating that following advice, she wasn't prepared to do all the coaching sessions outside of her office hours. The client replied, 'Your industry needs to evolve as other industries have evolved – it's backward that you're not willing to work flexible hours'. The coach suggested that the coachee find another coach.

Reflecting on your own practice:

- How would you have approached this conversation?
- Have you made clear your office hours with your clients?
- How do you deal with ad hoc requests from clients?
- To what extent is your working hours fit with your needs and the needs of others in your private life?
- What are the repercussions of your choices?
- Is there anything you wish to note to take to supervision or your coach or mentor?

Do you wish to add anything to your self-care plan?

Being in 'coach or mentor mode' all the time

Some coaches or mentors are in 'service mode' all of the time and even 'off duty' act like a coach – feeling an urge or obligation to coach or mentor friends around a challenge they're facing. Even though most coaches or mentors love their work, being a coach or mentor 24/7 is draining (or boring for others)! It's important to learn to switch off so your work doesn't become your life and so that you spend time with your friends and family, totally outside of your role as a coach or mentor. A doctor never consults out of the consulting room, nor should a coach or mentor if they want to be considered professional. Has your work become your life? The tools and techniques in the 'Be assertive around your boundaries' section in this chapter will be useful.

Failing to reach out to others for support and help

Strong support cycles have been found to be one of the most endorsed strategies by therapists to prevent burnout and foster resilience (Gupta et al., 2012). Seeking professional support, for example, peers, mentors, supervision, and a coach, is a critical factor for self-care (Dorociak et al., 2017). Those that don't reach out to others for support may feel isolated and at risk of burnout. How isolated do you feel? Is your supervision enough to support you? Are you seeing enough of old friends who can help you gain perspective and see the humour in your situation? Have you considered joining co-coaching forums? How else can you find the support to forget your work and have fun? Are you engaging in enough continuous professional development (CPD) to meet with other coaches and mentors? Pause now to consider if you wish to add anything to your self-care plan or to discuss with your supervisor.

Not living your values

Values are the principles by which you lead your life, and they are the things you hold dear and important in your life. Sometimes the role of the coach or mentor fits superbly with your values, but it might not. It might, for instance, be that you value laughter, fun, and action, and these values might be stifled as you carry out the role of a coach or mentor. When you live your values, you feel congruent, comfortable in your own skin, and you look authentic. If you are not living by your values, you may feel lost, in a battle with yourself, torn, stressed, and unhappy.

Reflecting on your own practice:

- How does my life as a coach or mentor meet my values?
- What values do I have that are *not* met by my role as a coach or mentor? How else am I making time to live those values?
- What values would people assume I have from how I'm living my life?
- What's the impact of my not living [insert your value] fully?
- What impact may this have on my family and friends?
- What's stopping me from living [insert your value]?
- What could be the benefit of my living more of my values?

Hopefully, as coaches or mentors, you know what your values are. If you don't, we would recommend that you reread chapter two and complete the values sort. Add any comment or actions into your self-care plan as appropriate now.

Ignoring your body

Coaching or mentoring is sedentary work. We are obliged to keep up with continuous professional development, and that often includes reading – that amounts to more sitting. Many coaches or mentors work from home, and this can mean working hours blur into working all hours. Access to food all day may make you graze too frequently or maybe on the wrong foods. It is important to build into our day reminders and regimes that adhere to good physical mastery: Exercise, good nutrition, rest, sleep hygiene. Our bodies give us warning signs when we need to stop and slow down, which we need to pay attention to. What is your body telling you? What is your inner voice trying to help you to do? As coaches or mentors, you may be self-employed. Are you taking holidays? Are you allowing yourself to be available while on holiday? Are you allowing enough time off to gain perspective and recharge?

As you think about your physical mastery, what wisdom comes to mind? What support do you need to think that through or take action? If this is an area in which you need to take action as you come to the physical mastery strategies, take some time to think through what you need.

Self-care strategies

Self-care is our responsibility, not only to ourselves but to our families, friends, clients, and the coaching or mentoring community. Our self-care strategies are likely to change as our life experiences change, and we need to create multifaceted strategies to meet the multifaceted antecedents of stress-related illnesses (Prochaska, Norcross & DiClemente, 1995). Your needs will be unique to you, so it is vital you choose a strategy that reflects your needs from your analysis. Select ones that you think will work for you, ones that will have the most value, keep you at your best.

If you are noticing warning signs of compassion fatigue or signs the stressors are building up and harming your happiness, your satisfaction, or your health, it is time to be proactive and kick-start some new habits. Habits don't form overnight; they require persistence. The latest research suggests a new habit takes far longer than the pop psychology writers would have us believe. Dr Phillippa Lally, a health psychologist at University College London, and her colleagues found that on average it takes 66 days before a new behaviour becomes automatic, and it may even take as long as 254 days (Lally et al., 2010).

Be assertive around your boundaries

We have an ethical responsibility to maintain boundaries – it is one of the Shared Global Values of coaching or mentoring in the industry. Keeping control over working hours, not thinking of work in personal time, is essential for self-care (Gupta et al., 2012) and ensuring separation from your clients' problems (Norcross, 2007). You probably know what motivates you, what drains you, and where your boundaries are challenged. How assertive are you on your boundaries?

Some people find using an assertiveness model helps them have a structure for their negotiations. Here is a model of negotiating with others, we call the DEAL Model (see Table 6.1).

In relation to each stage, good practice suggests:

- It is important not to be judgmental or even label things with positive or negative attributions – keep to descriptive phrases only. For example: 'I'm going to describe the situation as I see it …'
- Being specific is helpful. For example: 'When you do X, I feel Y, and the consequence is Z.' Most people do not make clear the repercussions of other people's actions. Most people are surprised when they hear an honest response to their actions or a situation, and they wake up to the issue and want to engage.
- It is essential to ask the other person to let you know how they see things and how they feel. Ask, too, for their ideas on how you can work together for an acceptable solution. For example: 'What is your perspective and what are your ideas for constructively moving this forward?'
- It is advantageous to work out how you will tell them how much better you will feel and what it could do for them if the outcome were to be acceptable to both of you. For example:
'Great, the benefits of doing this are …'
'I'm going to describe to you the situation as I see it …'
'My concerns are …'
'Great, the benefits of doing this are …'

Table 6.1 The DEAL Model

	Assertive Negotiation
D	Describe the situation objectively and accurately.
E	Express your concerns.
A	Ask for the other person for their perspective and their ideas for working for an acceptable change/solution.
L	List/state the benefits with the person to the situation and the relationship when the change is implemented.

Using the DEAL model, work through something you want to assert yourself on. Then pause for now to add to your draft plan anything that might be relevant.

Reflecting on your own practice:

- What are the optimal number of sessions for you in a day and a week?
- How well do you manage to have breaks in between sessions?
- How well do you use the time in between sessions?
- How do you make your coaching sessions fit within the best time for you to work?
- How well do you distance yourself from your clients? How can you find out what others do and what might work for you?
- If you work from home, how do you separate your work and living space?
- Do you talk to or meet clients after you have finished the coaching or mentoring assignment? If so, how well do you re-contract to redefine that relationship?
- How good are you at reducing your workload when you feel overwhelmed?
- Are you able to switch off outside of coaching?

Work through what to do if boundaries might be crossed or you might be under pressure to bend your rules. If boundaries are in danger of being crossed, how are you going to monitor this? Consider these points:

- How have you identified your limits and boundaries?
- How do you show respect to yourself and ask others to respect your limits?
- When and how does your agenda overlap with that of your clients?
- When might you project your concerns and issues onto your clients?
- When and how do you lay out boundaries and any areas of conflict of interest?
- Create audio of yourself explaining your boundaries. Listen to yourself to check how clear you are being.
- What mantra, what questions, what rules can you make to remind yourself of your boundaries?

Take time to reflect on your feelings: If things are making you uncomfortable, be prepared to assert yourself. What do you want to add to your self-care plan?

Taking supervision with a qualified supervisor

Supervision, as you know, is an essential method for increasing self-awareness in coaches or mentors and monitoring self-care. You have probably already experienced how supervision can throw up some ways in which the coach or mentor is becoming entangled, and often stressed, in the 'parallel processing' of their client's dysfunctional organisational culture. In a survey of 376 coaches,

70% had discussed unconscious processes in supervision (Turner, 2010). Those who regularly seek supervision have more positive outcomes than those who do not (Norcross, 2000.) The UK International Coach Federation (2018) list the following benefits of supervision for coaches ('coaches' can be used interchangeably with 'mentors'):

- Develop your coaching skills and your coaching practice to provide the highest standards of service to your clients.
- Address with an experienced supervisor, on a confidential basis, ethical issues that you may encounter during coaching.
- Accelerate your professional and personal development, as part of lifelong learning as a coach.
- Explore problems and dilemmas in a safe and confidential environment, and obtain an experienced second opinion on coaching situations that may arise.
- Develop skills, knowledge and build resilience and confidence as a new coach.

We urge all coaches and mentors to undergo regular supervision to ensure they are the best possible coach or mentor and to co-create on their self-care journey. The AC advises you to have at least one hour of supervision for every 15 hours of coaching or mentoring. The EMCC advises no less than one hour of supervision per 35 hours of practice, ensuring a minimum of four hours a year.

Examining how supervision is working for you:

- Is your supervision challenging you against the highest standards?
- Are you learning and growing substantially from each session?
- Do you feel supported?
- Are you feeling better after supervision?
- Do you have strategies to employ after supervision?
- How are you developing under the support of supervision?
- How is supervision helping you adapt to the situations you find yourself in?
- What different kind of supervisor might you next need?

What conversations do you need with your supervisor as a result of this analysis? What might you consider putting in your self-care plan?

You may also wish to engage in an Action Learning Set, which is typically a group of 5–7 peers (Pedler, Burgoyne & Brook, 2005). It is an opportunity for them to come together to find practical ways of addressing real-life challenges they face and to support their learning and development. There is normally a trained facilitator who guides the process of the attendees finding solutions to their challenges and issues through a structured process of insightful questioning combined with a balance of support and challenge from the group.

Engaging in continuous professional development

Dorociak et al. (2017) found engaging in professional development a funda-mental construct in self-care. Keeping up-to-date will help you alleviate the negative effects of stressors embedded in your role. CPD will give you courage and confidence. When was the last conference you attended? Are you read-ing the academic journals and magazines of the industry? Are you challenging yourself to teach and learn? What more could you do to engage with industry leaders and role models? Are you engaged with all the governing bodies, as each offers different events and training opportunities? What might be useful to look up and schedule into your self-care plan?

Developing and being with people who can help you see the humour

Humour is a mature adaptation: It involves emotional expression, but without discomfort or unpleasant side effects on others. Thus, staying in touch with humour has been found to be an effective self-care technique (Simionato & Simpson, 2018). You might brush off laughter as lightweight and irrelevant, but there is empirical evidence that laughter helps us deal with physical and emotional distress and helps us replace negative with positive affect (Nezu, Nezu & Blissett, 1988). Using humour in coaching and mentoring sessions can reduce tension and puts life into perspective. However, we need to use our judgement to determine when to use humour and to ensure it is used sensi-tively. If you want to have more humour in your life, we recommend watch-ing comedies, reading funny books, or hanging around with funny people. Seeing old friends can help you gain perspective and humour. What needs to go into your self-care plan to help you have/regain your humour?

Developing your physical mastery

Physical mastery involves physical activity, sleep hygiene, proper nutrition, avoidance of reliance on drugs or alcohol, and taking health screening and results seriously. Table 6.2 provides a helpful checklist for you to use as you think about the extent to which you are developing your physical mastery.

Reflecting on your own practice:

- What are your responses telling you?
- What information or help could you seek to help your physical mastery?

Pause now to add to your draft plan either your concerns to bring up with your coach or mentor, or ideas that you wish to implement.

Developing your spiritual and social mastery

Spiritual and social mastery involves feeling connected with others, with your faith if you have one, having a sense of belonging, having a social life, engaging

Table 6.2 Developing your physical mastery

Physical mastery – check-in		
Dimensions	*Questions*	*Answer*
Checking-in	Do you have regular health checks? Do you act on health advice?	
Exercise	Do you take appropriate exercise daily? Does your daily exercise regime include strength, aerobic, and stretching? Are you out walking in nature most days?	
Diet	How balanced is your diet (a variety of different types of food)? Do you eat at least five portions of fruit and vegetables daily? Do you avoid junk food?	
Drink	Do you have at least three alcohol-free days a week? Do you avoid alcohol binges? Are you keeping hydrated with water (8 glasses a day/2 litres)?	
Drugs	Do you self-medicate with prescribed or non-prescribed drugs? Are you addicted to prescription or non-prescription drugs?	
Sleep	Do you have between 7 and 9 hours sleep most nights? Are you sleeping well, or is your sleep disturbed? Do you wake to feel refreshed and ready to go?	
Breaks	Do you take short breaks throughout the day? Do you switch off from your electronic devices at regular intervals? Are you taking regular holidays?	
Energy	How well are you looking after your energy? On a scale of 1–10, how energetic do you feel by the end of the day? Do you feel exhausted?	

in recreational activities like hobbies, mindfulness, and living a life congruent with your purpose and values. Table 6.3 provides a helpful checklist for you to use as you think about the extent to which you are developing your spiritual and social mastery.

Table 6.3 Developing your spiritual and social mastery

Spiritual and social mastery – reflective questions		
Dimensions	Questions	Answer
A sense of purpose and meaning	To what extent do you feel a sense of purpose in work? How about in the rest of your life? Do you feel as if you belong to your workplace? Your friendship group? Your community? To what extent do you feel that your life is close to the ideal?	
Presence	To what extent are you rushing and/or pausing to appreciate the moment? To what extent are you able to concentrate and fully focus in the moment?	
Reflection	To what extent do you spend time reflecting? How often do you give and receive feedback? What do you do with the feedback?	
Support	Do you share problems at work with trusted colleagues or other people in your profession? Do you share problems at home with trusted friends? As you reflect on your support network, how broad is your support network?	
Connection	Are you prioritising social time with others? Are you prioritising time with your friends and family? What effort have you made lately with them? Do you involve yourself in community events? Do you involve yourself in social events at work?	
Fun	Do you have enough humour and laughter in your life? Are you spending enough time with people who make you laugh, people you really like, people you enjoy? Are you having enough 'play time'?	
Leisure	Have you got a hobby? How much time are you dedicating to it? What's stopping you? How can you carve out time to prioritise this?	
Faith	How well are you connecting to your faith? Are you in touch with your spirituality or adhering to your religious practices?	

Reflecting on your own practice:

- What needs further thought or discussion or action? And with whom?
- Do you need to connect with groups of people more? Specific people?
- Can you work out what you need and how you could be meeting that need?

Add anything relevant to your draft plan now.

Developing your emotional and mental mastery

This involves maintaining a positive inner voice, holding a positive and rational belief, self-compassion, being in touch with a wide range of feelings yet having emotional regulation at the same time. It also involves the ability to negotiate with others about the demands they place on you.

Burnout is rare, but anxiety, depression, stress-related illnesses are widespread. There are common antecedents embedded in our roles that can lead to these health issues. Table 6.4 provides a list of reflective questions to help you consider the relationship between emotional and mental mastery and your coaching or mentoring practice.

Reflecting on your own practice:

- What more could you do to self-regulate?
- Where have you been making compromises at the expense of your well-being?

Pause now to add to your draft plan anything that might be relevant for you right now.

Emotional regulation training

Learning how to regulate emotions and monitor emotional attachment to clients takes time and concerted attention. Researchers found therapists who reported higher work frustration also had higher burnout (Simionato & Simpson, 2018). Therefore, emotional regulation, the process of modulating one or more aspects of an emotional response (Gross, 1998), is crucial. There are many different approaches to emotional regulation training: just Google it and see what comes up in a web search. Google, too, Positive Psychology 'positive psychology program.com' and also the MOOC sites of free online courses.

Mindfulness training

Mindfulness is one technique which has been found to be a significant mediator between self-care and well-being (Richards, Campenni & Muse-Burke, 2010), acting as a protective buffer against stress and burnout. Mindfulness can be defined as the process of bringing a certain quality of attention to

Table 6.4 Developing your emotional and mental mastery

Emotional and mental mastery – reflective questions		
Dimensions	*Questions*	*Answer*
Emotional insight	What do you notice about your emotions after seeing your clients (think of current ones and past ones)? How are you reacting to people and events – are you finding emotional regulation difficult?	
Beliefs and mindset	How often do you look at your beliefs and mindsets and challenge them? What is the ratio of positive to negative self-talk coming from your inner voice?	
Self-regulation	Are you monitoring your feelings towards your clients and the people in their lives? How well are you acknowledging and managing your emotions? How easy is it for you to maintain emotional regulation during your sessions?	
Impact	Are you aware of the emotional toll your work is having on you? What kind of psycho-physical effort and cost do you have in maintaining appropriate emotional equilibrium after a session? Are you aware of the specific triggers that limit your well-being? How stressed or nervous do you feel? Do you think you could be depressed? Where have you been making compromises at the expense of your well-being?	
Relationships	Are you spending enough time with your family? Your wider family? Are you reaching out enough for help and support? Do you share your worries and feelings with another/others?	

moment-to-moment experience (Kabat-Zinn, 2003). Mindfulness training has been associated with reducing rumination and unrealistic expectations (Simionato & Simpson, 2018), enhancing emotional regulation, less return to depressive thinking following sad mood induction (Kuyken et al., 2010) while also reducing burnout (Krasner et al., 2009). Mindfulness not only positively impacts your well-being but it also positively affects the therapeutic relationship through enabling the coach or mentor to be calm, alert, and present with a sense of curiosity with clients and openness and detachment. Once the coach or mentor is relaxed, clients can enter a state of calmness.

In chapters 2 and 4, we touched on mindfulness in more detail, and there are many mindfulness training courses advertised on the web that can be taken virtually and are reasonably priced. Look up some mindfulness courses online or consider taking a course run from anywhere in the world with a virtual group. Mindfulness has really helped us to develop our coaching and mentoring presence.

Cognitive behavioural therapy

You might consider having cognitive behavioural therapy (CBT), which is particularly useful for challenging ideologies, beliefs, and assumptions, and checking the quality of your thinking. We need to be aware of our thinking errors, such as if we are overthinking or taking responsibility for our clients' issues and worries. Remind yourself that we are human and prone to predictable errors in judgement; this is normal. We need to recognise when errors arise and restructure our thoughts by busting the assumptions. Just as Wayne Dyer (2010), an American philosopher and author, said: 'change the way you look at things and the things you look at change'. If we do not recognise and restructure these thoughts, they can affect you as much as your clients. It is common amongst therapists to incorrectly blame themselves for adverse events, adopting personal causality (Norcross & VandenBos, 2018).

Reflecting on your practice:

- What is distorting your thinking?
- How can you make sure the evidence you are collecting is reliable and trustworthy?
- How can you test the claim? For example, if we take the example 'I can't fail with any of my clients', challenge yourself about whether that is really true. Is it only your fault if they fail? What other variables could lead to the session failing?
- Are you setting unrealistic expectations?
- How could you reframe that belief so you are not entirely responsible for the outcome?

If you want to dive deeper into your own thinking, we suggest you reread the tools and techniques in section two of chapter 2, Locus of Control. Your General Practitioner is the best option for a referral to a CBT specialist.

Developing your environmental mastery

Your environmental mastery can impact your stress levels and health as well as your ability to focus on clients in the right way and to live a life in line with your values. Table 6.5 provides a list of reflective questions to help you consider the relationship between environmental mastery and your coaching or mentoring practice.

Reflecting on your own practice:

• Is there anything from your responses that you think might help you develop environmental mastery that impacts on your stress levels and well-being and that you can build into your self-care plan?

Table 6.5 Developing your environmental mastery

Environmental mastery – check-in		
Dimensions	*Questions*	*Answer*
Checking-in	To what extent are you aware of the relationship between the forces/influences, inhibitors, and facilitators in your professional environment?	
Economic	How well acquainted with the economics of our industry are you? How secure are you that you know your market value and know what to charge?	
Social	Consider how you deal with social changes and expectations of language and how you approach changing situations at work (for example, with a gender-neutral person, or with a blind person or autistic person).	
Ethical and Environmental	What ethical standards and/or code to you adhere to in your practice? What more would you like to consider in creating your ethical stance on the environment?	
Political and Legal	To what extent do professional standards impact on your practice? How do you manage clients' data protection? What is the industry standard for professional indemnity?	
Technology	How well have you experimented with technology – to find the most reliable and fast service or to work with clients in virtual sessions? How well do you turn away from technology – do you turn off your phone/computer to give yourself space?	

Self-care plans

We've suggested that you might like to create a self-care plan in any way that works for you. It might be summarised with a mantra, a quote, or a picture, but we think a structured approach can also help you think through the elements that will make it a robust plan. You may wish to begin with an initial analysis of your current self-care, set out in Table 6.6. This may then inform your self-care plan (see Table 6.7).

We have set out a structure (in Table 6.6 and 6.7) that might help prompt you to create a plan that will be feasible and will help you take committed actions of self-care. This is something that can be regularly updated after you've reflected what's working well and not so well. The aim is to create a plan that will be sustainable.

A synopsis of your self-care needs:

1. Developing and setting boundaries.
2. Undergoing regular supervision and other support/challenge.
3. Engaging in CPD – your personal and professional development.
4. Staying in touch with humour.
5. Developing physical mastery.
6. Developing emotional and mental mastery.
7. Developing spiritual and social mastery.
8. Developing environmental mastery.

Table 6.6 Self-care analysis

Self-care analysis		
Self-care strategy	*Give yourself a mark, 1–10, where 10 is strong need of attention*	*Reflection*
Developing and setting boundaries		
Undergoing regular supervision and other support		
Engaging in CPD		
Staying in touch with humour		
Developing physical mastery		
Developing spiritual and social mastery		
Developing emotional and mental mastery		
Developing environmental mastery		

Table 6.7 Self-care plan

Self-care plan	
My purpose in having a self-care plan is:	My aim in this self-care plan is to:
What are my common pitfalls (i.e. empathic over-arousal, not seeking support)?	
What do I need to watch in terms of developing and setting boundaries?	How shall I cater for this need?
What do I need to watch in terms of supervision?	How shall I cater for this need?
What do I need to watch in terms of CPD?	How shall I cater for this need?
How am I going to develop my *physical* mastery? • • •	How am I going to develop my *emotional and mental* mastery? • • •
How am I going to develop my *social and spiritual* mastery? • • • •	How am I going to develop my *environmental* mastery? • • • •
What negative coping strategies do I want to stop using? • • •	

Obstacles to maintaining my self-care strategies	What assumptions am I making that I need to check out?
• • • •	

How feasible and sensible is this plan? How much do I really want to do the actions? Do I believe I will do them and if not – what do I know that might work for me in seeking help to overcome the obstacles or the way I might forget, derail, or ignore the plan?

Whom do I need to ask for support?

How will I remind myself to practice self-care?

If I implement this plan, how would I feel? What would the other benefits be?

Reflection (1 month later). What is working? What's not working? Is this plan still important to me?

Reflection 2 months later

Reflection 3 months later

Reflection 4 months later

Closing remarks

Time spent on your self-care will enable you to continue to grow and transform so that you can deal with the issues clients will throw at you.

Self-care will maintain your confidence and separateness so that your clients' feelings/thoughts do not impose on yours, and your feelings/thoughts do not impose on theirs. Only the mature and confident individual can accomplish this. Undoubtedly, 'stuff' happens to all of us that can knock our confidence and perspective, leaving us doubting our wisdom.

Of course, we don't want to be entirely sure of ourselves in a session, or else it loses the creativity, the genuine search, and real moments of not-knowing that lead to insights for clients. The work in this self-care helps you become comfortable with not knowing, not being the expert, the experienced, wise person, the one paid to help sort out this mess. You won't accept, nor rebuff, the expectations others have of you unless they fit within your professional practice. But it takes a steady, stable, reliable hand and head to remain true to yourself and your practice in the midst of high drama, and high drama is there in most sessions if we care to notice!

Engaging in the self-care mentioned in this chapter will help you to continue to mature, to grow, and transform. This will enable you to put to one side, as much as is possible, what is going on in your life, your predispositions, your affections, your anxieties, and engage with your coach in a fresh way, untainted by your lenses. How marvellous you will feel when you can respond with equanimity to silence, things not working, things working well, praise, criticism, cancellations, scores that clients might throw at you!

In the meantime, we wish you all the very best in your pursuits and your learning agility – we know the great impact you can have on another human being, and that is so precious.

QUESTIONS FOR REFLECTION

1. How can you become an even more reflective practitioner?
2. Having done this reflection, what do you conclude?
3. What have you learned about yourself?
4. How will you remind yourself to self-care?
5. How are you going to develop your physical, emotional, social, spiritual, and environmental mastery?

Additional reading and resources

Dorociak, K.E., Rupert, P.A., Bryant, F.B. & Zahniser, E. (2017). Development of the professional self-care scale. *Journal of Counselling Psychology*, 64(3), p. 325.

Norcross, J.C. & VandenBos, G.R. (2018). *Leaving it at the Office: A Guide to Psychotherapist Self-Care*. New York: Guilford Press.

Trotter-Mathison, M. & Skovholt, T. (2014). *The Resilient Practitioner: Burnout Prevention and Self-Care Strategies for Counsellors, Therapists, Teachers, and Health Professionals*. Abingdon: Routledge.

References

Alexander, G. (2006). Behavioural coaching–The GROW model. *Excellence in Coaching. The Industry Guide* (pp. 61–72). London, UK: Kogan Page.

Casserley, T. & Megginson, D. (2008). *Learning from Burnout*. London: Routledge.

Decety, J., Yang, C.Y. & Cheng, Y. (2010). Physicians down-regulate their pain empathy response: an event-related brain potential study. *Neuroimage*, 50(4), pp. 1676–1682.

Dorociak, K.E., Rupert, P.A., Bryant, F.B. & Zahniser, E. (2017). Development of the professional self-care scale. *Journal of Counseling Psychology*, 64(3), pp. 325–334.

Dyer, W.W. (2010). *The Power of Intention*. New York: Hay House, Inc.

Gross, J.J. (1998). The emerging field of emotion regulation: an integrative review. *Review of General Psychology*, 2(3), p. 271.

Gupta, S., Paterson, M.L., Lysaght, R.M. & Von Zweck, C.M. (2012). Experiences of burnout and coping strategies utilized by occupational therapists. *Canadian Journal of Occupational Therapy*, 79(2), pp. 86–95.

Hochschild, A. (1983). *The Managed Heart*. Berkeley, CA: University of California Press.

Hojat, M. & LaNoue, M. (2014). Exploration and confirmation of the latent variable structure of the Jefferson scale of empathy. *International Journal of Medical Education*, 5, p. 73.

ICF (International Coaching Federation). (2015). *Code of Ethics*. Accessed on 19th November 2018 at: https://coachfederation.org/code-of-ethics.

International Coach Federation. (2018). *Coach Supervision*. Accessed on 19th November 2018 at: https://www.coachfederation.org.uk/profession al-development/coach-supervision/.

Lally, P., Van Jaarsveld, C.H., Potts, H.W. & Wardle, J. (2010). How are habits formed: modelling habit formation in the real world. *European Journal of Social Psychology*, 40(6), pp. 998–1009.

Kabat-Zinn, J. (2003). Mindfulness-based interventions in context: past, present, and future. *Clinical Psychology: Science and Practice*, 10(2), pp. 144–156.

Karpman, S. (1968). Fairy tales and script drama analysis. *Transactional Analysis Bulletin*, 7(26), pp. 39–43.

Kets de Vriers, M.F.R. (2013). The dangers of codependant mentoring. *Harvard Business Review*. Accessed on 12th September 2018 at: https://hbr.org/2013/12/the-dangers-of-codependent-mentoring.

Krasner, M.S., Epstein, R.M., Beckman, H., Suchman, A.L., Chapman, B., Mooney, C.J. & Quill, T.E. (2009). Association of an educational program in mindful communication with burnout, empathy, and attitudes among primary care physicians. *JAMA*, 302(12), pp. 1284–1293.

Kuyken, W., Watkins, E., Holden, E., White, K., Taylor, R.S., Byford, S., Evans, A., Radford, S., Teasdale, J.D. & Dalgleish, T. (2010). How does mindfulness-based cognitive therapy work?. *Behaviour Research and Therapy*, 48(11), pp. 1105–1112.

Newell, J.M., Nelson-Gardell, D. & MacNeil, G. (2016). Clinician responses to client traumas: a chronological review of constructs and terminology. *Trauma, Violence, & Abuse*, 17(3), pp. 306–313.

Nezu, A.M., Nezu, C.M. & Blissett, S.E. (1988). Sense of humor as a moderator of the relation between stressful events and psychological distress: a prospective analysis. *Journal of Personality and Social Psychology*, 54(3), p. 520.

Norcross, J.C. (2000). Psychotherapist self-care: practitioner-tested, research-informed strategies. *Professional Psychology: Research and Practice*, 31(6), p. 710.

Norcross, J.C. & Guy, J.D. (2007). *Leaving it at the Office: A Guide to Psychotherapist Self-Care*. New York: Guilford Press.

Norcross, J.C. & VandenBos, G.R. (2018). *Leaving it at the Office: A Guide to Psychotherapist Self-Care* (2nd ed.). New York: Guilford Press.

Omoto, A.M., Malsch, A.M. & Barraza, J.A. (2009). Compassionate acts: Motivations for and correlates of volunteerism among older adults. In *The Science of Compassionate Love: Theory, Research, and Applications. Mental Health, Religion & Culture*, 14(9), pp. 257–282.

Pedler, M., Burgoyne, J. & Brook, C. (2005). What has action learning learned to become? *Action Learning: Research and Practice*, 2(1), pp. 49–68.

Preckel, K., Kanske, P. & Singer, T. (2018). On the interaction of social affect and cognition: empathy, compassion and theory of mind. *Current Opinion in Behavioral Sciences*, 19, pp. 1–6.

Prochaska, J.O., Norcross, J.C. & DiClemente, C.C. (1995). *Changing for Good*. New York: Avon.

Rabkin, J.G. & Struening, E.L. (1976). Life events, stress, and illness. *Science*, 194(4269), pp. 1013–1020.

Richards, K., Campenni, C. & Muse-Burke, J. (2010). Self-care and well-being in mental health professionals: the mediating effects of self-awareness and mindfulness. *Journal of Mental Health Counseling*, 32(3), pp. 247–264.

Roger, C.R. (1951). *Client-Centered Therapy: Its Current Practice, Implications and Theory*. Boston, MA: Houghton Mifflin.

Schwebel, M. & Coster, J. (1998). Well-functioning in professional psychologists: as program heads see it. *Professional Psychology: Research and Practice*, 29(3), p. 284.

Shostrom, E.L. (1965). *Three approaches to psychotherapy (Part I)[Film]*. Orange, CA: Psychological Films.

Simbula, S. & Guglielmi, D. (2010). Depersonalization or cynicism, efficacy or inefficacy: what are the dimensions of teacher burnout? *European Journal of Psychology of Education*, 25(3), pp. 301–314.

Simionato, G.K. & Simpson, S. (2018). Personal risk factors associated with burnout among psychotherapists: a systematic review of the literature. *Journal of Clinical Psychology*, 74(9):1431–1456.

Solon, O. (2012). Compassion over empathy could help prevent emotional burnout. Accessed on 11th October 2018 at: https://www.wired.co.uk/article/tania-singer-compassion-burnout.

Turner, E. (2010). Coaches' views on the relevance of unconscious dynamics to executive coaching. *Coaching: An International Journal of Theory, Research and Practice*, 3(1), pp. 12–29.

Williams, N. (2014). Managing transference and countertransference. Accessed on 17th October 2018 at: https://tpcleadership.com/uk/blog-post/managing-transference-and-countertransference-html/.

Young, E. (2016). How sharing other people's feelings can make you sick. *New Scientist*. Accessed on 19th October 2018 at: https://www.newscientist.com/article/mg23030732-900-how-sharing-other-peoples-feelings-can-make-you-sick/.

Zammuner, V., Lotto, L. & Galli, C. (2003). Regulation of emotions in the helping professions: nature, antecedents and consequences. *Australian e-Journal for the Advancement of Mental Health*, 2(1), pp. 43–55.

7   Final thoughts

Introduction

At the beginning of this book, we presented a relatively bleak picture of the world we live in today. Characterised by increased pressure and demands on all aspects of life, the 24/7 environment and culture surreptitiously facilitates permanent connectivity and information overload, leading to stress and burn-out and the growing prevalence of physical and mental ill health. We live in an era of unprecedented opportunity, whereby access to education, information, resources, careers, technology, and travel are all within reach. However, with opportunity comes responsibility, as the line easily blurs between opportunity and overwhelming choices. The role of the coach or mentor has never been more vital. Supporting clients to develop their ability to cope, adapt, and thrive by helping to cultivate a deep understanding of oneself, clients can positively impact their physical, mental, and social well-being. At the core of this book is our Four-Stage Model for Work-Life Balance, developing clients' self-aware-ness, self-insight, capability, and capacity to influence their work-life balance. In this final chapter, we revisit some of the core themes that have emerged in our research and practice, addressing the growing need to make space and time for quality thinking and dialogue.

Taking responsibility for our work-life balance

Achieving the desired work-life balance requires that clients take responsibility for the ongoing assessment and evaluation of all areas of their lives and manage their own time to make their own choices. Attending to all areas of our lives and understanding which areas may need greater attention at different times requires a high degree of self-insight, self-awareness, situational awareness, and an understanding of what we can and can't influence and control. Often, we hear clients and colleagues asking, 'Where do we start?' There is not always an obvious starting point. Sometimes addressing an immediate issue, a serious setback at home or work is needed before embarking on a long and often pro-found journey of self-insight and discovery. Setbacks can be pivotal moments that can lay a heavy toll on clients' ability to cope. Their work-life balance, energies, and supplies will determine their ability to manage and overcome the setbacks they encounter.

In our research and practice, we have found that several themes have emerged which might be regarded as prerequisites for achieving work-life balance and well-being:

- The degree to which we hold a positive view of self and our self-insight, knowledge skills, behaviours.
- The ability to state our life strategy and the ability to define and incrementally move towards life success.
- The ability to seek and express meaning and purpose, and to understand the way we experience connectedness.
- Taking responsibility for our emotions, understanding and regulating our emotions, and understanding the emotions of others.
- Managing our health and energy levels.
- The ability to cope with pressure and adversity so that we can bounce back in the face of difficult conditions, change, or pressure.
- The ability to analyse and manage our environment, appreciate potential resources, access resources, and navigate external routes to help meet our needs and support all areas of our life.
- Having support networks at home, work, and in our broader network to meet our needs and the needs of others.
- Making informed and purposeful choices and negotiating with self and others.

We explained that the themes can be broadly grouped into four areas as illustrated in our Four-Stage Model for Work-Life Balance.

Coaching or mentoring can be hugely influential in supporting clients to overcome barriers and challenges, including negative self-talk and self-defeating behaviours. By addressing self-esteem and locus of control, we can help our clients take control of their work-life balance. Uncovering your clients' beliefs about success in general and analysing how close they are to what success looks like for them, will enable your clients to work towards success and life satisfaction. Helping to keep clients focused, work towards a goal, and keep forward momentum, often results in greater well-being and the ability to thrive.

In turn, this increases resilience levels, developing mental, emotional, social, and environmental mastery. The six-mastery model of resilience focuses attention on understanding the different needs of individuals, individual psychological characteristics, how individuals interact within diverse environments, and how these different variables may influence resilience levels. Your coaching or mentoring sessions provide a space where your clients' work-life balance issues can be addressed, helping them to be at their most effective, productive, and positive. This increases their capacity to cope and bounce back from change and pressures, adopting a flexible and adaptive approach to the challenges they face. Typically, clients who develop their resilience are more able to reach out to others, buffering their support system and reducing feelings of isolation. Developing resilience requires a consistent long-term commitment to working towards six masteries – mental, emotional, physical, social, spiritual, and environmental.

Decision-making and negotiation are critical skills in achieving the desired work-life balance. Clients' ability to see and think through options can be significantly hindered by the environment and their own mental state. Experiencing short-term emotions can get in the way of our ability to decide and take action. We might choose the path of least resistance because we lack energy and the capacity to choose a road which requires greater effort and application. Encouraging your clients to engage in conversation with others provides the opportunity to access information, consider different scenarios and their implications, develop new and alternative options, and think through possibilities before making a decision. Negotiation is a crucial skill that clients increasingly need to have in order to navigate aspects of work and non-work, elucidating and resolving issues such as pay, role, responsibilities, work conditions, and alignment between individual, line manager and organisational expectations. We all negotiate continuously in our day-to-day lives, even when we don't think of ourselves as doing so. Assisting clients in developing their negotiation skills can impact on all areas of life: A pay rise, changing working patterns, childcare responsibilities, moving house, or supporting an elderly parent. The ability to negotiate is, therefore, an important skill to have when working towards greater work-life balance.

Quality time, thinking, and dialogue

People often talk about quality – the quality of life, quality time, quality thinking, and quality dialogue. But what does this mean in reality? Usually, clients mean space – the physical and mental time to recuperate their energies. Evidence shows that reflective space is hugely beneficial in all aspects of our lives. Reflective space enables quality time, deep thinking, and focused dialogue; the role of the coach or mentor facilitates this space and enables depth of thinking and dialogue, which can be both restorative and transformative.

For coaches or mentors, supervision, peer groups, action learning sets, and communities of practice all provide a reflective space and the opportunity to engage in reflective thinking and dialogue. The benefits of supervision are wide-ranging; for many coaches or mentors, the core purpose of supervision is to enhance their well-being and develop their practice. This might include:

- Increasing self-insight and self-awareness.
- Developing skills and understanding capacity and capability.
- Processing experiences when working with clients.
- Developing the quality of conversation between the coach or mentor and their clients.
- Exploring problems and dilemmas in a safe and confidential environment and obtaining an experienced second opinion on situations that may arise.

Understanding, evaluating, and selecting self-care strategies to address current and future needs are important steps in looking after yourself. The self-care plan outlined in the previous chapter is a useful starting point and will help you to appreciate the extent to which you are looking after yourself. We encourage you to think about your needs as well as those of your clients.

Closing remarks

No silver bullet can cut through the complexities of our lives as they are today. The more complex our lives become and the greater the struggles and pull between wants and needs, the more we experience conflict and strain. Work–life balance requires the ongoing assessment and evaluation of all areas of our lives. We suggest that regardless of the origins and approach to our coaching or mentoring practice, we can all draw from the whole range of traditions and methods to assist our clients. We hope that the theory, tools, techniques, and case studies provided in this book enable you to work with your clients to achieve their desired work–life balance.

Index

Page numbers in *italics* refer to figures. Page numbers in **bold** refer to tables.

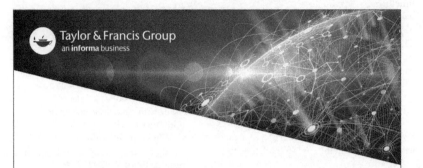